Golden Thoughts of Mother, Home & Heaven

GENE FEDELE

Gene Fedele

"ASTRA PETAMUS"
LET US SEEK HEAVEN!

Bridge-Logos

Gainesville, Florida 32614 USA

All Scriptures are from the **King James Version** unless otherwise indicated.

Golden Thoughts of Mother, Home & Heaven
Edited by Gene Fedele

Copyright 2003
Bridge-Logos
Library of Congress Catalog Number: Pending
International Standard Book Number: 0-88270-9453

Published by:
Bridge-Logos
Gainesville, FL 32614
bridgelogos.com

Presented to

Contents

Author's Preface .... Gene Fedele 11
My Dying Son .... Gene Fedele 14
Mother, Home, and Heaven .... Mary J. Muckle 17
Mother, Home, and Heaven .... Anonymous 18
Mother, Home, and Heaven .... John McCoy 19

MOTHER?

Mother .... Fanny Crosby 25
Christian Mother .... John Newton 26
Mother and Child .... Charles Kingsley 27
The Mother at Home .... Mother's Treasury 28
The Mother's Opportunity .... Anonymous 33
A Mother's Prayer .... Anonymous 35
Words for the Christian Mother .... Mother's Magazine 35
The Influence of a Christian Mother .... Dean Kirman 40
The Mother's Power .... Mrs. A. G. Whittelsey 41
Mother's Vacant Chair .... T. De Witt Talmage 42
Working and Waiting .... Anonymous 43
Appeal to Mothers .... Christian Treasury 45
A Mother's Love .... James Montgomery 46
The Mother's Charge .... Lydia H. Sigourney 46
Mother's Empire .... H. H. Birkins 46
My Mother's Bible .... Bishop Gilbert Haven 48
Maternal Instruction .... John S. C. Abbott 51
Consequences of Neglect .... John S. C. Abbott 53
A Mother's Influence .... John B. Gough 54
Maternal Influence .... Sunday at Home 55
The Mother of John Quincy Adams .... Sunday at Home 56
To a Bereaved Mother .... John Quincy Adams 57

Responsibility of Mothers .... T. De Witt Talmage 59

Mother's Comfort .... Elizabeth Prentiss 60

Recollections of My Mother .... Horace Greeley 60

My Mother's Picture .... William Cowper 61

Dying Child and Her Departed Mother .... Henry Harbaugh 62

Jesus to His Mother .... J. R. Miller 63

President Garfield's Mother .... J. R. Miller 64

The Little Mother .... S. B. Shaw 66

He Never Forgot His Mother .... Mrs. A. G. Whittelsey 68

The Love of God .... Mother's Gift 73

Teach Your Children to Love .... Jean Paul Richter 74

To My Mother .... Thomas Moore 75

The Mother's Work .... Henry Ward Beecher 75

My Mother's Bible .... George P. Morris 76

A Tender Mother .... George Eliot 77

The Young Mother .... Mother's Magazine 78

The Mothers of Two Great Men .... Christian Miscellany 81

Washington Loved His Mother .... Mother's Magazine 82

Advice to Mothers .... Celesta 83

Maternity .... Christian Miscellany 85

The Righteous Mother Comforted .... Mother's Journal 85

A Mother May Forget .... Mary Winslow 89

I Love My Mother .... "Aunt Mary" 91

My Grandmother .... Mrs. S. B. Phelps 91

Mother .... Elizabeth Prentiss 95

Sir Isaac Newton's Mother .... Jabez Burns 98

Suzannah Wesley and Her Children .... Jabez Burns 100

Richard Knill's Mother .... Jabez Burns 102

The Mother of Andrew Jackson .... Jabez Burns 104

Maternal Influence of Philip Henry .... Jabez Burns 105

Maternal Influence .... J. S. Law 106

A Sick Daughter to Her Mother .... Mrs. Davidson 107

A Good Daughter .... Dr. Palfrey 109

HOME

Home .... Fanny Crosby 113

Family Worship .... V. A. Boardman 114

Parental Authority .... Mother's Treasury 115

Care for the Soul .... John Bunyan 117

The Family Gathering .... William Sprague 117

Increasing Love of Christ .... Edward Payson 119

Hints to a Happy Home .... V. T. Moore 119

Comfort Out of Trouble .... John Willison 120

Masters of Families .... William Jay 121

Heart Religion .... J. C. Ryle 121

Education of Children .... Cotton Mather 123

The Sabbath School .... Asa Bullard 126

The Happy Family .... William Jay 127

Not One Child to Spare .... Ethel L. Beers 128

Babies and Their Rights .... Margaret Sangster 130

Family Prayer .... William Jay 132

Courtesies to Parents .... Sunday School Times 132

Family Government .... V. T. Moore 134

The Husband's Part .... J. R. Miller 143

The Wife's Part .... J. R. Miller 148

The Parent's Part .... J. R. Miller 156

The Children's Part .... J. R. Miller 164

The Aim and Object of Life .... C. H. Spurgeon 175

Making the Most of Each Day .... Philip Doddridge 177

The Happiest Home .... Anonymous 179

Home .... James Montgomery 180

True Godliness .... William Jay 181

Design of the Family .... V. T. Moore 181

The Old Folks .... The Congregationalist 182

The Home of Childhood .... Samuel D. Burchard 184

Home Training of Children .... D. L. Moody 189

Knowing Christ .... Octavius Winslow 191

The Beautiful Home .... Oliver Wendell Holmes 192
Study Christ's Life .... Elizabeth Prentiss 193
Home Happiness .... F. S. Cassady 193
My Heart Shall Be Glad .... J. R. Miller 196
Happiness in the Home .... Christian Parlor Magazine 196
The Old Home .... Alfred Tennyson 197
Home Shadows .... Robert Collyer 198
Let the Little Children Come .... J. R. Miller 200
Religion in the Family .... Ladies' Repository 201
Home Affection .... H. C. Dane 202
Home Instruction .... Hon. Schuyler Colfax 205
Home Sweet Home .... Saturday Evening Post 206
Family Religion .... Mother's Magazine 208
I Was a Wandering Sheep .... Horatius Bonar 209
The Power of Home .... R. S. Storrs 210
The New Song .... Elizabeth Prentiss 210
The Light of Home .... Sarah J. Hale 212
Sweet Ties of Home .... Margaret Sangster 212
Home Religion .... Mother's Treasury 213
Family Prayers .... Christian at Work 216
Home and its Queen .... Scribner's Monthly 217
A Cheerful Home .... Friend's Intelligencer 219
Conversation in the Home .... Churchman Magazine 220
Speak Cheerful Words .... Ladies' Repository 221
A Happy Home Defined .... James Hamilton 224
The Family .... Bayard Taylor 224
Make Home Life Beautiful .... B. G. Northrup 225
Building a Home .... T. De Witt Talmage 226
Joys of Home .... Sir John Bowring 229
The Children's Bedtime .... Jane Ellis Hopkins 230
Man's Earthly Love and Joy .... Donald Mitchell 232
Home Truths .... Thomas Guthrie 235
Sweet Home .... Golden Gems of Life 237
Children in the Home .... S. C. Ferguson 239
Our Baby .... Anson D. F. Randolph 239

The Home Circle .... Golden Gems of Life 241
Character Formed at Home .... E. H. Chapin 242
True Hospitality .... Sir Arthur Helps 244
Christianity at Home .... John Angell James 245
Tell Your Wife .... Pacific Rural Press 246
The Little Children .... Henry Longfellow 247
A Worthy Ambition .... John B. Gough 249
Influence of Character .... William Taylor 250
Model Homes .... Samuel Fallows 251
H-O-M-E .... T. De Witt Talmage 252
The Trials of Home .... W. K. Tweedie 252
Family Prayer .... Matthew Henry 256
Home Memories .... J. R. Miller 257
Raising Our Children .... Matthew Henry 258
Home: A Divine Institution .... W. K. Tweedie 259
Patience With Children .... C. H. Spurgeon 260
Christ Our Home .... J. C. Ryle 260
Brave Children of God .... D. L. Moody 261
The Christian's Home .... Thomas Guthrie 262
Home is Like Heaven .... Golden Gems of Life 262

HEAVEN?

Heaven .... Fanny Crosby 265
Assurance of Heaven .... Isaac Watts 266
Fountain of Consolation .... J. G. Pike 266
The Gardener and the Rose .... C. H. Spurgeon 267
Trials and Afflictions .... R. M. M'Cheyne 268
The Christian's Future Happy Home .... J. G. Pike 268
Lord, it Belongs Not to My Care .... Richard Baxter 269
A Clearer Vision .... Edward Payson 271
Fullness of Joy in Heaven .... J. G. Pike 271
The Heavenly Home .... The Mother's Journal 272
Dying Meditations .... John Willison 276

Eternal Holiness and Happiness .... J. G. Pike 277
Complete Perfection .... J. G. Pike 278
Christ's Second Coming .... R. M. M'Cheyne 279
Death is Gain .... Samuel Rutherford 279
Desire After Heaven .... William Jay 280
Realities of Eternity .... J. G. Pike 280
Preparing for the Happiness of Eternity .... Joseph Addison 282
Directions for Mourners .... John Willison 283
Knowledge in Heaven .... Isaac Watts 283
Sown in Weakness .... E. H. Bickersteth 284
Raised in Power .... E. H. Bickersteth 285
To Be With Christ .... Richard Baxter 286
In View of Glory .... Edward Payson 286
Dying Testimony of Believers .... Various 288
The Way to Heaven .... Jonathan Edwards 300
Perfection of the Soul .... Joseph Addison 303
No Cross, No Crown .... John Bunyan 303
He Cares for You .... J. G. Pike 304
John Sudlow .... Anecdotes for the Young 305
My Little Playmate and Her Grandfather ...... Theodore Thinker 306
The House of God .... Jonathan Edwards 309
The Departed Child .... Samuel Rutherford 309
Soul and Body Glorified in Heaven .... John Bunyan 310
The Pearly Gates Ajar .... Emily Judson 312
Employment in Glory .... Jonathan Edwards 313
Future Usefulness .... Horatius Bonar 314
Meditating on Future Life .... John Calvin 314
Glimpses Through Life's Window .... J. R. Miller 316
Use of Afflictions .... R. M. M'Cheyne 323
In Mother's Place .... Anonymous 324
Precious Comfort From Sickness .... C. H. Spurgeon 325
How Sin Appears in Heaven .... Edward Payson 326
Patience Under Trials .... William Jay 327
Eternal Choice .... J. G. Pike 329
The Happy Blind Girl .... J. C. Ryle 330

The World to Come .... American Tract Society 332

Consider What Heaven Is! .... Edward Reynolds 336

Glimpses at Immortality .... J. R. Miller 336

Comfort for the Bereaved .... John Chrysostom 339

Beating Me Home .... Annie Johnson Flint 343

Look Upwards .... Jonathan Berridge 345

Death of the Little Scholar .... Charles Dickens 345

The Last Enemy .... E. H. Bickersteth 347

Having an Eternal View .... J. G. Pike 348

Earthly Affections and Hope of Heaven .... William Gurnall 349

Heaven, A Place .... D. A. Harsha 350

Entering the Celestial City .... John Bunyan 354

Life Through Death .... Horatius Bonar 354

The Joys of Earth are Fleeting .... Harriet E. Francis 355

Time and Eternity .... John Flavel 357

Contrast Between Earth and Heaven .... James Hamilton 357

The Blood of the Lamb .... Octavius Winslow 358

The Word Made Flesh .... Horatius Bonar 359

We Shall See in Heaven .... Ladies' Repository 360

The Blessing of Affliction .... Golden Gems of Life 362

To A Better Land .... R. M. M'Cheyne 363

Jesus Knew it All! .... Octavius Winslow 363

Dealing With Sorrows .... J. R. Miller 365

It is Well With Your Child .... C. H. Spurgeon 366

Nothing is Forgotten .... Charles Dickens 368

Go Tell Jesus! .... Octavius Winslow 368

No Pain in Heaven .... Isaac Watts 369

Blessing Beyond Our Losses .... J. R. Miller 371

Oh, Come Thou Down to Me .... Elizabeth Prentiss 372

God's Relationship to Children .... John Guthrie 373

Heavenly Homesickness .... C. H. Spurgeon 374

Living for Immortality .... J. R. Miller 375

Children Before the Throne .... Thomas Boston 375

Little Ones in Heaven .... Robert Ferguson 377

What Really Matters .... J. R. Miller 377

The Triumphant Death-bed Scene .... Mother's Magazine 378

Saints Among Us .... Elizabeth Prentiss 380

A Mother's Comfort .... Anonymous 381

With Great Delight .... Elizabeth Prentiss 382

A Sweet Sorrow .... Philip Schaff 383

Perfection .... Edgar Guest 384

Gateway to Glory .... J. R. Miller 385

The Bloom Falling Into Christ's Lap .... Samuel Rutherford 387

Hard Couch of Sorrow .... Henry Law 388

Behold Your King .... Elizabeth Prentiss 389

A Dying World .... J. C. Ryle 389

Awake From Your Sleep! .... John Wesley 390

Flee From the Wrath to Come .... John Wesley 391

Your Inheritance .... Octavius Winslow 391

Life in Jesus .... Mary Winslow 392

Heavenly Prayer .... D. A. Harsha 393

The Mother's Jewels .... M. C. Bowman 393

God's Everlasting Goodness .... Elizabeth Prentiss 395

Home at Last! .... Mother's Journal 396

The Glory of Heaven .... D. A. Harsha 397

Infants in Glory .... Various 399

No Night There .... Margaet Sangster 401

Just Like the Plan! .... James McConkey 402

Blessed Are the Dead Which Die in the Lord ...... E. H. Bickersteth 403

Daily Trials .... John Newton 406

A Well Founded Hope .... George Herbert 406

Victory Over Death .... Horatius Bonar 407

The Christian in Glory .... C. H. Spurgeon 407

Night of Weeping, Joy in the Morning .... Horatius Bonar 409

Satisfied! .... Elizabeth Prentiss 409

Sanctified Affliction .... Watchman and Reflector 410

Sunshine for the Sorrowing .... Theodore L. Cuyler 412

A New Creation .... Horatius Bonar 414

Thoughts of Heaven .... William Pierce 415

The Way to Heaven .... J. R. Miller 416

Ties Not Broken in Heaven .... Henry Harbaugh 418

Jesus, Come to Me .... Bernard of Clairvaux 418

The Christian in Heaven .... John S. C. Abbott 419

Sympathy of the Two Worlds .... C. H. Spurgeon 419

Our Departed Friends in Glory .... D. L. Moody 420

Two Funerals .... C. H. Spurgeon 421

Delights of Heaven .... Isaac Watts 421

Our Friends in Heaven .... Jonathan Edwards 423

Degrees of Bliss in Glory .... J. R. MacDuff 425

The King Calls His Children .... Cotton Mather 426

Seeing Friends Again .... Cyprian 426

Would You Call Him Back? .... S. I. Prime 427

Death of a Good Man .... C. H. Spurgeon 429

Sir Isaac Newton .... Philip Doddridge 429

Echoes From Heaven .... John Cumming 430

Assurance of Present and Future Happiness ...... William McEwen 430

Death Has Lost its Terror .... Philip Schaff 431

Splendor of Eternal Glory .... James McConkey 432

Heaven in My Heart .... Richard Baxter 433

We Reap What We Sow .... J. C. Ryle 433

Eternal Life in Christ .... J. R. Miller 434

The Little Girl and the Ferryman .... D. L. Moody 436

Present, Past, and Future .... Daniel Webster 437

The Whole Family in Heaven .... John Angell James 438

Happiness in Heaven .... William McEwen 441

Christ First! .... Charles Dickens 442

Heavenly Thoughts .... D. L. Moody 442

Always Ready! .... J. R. Miller 443

Present With the Lord .... Isaac Watts 444

My Soul! .... George Matheson 445

Where Will You Be? .... J. C. Ryle 446

List of Authors

Abbott, John S.C.
(1805-1877) 51, 53, 419

Adams, John Quincy (1767-1848) 56, 57

Augustine, Aurelius (354-430) 290, 350

"Aunt Mary" 91

Baxter, Richard (1615-1691) 259, 269,
286, 297, 308, 350, 425, 433

Beecher, Henry Ward
(1813-1887) 75, 127, 241, 359

Beers, Ethel L. (1827-1879) 128

Bernard of Clairvaux (1090-1153) 418

Berridge, John (1716-1793) 345

Bickersteth, E. H.
(1825-1906) 284, 285, 347, 380, 403

Birkins, H. H. 46

Boardman, V. A. 114

Bonar, Horatius (1808-1889) 209, 314,
354, 359, 407, 409, 414

Boston, Thomas (1676-1732) 375

Bowman, M. C. 393

Bowring, Sir John (1792-1872) 229

Brooks, Thomas (1608-1680) 410, 431

Bunyan, John (1628-1688) 117, 293,
303, 310, 347, 354

Burchard, Samuel T. (b. 1808) 184

Burns, Jabez (1805-1876) 98, 100, 102,
104, 105

Calvin, John (1509-1564) 314, 399, 427

Cassady, F. S. 193

Celesta 83

Chapin, E. H. (1814-1880) 242

Chrysostom, John (347-407) 339

Colfax, Hon. Schuyler
(1823-1885) 205

Collyer, Robert (1823-1912) 198

Cowper, William
(1731-1800) 53, 61, 420

Crosby, Fanny (1820-1915) 25, 113, 265

Cumming, John (1807-1881) 430

Cuyler, Theodore L. (1822-1909) 412

Cyprian (200-258) 426

Dane, H. C. 202

Davidson, Mrs. 107

Dickens, Charles
(1812-1870) 95, 345, 368, 442

Doddridge, Phillip (1702-1751) 177, 429

Dwight, Timothy (1752-1817) 209

Edwards, Jonathan (1703-1758) 210,
298, 300, 309, 313, 423

Eliot, George (1819-1880) 77

Fallows, Samuel (1835-1922) 251

Fedele, Gene 13

Ferguson, S. C. 239

Ferguson, Robert (1842-1895) 377

Flavel, John (1630-1691) 357

Flint, Annie Johnson (1866-1932) 343

Francis, Harriet E. 355

Garfield, James A. (1831-1881) 64, 412

Gough, John B. (1817-1886) 54, 249

Greeley, Horace (1811-1872) 60

Greeley, Horace (1811-1872) 60

Goodwin, Thomas (1600-1680) 306

Gurnall, William (1617-1679) 349

Guthrie, Thomas (1803-1873) 235, 262

Guthrie, James (1612-1661) 294, 373

Hale, Sarah J. (1788-1879) 34, 212

Hamilton, James (1814-1868) 224, 357

Harbaugh, Henry (1817-1867) 418

Harsha, D. A.
   (b. 1827) 350, 383, 393, 397
Haven, Bishop Gilbert (1821-1880) 48
Helps, Sir Arthur (1813-1875) 244
Henry, Matthew (1662-1714) 206,
         247, 256, 258, 298, 415
Herbert, George (1593-1633) 406
Hodge, Archibald Alexander (A. A.)
   (1823-1886) 238
Holmes, Oliver Wendell (1809-1894) 192
Hopkins, Jane Ellis 230
James, John Angell (1785-1859) 245, 438
Jay, William (1769-1853) 121, 127,
        132, 181, 280, 327, 414
Kingsley, Charles (1819-1875) 27
Kirman, Dean 40
Law. J. S. 106
Lincoln, Abraham (1809-1865) 55
Longfellow, Henry (1807-1882) 247
Luther, Martin (1483-1546) 290
M'Cheyne, Robert Murray
   (1813-1843) 268, 279, 282,
        323, 363
MacDuff, J. R. (1801-1871) 425
Mather, Cotton (1662-1727) 123, 426
Matheson, George (1842-1906) 444
Matthews, J. M. 48
McConkey, James (1858-1937) 402, 432
McCoy, John 19
McEwen, William 430, 441
Miller, James Russell (J. R.),
   (1842-1912) 63, 64, 143, 148,
        156, 164, 196, 200, 257, 316,
        336, 365, 366, 371, 375, 377,
        385, 416, 434, 443
Mitchell, Donald 232
Montgomery, James 46, 180
Moody, Dwight L. (1837-1899) 189,
        261, 420, 436, 442
Moore, Thomas 75

Moore, V. T. 119, 134, 181
More, Hannah (1745-1833) 211
Morris, George P. 76
Muckle, Mary J. 17
Newton, Sir Isaac (1642-1727) 98, 429
Newton, John
   (1725-1807) 26, 55, 325, 399, 406
Northrop, B. G. 225
Palfrey, Dr. 109
Payson, Edward (1783-1827) 119, 271,
        286, 299, 326
Pearce, William (1764-1825) 415
Perkins, William (1558-1602) 400
Phelps, Mrs. S. B. 91
Pike, John Gregory (J. G.),
   (1784-1854) 266, 268, 271, 277,
        278, 280, 304, 329, 348,
Prentiss, Elizabeth
   (1818-1878) 60, 95, 193, 204,
        210, 222, 372, 380, 382, 387,
        389, 390, 395, 399, 404, 409,
Prime, Samuel I. (1812-1855) 427
Randolph, Anson D. F. 239
Randolph, John (1773-1833) 58
Reynolds, Edwards (1599-1676) 336
Richter, John Paul (1763-1855) 74
Romaine, William
   (1714-1795) 356
Rutherford, Samuel (1600-1661) 279,
        294, 309, 387, 412
Ryle, John Charles (J. C.),
   (1816-1900) 121, 260, 330,
        389, 433, 445
Sangster, Margaret
   (1838-1912) 130, 212, 401
Schaff, Philip (1819-1893) 383, 431
Shakespeare, (1564-1616) 323
Shaw, S. B. 66
Sigourney, Lydia H. (1791-1865) 46
Smyth, Thomas 400

Sprague, *William (1799-1856)* *117*

Spurgeon, *Charles Haddon (C. H.)*,
(1834-1892) *175, 191,*
260, 267, 325, 366, 374,
407, 419, 421, 429

Storrs, *R. S.* *210*

Talmage, *T. De Witt*
(1832-1902) *42, 59, 226, 252,*

Taylor, *Bayard (1825-1878)* *224*

Taylor, *William* *250*

Tennyson, *Alfred (1809-1892)* *197*

Thinker, *Theodore* *306*

Toplady, *Augustus (1740-1778)* *401*

Tupper, *M. F.* *256*

Tweedie, *W. K.* *252, 259*

Watts, *Isaac (1674-1748)* *266, 283, 369,*
421, 444

Webster, *Daniel (1782-1852)* *437*

Wesley, *John (1703-1791)* *390, 413*

West, *Benjamin (1738-1820)* *45*

Whittelsey, *Mrs. A. G.* *41, 68*

Willison, *John*
(1680-1750) *120, 276, 283*

Winslow, *Mary (1610-1687)* *89, 392*

Winslow, *Octavius*
(1808-1878) *191, 358, 363, 368, 391*

Dedication

To my mother, Sharon, whose constant love, selfless giving and maternal instruction helped set my feet, at an early age, along the "narrow path." She has, as both a mother and grandmother, served her family with joy and dedication.

To my grandmother, Alice, who was a blessed example to me of what is wholesome and pure, in my formative years. Her love and devotion to her children and grandchildren are exemplary, and have never faded throughout her nearly ninety years on earth.

To the mother of my children, Kerri, whose virtue and character is, indeed, a "masterpiece in progress" of the sanctifying work of the Holy Spirit. She has triumphed over many of the trials of motherhood with Christian joy and fortitude—developing a deeper relationship with her Savior along the way. Her pious, maternal influence has ushered one child into Glory and is leading the hearts of three more on that same blessed path. Her quiet resignation to the will of God and loving devotion to the "highest of callings"—motherhood—are sources of inspiration to many.

Their exists no sweetness as a mother's rosy cheek, no softness as a mother's warm embrace, and no comfort as a mother's gentle voice. In the words of Bishop John Newman, "O mothers! You are the guardians of infancy, the instructors of childhood, the companions of youth, and the partners of manhood. As are our mothers, so are our homes, our churches, our world."

Many of the world's godly men and women throughout history were raised by pious mothers who ceased not to pray for them and teach them the love of God through Jesus Christ. O, think of the blessings that would be absent from each age of Christiandom had not Monica been on her knees for decades, faithfully pleading with the Lord for the soul of her beloved Augustine; or if Suzannah had not devoted an hour each day with little John on her lap relating gospel truths and the love of the Savior to Wesley's heart and mind. And we can include Bernard, Newton, Edwards, Watts, Spurgeon, Garfield, Miller, Doddridge and so many others who bear witness to an early life influenced by a godly, devoted mother.

Home is, in many wonderful ways, a heaven begun below. It is at the same time, the scene of earth's dearest ties. Each time a man and woman exchange the sacred vows of conjugal commitment and christen the hearth of their earthly abode; each time the new-born babe takes comfort within the warm bosom of its mother; each time the family altar is erected and sanctified to the Lord; a taste of heavenly blessing descends upon the inhabitants of the Christian home. Were it not for the tenderness, contentment, and communion of the home, the whole fabric of society in any generation would disintegrate. Many of the greatest saints of old received lasting impressions in a godly home; John the Baptist and the Prophet Samuel were sanctified from the womb; Timothy knew the Scriptures from the earliest age; Isaac Watts was nine years old when he received Christ—Jonathan Edwards was seven, and Matthew Henry was eleven! Rev. Samuel Burchard says it well, "The Christian home, implying marriage, mutual affection, piety, gentleness, refinement, meekness, forbearance, is our ideal of earthly happiness—a beautiful and impressive type of heaven."

Oh! To be a whole family in heaven! Should that not be our aim within the familial circle? Should we not strive to erect a sort of domestic "Beulah Land" within the home, that all inhabitants might experience glimpses of that immortal life? Should we not be developing those imperishable qualities in our families and ourselves that we might approach that fairer land with confidence and anticipation? Yes, it was the Savior himself that promised, "Where I am, there may ye be also." There will be reunited homes in heaven, and the long-parted will embrace in everlasting love and peace, to never part again.

The well-known minister and evangelist of the late nineteenth century, Rev. Theodore Cuyler, speaks so eloquently of the blessed union of mother, home and heaven with these words: "The *Mother* is the fountainhead of the *Home*. The home is the fountainhead of society and the Church of Christ. And no influences in the universe contribute so much towards guiding souls *Heavenward* as the *Home* and the *Mother*."

It has been my desire for many years to see this present work published and in the families of God's people. The purpose of the book is for home reading and family devotions. The idea of this work is not unique to me though. Two books of a similar nature were published in the later part of the nineteenth century. The first was *The Golden Chain That Links Mother, Home, and Heaven;* introduced in 1872 by Mary Newman. This was followed by *Golden Links On Mother, Home, and Heaven,* which was published by E. B. Treat in 1878. Both contain a wealth of striking thoughts on this "trinity" of subjects by various well-known Christian authors from centuries past. I became acquainted with *Mother, Home, and Heaven* when I purchased a copy of the Treat edition about five years ago. My soul was greatly blessed each time I opened the volume in devotional meditation. Since that time, I have purchased numerous copies as gifts for friends and family.

Working with the publishers at Bridge-Logos, we decided it was time to publish an edition of *Mother, Home, and Heaven,*—these "blessed themes of humanity,"—that this generation of believers might also be blessed and encouraged in the Christian journey. This new edition follows the general format of the nineteenth century editions, but with substantial improvements. Prose and poetry from the pen of many famous Christian authors of the past four centuries, and beyond, will encourage your heart and lift your soul. The multitude of engravings, which come primarily from my private library, lend a design contemporary to the era of the writers and complimentary to the wholesomeness of their writings.

I felt it fitting to begin this collection of writings with an excerpt from my own pen, *My Dying Son,* written the day after my eight-year old son, Christopher, left this world for his mansion above. It was written as my heart's expression of the events surrounding the last moments of his life on earth. It is my hope and prayer that you find solace in the precious truths of this book as you tread along the pathway of this life on your way to the next.

Gene Fedele, Editor

My Dying Son!

From A FATHER'S JOURNAL
June 22, 1998, the day after my 8 year-old son, Christopher, entered glory.

—*Gene Fedele*

ehold, in a somber hospital chamber, stands in agony of sorrow, a small gathering of family and friends, tearfully awaiting the beautiful, earthly form of my son to fade in death. We have done all that man and medicine could offer for my little buddy, but the end seems near. Cruel enemy, this enemy of death, who robs me of my only son and my best friend! A ruthless foe that has stolen the dreams and hopes of a young boy, and denied his loved ones the joy of future years.

There beside his bed of pain, I stand, overcome with grief and a breaking heart. I know there is nothing more I can do, but give up my cherib to God. O, the suffering! How can I bear it! I manage a parting kiss upon his brow as I whisper in his ear, "Cling to Jesus' hand, my son, when He comes for you. He will take you to your heavenly Father, for the work of your earthly father is done." I clasp my hands around his limp fingers, praying for supernatural strength to endure this lot given me; to bear up under the heavy burden of affliction cast upon my heart, and say with my Savior, "If possible, let this cup pass from me; nevertheless, not my will but thine be done."

Tears stream down my cheeks onto his forehead, as though they might soothe the pain of this dismal scene. My ear is peaked to catch the sound of each struggling breath, growing fainter every moment. Fear grips my soul as I wonder, "Will the next one be his last?" The many years of suffering have now come to these last few breaths . . . until at last he is gone! My beautiful boy is dead! I can truly feel the final quiet breath release his soul into glory. His lovely face now fixed in the slumber of death brings forth expected sobs of sorrow. My fingers gently close the lids that adorn his bright-blue orbs of delight—an image forever fixed in my mind. The cold reality that I will never again gaze into these eyes, or hear sweet words from these lips, or feel the warmth of this hand in mine, is too much to bear! My heart is crushed and I am stricken in grief! O Jesus, stand by me now!

I feel the warmth drain from his flesh and this cold, gray temple must soon be taken away. His spirit for sure has fled and left me behind with a deafening silence. My mind is easily fooled that this is not real, and he will arise and come home. O, this is too agonizing to bear! I can do nothing but shed tears of bitter anguish and sorrow!

It is true, I have often gazed into those deep blue eyes, searching for scenes of future years. I scanned his fine countenance and, in my imagination, strength of body and spirit reigned in eager service to the King. The experience of a father's delight in the glowing enthusiasm of youth transformed into the gentle and quiet strength of godly manhood will not be mine to know. The hand of a most wise and loving Father hath seen fit, in His mercy and wisdom, to deliver this precious seedling of promise from the clutches of a sin-cursed world. Could it be that such a good Father calls to Himself one of whom the world is not worthy? O blessed Lord, may my tears of sorrow be turned to tears of joy, for my son has entered thine everlasting abode where all embrace perfect peace and heavenly rest.

Beloved Savior, I release to you my only son, my hero and my treasure into the glorious company of a shining, holy multitude encircling thy brow. My breast draws warmth from anticipation of my son's sweet, eternal embrace awaiting me in that fairer land. Though my broken heart pounds from the empty pangs of grief and lost dreams, I rest my all on the promises of my blessed and victorious Savior who says, "Blessed are they who mourn, for they shall be comforted."

Mother, Home, and Heaven

Mary J. Muckle

here are three words that sweetly blend,
    That on the heart are graven;
A precious soothing balm they lend;
    They're Mother, Home, and Heaven!

They twine a wreath of beauteous flowers,
    Which, placed on memory's urn,
Will e'en the longest, gloomiest hours
    To golden sunlight turn!

They form a chain whose every link
    Is free from base alloy;
A stream where whosoever drinks
    Will find refreshing joy!

They build an altar where each day
    Love's offering is renewed;
And peace illumines with genial ray
    Life's darkened solitude?

If from our side the first has fled,
    And Home be but a name,
Let's strive the narrow path to tread,
    That we the last may gain!

Mother, Home, and Heaven

The sounds that fall on mortal ear,
    As dewdrops pure at even,
That soothe the breast, or start the tear,
    Are mother, home, and heaven.

A mother—sweetest name on earth,
    We lisp it on the knee
And idolize its sacred worth
    In manhood's infancy.

A home—that paradise below,
    Of sunshine and of flowers,
Where hallowed joys perennial flow,
    By calm, sequestered bowers.

And heaven—the port of endless peace,
    The haven of the soul,
When life's corroding cares shall cease,
    Like sweeping waves, to roll.

O, weep not, then, though cruel Time
    The chain of love has riven;
To every link, in yonder clime,
    Reunion shall be given.

O, fall they not on mortal ear
    As dewdrops pure at even,
To soothe the breast, or start the tear,
    A mother, home, and heaven?

Mother, Home, and Heaven

John McCoy

child, speaking to a friend of his home, was asked; "Where is your home?" Looking up with loving eyes at his mother, he replied, "Where mother is." Home! What a hallowed name! How full of enchantment and how dear to the heart! Home is the magic circle within which the weary spirit finds refuge. It is the sacred asylum to which the care-worn heart retreats to find rest from the toils and cares of life. Home! That name touches every fiber of our soul. Nothing but death can break its spell. And, as dear as home can be, is the mother that presided over it, and that we loved. Long years may have flown since we saw that home, and since the dearest of all earthly friends has slept the long and silent sleep of death, but that home and that mother will never cease to awaken the sweetest recollections of our lives. "Home, Sweet Home!"

Some years ago twenty thousand people gathered in the old Castle Garden, New York, to hear Jenny Lind sing, as no other songstress ever had sung the sublime compositions of Beethoven, Handel, etc. At length, the Swedish Nightingale thought of her home, paused and seemed to fold her wings for a higher flight. She began, with deep emotion, to pour forth, "Home, Sweet Home." The audience could not stand it. An uproar of applause stopped the music. Tears gushed from the eyes of that vast multitude like rain. After a moment, the song came again, seemingly as from heaven—almost angelic, "Home, Sweet Home!" That was the word that bound, as with a spell, twenty thousand souls.

Home of my childhood! We are folded again in mother's arms. She is again leaning over us, and bathing our forehead and cooling our fevered brow. But, alas! that mother is no longer in that home. She has gone to live with the angels. But there is another home, a home beyond the stars, and mother has gone to live, "Where they know not the sorrows of time."

> Up to that world of light,
>   Take us, dear Savior;
> May we all there unite,
>   Happy, forever.
> Where kindred spirits dwell,
>   There may our music swell,
> And time our joys dispel—
>   Never—no, never.

Heaven is the home that awaits us beyond the grave. At the best estate, we are only pilgrims here. Heaven is our eternal home. Death will never knock at the door of that mansion. Parents rejoice very much when, on Christmas day, or on Thanksgiving day, they have their children at home, but there is almost always a son or a daughter absent from the country, or from the world. But, oh! How glad we will be when we are all at home, all safe at home. Once there, let earthly sorrows howl like storms, and swell like seas. Home! Let thrones decay and empires wither. Home! Let the world die in earthquake struggles and be buried amid the procession of planets and dirge of spheres. Home! Let everlasting ages roll in irresistible sweep. Home! No sorrow, no crying, no death, but home, sweet home. Beautiful home! Everlasting home! Home with each other! Home with the angels! Home with God! Home with mother! Home! Home! By the grace of the dear Master, may we all get home.

> I sit and think, when the sunset's gold
>   Is flushing river and hill and shore,

I shall one day stand by the water cold,
*   And listen to the sound of the boatman's oar;*
I shall watch for a gleam of the snowy sail,
*   I shall hear the boat as it gains the strand;*
I shall pass from sight, with the boatman pale,
*   To the better shore of the spirit land.*
I shall know the loved who have gone before;
*   And joyfully sweet will the meeting be,*
When over the river, the peaceful river,
*   The angel of death shall carry me.*

Adieu, reader. Here we lay down our pen, but here we do not end our meditations. Our thoughts, and feelings, and hopes crowd onward still.

*Timothy, with his mother, Eunice, and
his grandmother, Lois.*

MOTHER

*"Strength and honor are her clothing; and she shall rejoice in
time to come. She openeth her mouth with wisdom;
and in her tongue is the law of kindness. She looketh well to the
ways of her household, and eateth not the bread of idleness.
Her children rise up and call her blessed; her husband also, and he
praiseth her. Many daughters have done virtuously, but thou
exceedeth them all. Favor is deceitful, and beauty is vain; but a
woman who fears the Lord, she shall be praised."—Proverbs 31:25-30*

*"I thank God...when I call to remembrance the genuine faith
that is in you, which first dwelt in your grandmother Lois and your
mother Eunice, and I am persuaded is in you also."—2 Timothy 1:5*

*"Suffer the little children to come unto me, and forbid them not,
for of such is the Kingdom of heaven."—Matthew 19:14*

*"Lo, children are a heritage of the Lord; and the fruit of the womb
is His reward."—Psalm 127:3*

*"And she [Hannah] said, "O my lord! As your soul lives, my lord [Eli],
I am the woman who stood by you here, praying to the Lord.
For this child I prayed, and the Lord granted me my petition
which I asked of Him. Therefore I have lent him to the Lord;
as long as he lives he shall be lent to the Lord."—1 Samuel 1:26-28*

*"My son, keep your father's command, and do not forsake the
law of your mother. Bind them continually upon your heart;
tie them around your neck. When you roam they will lead you,
when you sleep they will keep you; and when you awake they
will speak with you."—Proverbs 6:20-22*

*"Let your father and your mother be glad, and let her who bore
you rejoice."—Proverbs 23:25*

MOTHER?

By Fanny J. Crosby

The light, the spell-word of the heart,
    Our guiding star in weal or woe,
Our talisman—our earthly chart—
    That sweetest name that earth can know.

We breathed it first with lisping tongue
    When cradled in her arms we lay;
Fond memories round that name are hung
    That will not, cannot pass away.

We breathed it then, we breathe it still
    More dear than sister, friend, or brother,
The gentle power, the magic thrill,
    Awakened at the name of *mother*.

Christian Mother

John Newton

think a prudent and godly woman, in the capacity of a wife and a mother, is a greater character than any hero or philosopher of ancient or modern times. The first impressions which children receive in the nursery, while under the mother's immediate care, are seldom so obliterated but that sooner or later their influence conduces to form the future life. Though the child that is trained up in the way that he should go, may depart from it for a season, there is reason to hope he will be found in it when he is old. The principles instilled into the mind in infancy may seem dormant for a while, but the prayers with which the mother watered what she planted there, are, as some old writers say, "upon the Lord's file." Times of trouble recall those principles to the mind, and the child so instructed has something at hand to recur to. Thus it was with me. I was the only son of my mother—she taught me, she prayed for me and over me. Had she lived to see the misery and wickedness to which I plunged myself afterwards, I think it would have broken her heart. But in the Lord's time her prayers were answered. Distress led me to recollect her early care, and therefore I was led to look the right way for help. But a religious education implies much more than teaching a catechism and a few hymns. Happy and honored is the woman that is qualified to instruct her children, and does it heartily, in the spirit of faith and constant prayer.

We often speak of the birth of a child, as a matter of course, of no great moment but to the parents and relations. But indeed the birth of a child, whether in a palace or a workhouse, is an event of more real importance than the temporal concerns of an entire kingdom! When a child is born, an immortal soul is born. In that hour a new being enters upon a state of existence which will never end, and it is a being whose capacity for happiness or misery, is proportioned to its duration. To have the charge of such beings, to form their minds in their tender years, to bring them up in the nurture and admonition of the Lord, and at last to present them to Him, enables us to say, "Here am I, and the children Thou hast given me"—oh, what a blessing!

Have you read, or have I formerly mentioned to you, what a good old woman from the last century said, upon her dying bed? It was to this purpose: "I have been the mother of sixteen children; I nursed them all myself; and I know now that they are all either with Christ, or in Christ; and I believe I never gave one of them breast without putting up a prayer in my heart, that I might not nurse a child for the devil."

Mother and Child

Charles Kingsley

hat more beautiful sight is there in the world? What more beautiful and what more lovely? That man must be far from the Kingdom of God—he is not worthy to be called a man at all—whose heart has not been touched by the sight of his first child on its mother's bosom.

The greatest writers who have ever lived have tried to paint the beauty of that simple thing—a mother with her babe—and have failed. One of them, Rafaelle by name, to whom God gave the spirit of beauty in a measure in which He never gave it, perhaps, to any other man, tried again and again, for years, painting over and over that simple subject—the mother and her babe—and could not satisfy himself. Each of his pictures is most beautiful, each in a different way; and yet none of them is perfect. There is more beauty in that simple, every-day sight than he or any man could express by his pencil and his colors. And yet it is a sight which we see every day.

And as for the wonder of that sight—the mystery of it, I tell you this—That physicians, and the wise men who look into the laws of nature, of flesh and blood, say that the mystery is past their finding out; that if they could find out the whole meaning and the true meaning of those two words, mother and child, they could get the key to the deepest wonders of the world; but they cannot.

And philosophers who look into the laws of soul and spirit say the same. The wiser men they are, the more they find in the soul of every new-born babe, and its kindred to its mother, wonders and puzzles past man's understanding.

Yet it is the most common, everyday sight. That only shows once more what I so often try to show you, that the most common, everyday things are the most wonderful. It shows us how we are to despise nothing which God has made—above all, to despise nothing which belongs to human nature, which is in the likeness and image of God.

The Mother at Home

Mother's Treasury

rchbishop Leighton says, "Fill the bushel with good wheat, and there will be no room for chaff and rubbish." This is a good thought for every mother while tending her children, and watching the growth of their power in body and mind.

"As soon as they are born," the Bible says, "children go astray, speaking lies." So soon, therefore, will a Christian mother begin to "train her child in the way he should go," that good habits may be formed, ready to carry out good principles as the child grows old

enough to understand the reason for his conduct.

Good moral habits are essential to the healthfulness of the home, and these may be best taught by the watchful mother's training. One important part of her work is to remove hindrances out of her children's way to health and happiness. No dirt, or dirty habits for example, should be permitted. Washing their hands and faces many times in the day will often remove a sense of discomfort which makes them fretful, as also will giving them food at regular periods. Ragged dress and broken fastenings add a feeling of degradation that a careful mother will prevent as far as possible by keeping their clothes whole, neat, and clean. Making their own clothes, we may here remark, gives useful employment to girls and is an important aid in training them up to thrifty habits. Many families go in rags because they never learned to sew; while the same wages in the hands of those who know how to employ that useful "one-eyed servant," the needle, keep the household looking always respectable.

Children should also have time to play. Happiness is a great promoter of health. The Bible mentions "boys and girls playing in the streets," as one sign of national prosperity. They do not need expensive toys. A little French prince turned from his new year's present of toys from an empress grandmother to watch some peasants making dirt pies, and, it is said, begged the queen his mother to allow him to join in the sport which seemed so charming to his childish eye, as offering some scope to his ingenuity. A few old bits of wood, or scraps of broken crockery, stones, and oyster-shells, afford inexhaustible amusement, cost nothing, and do not spoil. If the mother will now and then put in a word to show an interest in her little ones' games, her own spirit will be refreshed and cheered by their light-heartedness.

Children are wonderful imitators, so it is comparatively easy to lead them early in good ways. They are never so happy as when trying to do what they see older people do. Their playing chiefly consists in copying elders. The little cottager "makes believe" to go to market, to plant a garden, to wash, to build, to cook, and to teach in school. The boys are never merrier than when imitating horsemen, or in some other way aspiring to be like their elders. Many of these games bring the bodily organs into excellent exercise, and strengthen and build up the system wonderfully. These amusements often truly prepare the children for the actual business of life, so that they soon become helpful to their parents. They should be watched and encouraged therefore in their play to habits of thoughtfulness and self-reliance.

Let it be remembered also, that while by all means it is well to send children to school, the largest portion of their education, whether for good or evil, is carried on at home, often unconsciously, in their amusements and under the daily influence of what they see and hear about them. It is there that "subtle brains and little fingers" find scope and learn to promote the well-being of the community. We cannot tell what duties our children may be called to perform in after-life. Many of England's greatest men were born poor cottagers. But we can, in a great measure, preserve their brains and limbs from injury. We can cultivate their faculties and teach them to exercise all their senses, to use their hands diligently and skillfully, to observe with their eyes and to listen to good instruction. In short, we can, by God's help, teach them "to choose the good and refuse the evil," as the prophet says. We can encourage them to be apt to learn, so that they may with readiness set about any duty which God may place before them.

Are the children naughty? Must they be punished? "The Lord loveth the son whom He chasteneth." "As many as I love I rebuke and chasten," are texts which will mitigate the anger of both father and mother, and teach them to adopt such means of correction as shall improve, instead of harden, their children's minds. Is a little daughter lame and sickly? Does a son get into a hard place? "Like as a father pitieth his children, so the Lord pitieth them that fear Him." "As one whom his mother comforteth, so will I comfort you," saith the Lord.

Does work fail and removal among strangers seem inevitable? The children's conclusion that "Father will see about it," "Mother will be with us," are phrases full of deeper meaning to their parents' ears as they raise their hearts to God, and remember, "Thou compassest my path;" "Thou knowest my way;" "Though I walk through the midst of trouble Thou wilt revive me."

> *"Within Thy circling power I stand,*
> *On every side I find Thine hand*
> *Awake, asleep, at home, abroad,*
> *I am surrounded still by God."*

In whom is there so much trust as in a father's love? Talk about duty to children, there is no pleasure sweeter than that of training them up in the nurture and admonition of the Lord—repaid as it is by their fervent friendship in after-life, and the hope of presenting them washed in the Savior's blood and faultless before the great throne at the last day.

AGE MAY WEAR and waste a mother's outward beauty, strength, senses and estate; but her relation as a mother is as the sun when he goes forth in his might, for it is always in the meridian and knows no evening.

—*Jewels for the Household*

The Mother's Opportunity

others, you are the divinely-appointed teachers and guides of your children, and any attempt to free yourselves from your duty is in direct opposition to the will of God. If you neglect them, the consequences are swift and sure, and how fearful they are. Let those broken-hearted mothers tell who have bowed in anguish over their lost sons; who, neglecting them in childhood, have at last seen them dead to every manly virtue.

Let me say to you who still have the opportunity to do so, train your children, whether boys or girls, to usefulness. Give them something to do. And as soon as they can walk, teach them to bring any little thing to you. And as they grow older, let them do all they can to help you. Spend most of your time with your young children. Sleep near them. Attend to washing and dressing them. Let them eat at the table with father and mother. Read, talk, play, walk with them, and be their companion and guide in all things and at all times. When the father can leave his work to take a little recreation, let him take it with the children, making it a special holiday. Don't be in haste to send them to school, but teach them at home. Oral instruction can be given while you are doing your work, and for a while will be of much more benefit than many hours of study. As soon as they want playmates, see that they have those of their own age, who have been well cared for at home, and are truthful. Let them play in or near the house, that you may observe the character of their intercourse. Never send children to school to get rid of the care or trouble of them at home, but when the right time comes, let them see that it is wholly for their good that you part with them. If possible, go often to the school-room yourself, nothing gives children so much encouragement. Always allow them to tell you all that has happened to interest or annoy them while absent from home. Never think anything which affects the happiness of your children too small a matter to claim your attention. Use every means in your power to win and retain their confidence. Do not rest satisfied without some account of each day's joys or sorrows. It is a source of great comfort to the innocent child to tell all its troubles to mother, and you must lend a willing ear. For you know that as soon as they cease to tell you all these things, they have chosen other confidants, and therein lies the danger. O mother! This is the rock on which your son may be wrecked at last. I charge you to set a watch upon it. Be jealous of the first sign that he is not opening all his heart to you.

Boys who are thus cared for and trained find more to please and amuse them at home than away. They are therefore saved from temptation. But if they are neglected until they arrive at the age when they would wish to go out evenings, there is small hope that any but arbitrary measures will prevent or secure obedience, and then it hardly can be called obedience. It is much more pleasant to apply the "ounce of prevention" than the "pound of cure" in such cases. When boys know that their society is valued highly at home, and that all its pleasures are marred by their absence, they will willingly stay if they can have something to occupy their time.—*Anonymous.*

O wondrous power! How little understood!
Entrusted to the mother's mind alone,
To fashion genius, form the soul for good.
—*Sarah J. Hale*

A Mother's Prayer

The sweetest sound heard through our earthly home,
    The brightest ray that gleams from heaven's dome,
The loveliest flower that e'er from earth's breast rose
    That purest flame that, quivering, gleams and glows,
Are found alone, where kneels a mother mild,
    With heart uplifted, praying for her child.
The stream of tears can never cease to flow
    Long as life's sun shall shine on us below;
And many angels have been sent by God
    To count the tear-drops wept upon life's road;
But of all the tears that flow, the least defiled
    Are when a mother prays beside her child.
Because it is to mortal eyes unseen,
    Ye call it foolishness, a childish dream,
In vain, ye cannot rob me of that thought,
    That legend with such heavenly sweetness fraught,
That blessed angels have for ages smiled
    To see a mother praying for her child.—*Anonymous.*

Words for the Christian Mother

Mother's Magazine

others, your children are not given, but only lent to you, to be educated for God. That little immortal now slumbering in your arms, in all the loveliness of helpless infancy, will live forever. Forever that existence will be prolonged, either in a state of the most insupportable and never-ending agony, "Where the worm dieth not, and the fire is not quenched," (Mark 9:44) and "tormented day and night, forever and ever," (Rev. 20:10) their voices "calling upon the rocks and the mountains to fall upon them, and hide them from the wrath of the Lamb" (Rev. 6:16); or their exulting notes will be heard on high among "harpers with their harps, and singing a new song before the throne," (Rev. 14:2) "saying, Salvation to our God which sitteth upon the throne, and unto the Lamb." (Rev. 7:10)

Consider well these things, Christian Mothers! And decide what shall be your motives in training and educating your children. Here pause, and decide what is the supreme good you most earnestly seek as well as desire for them. Halt no longer between two opinions. Attempt not to reconcile opposing kingdoms of "the Prince of Peace," and the "Prince of this world,"—for our blessed Redeemer has explicitly declared that "the Prince of this world hath nothing in him," and that "no man can serve two masters."

Some mothers have no hesitation in confessing theoretically, that religion is the most valuable possession, and the most to be desired for their children. But if a mother practically appears more anxious for her child to acquire wealth or distinction, to become an accomplished and scientific scholar, than a real devoted Christian,—if she testify more solicitude that her child should possess great skill in any of the arts, for instance, in music or painting; than a knowledge of God, the Creator, Redeemer, and Preserver,—and if she accustom that child to refer to the praise of man as the object to be desired,—that mother may indeed teach her child the letter of God's Word, but she must not expect to see him influenced by its Spirit as the effect of her instructions.

Is it not astonishing that any professedly Christian mother should ever employ the unhallowed stimulant of emulation in the education of her children, when she finds it classed in evil company by an uninspired penman?

If you wish to sacrifice your children upon the altar of the "Prince of this world," then you will undoubtedly use every effort and every stimulant to make them shine in the sphere for which you are training them. Here, again, I conjure you to pause! While the light footsteps of fashion's thoughtless votary tread only upon the rose-leaves strewn along their path, they are content; but when thorns pierce their tender feet, how bitterly do they suffer from those bleeding wounds! Bear in mind that the brilliant talents, cultivated in their utmost extent, and the best stored mind, without "a new heart," are but a fragrant and gorgeous wreath, crowning the victim sacrificed on the altar of this world. Remember too, that the most amiable temper, and most fascinating presence, though they may be lovely ornaments on earth, will not avail in the sight of God. Though your ear be continually greeted with your child's praises, yet remember that "without holiness" that child "cannot see the Lord."

Oh, mothers! I would implore you, if possible, to dismiss the world from your thoughts, so far as regards the raising of those little immortals entrusted especially to you. Set up a different standard for your children from that of the world. Teach them to compare themselves with the requisitions of the Word of God, and not with the world around them. In this you will plant in their bosom the fairest flower of heavenly growth—humility. If you wish your child to be meek and submissive, do not set before him the low motive of such and such conduct being attractive, and likely to obtain the praise of men; but encourage lovely traits of character upon the lofty principle of imitating the example of Christ. Do not correct a proud and haughty spirit by telling your child that no one will love or admire him if he is proud—but tell him that "God resists the proud," and condemns pride in every form. Talk not to them of wishing them to have a name in the world—do not wish it, but instruct them to live above the world. Teach them not worldly wisdom, for "the wisdom of the world is foolishness with God."—but endeavor to inculcate in them an habitual indifference to "the friendship of the world," warning them that "it is enmity to God." Should they possess its dangerous friendship, they would almost inevitably prize it beyond its value.

Christ says, "Without me ye can do nothing." How fervent and frequent therefore should be a mother's prayers! This is in fact her first privilege as well as duty, and one which ought to commence even before the birth of her first-born babe, humbly to implore divine assistance to enable her to faithfully discharge the important obligations which its expected birth will devolve upon her. Mothers! Pour out your souls in prayer for your beloved children—pray that they make "their calling and election sure." Pray fervently, in firm dependence on Him, who has promised, "All things whatsoever ye shall ask in prayer, believing, ye shall receive." (Matt. 21:22) See also James 1:6-8.

Teach your children that "they must set their affections on things above." Refer them to Matthew 6:2, where our Redeemer condemns the desire "to have glory of men," saying "truly I say unto you, they have their reward." Pause! and consider well what that reward is!

Dear Heavenly Father, impress these truths upon every mother's heart. Aid them to fulfill all your commands to "train up their children in the way they should go;" to teach them your laws, "when they sit in the house, and when they walk by the way, when they lie down, and when they rise up;" and when their fretful hearts prompt them to exclaim, "Who is sufficient for these things?" May they remember that "Thy grace is sufficient for them, and Thy strength made perfect in

weakness." Hear us, O God! Increase our diligence in action, increase our fervor in prayer, and above all we implore you to "increase our faith."

The Influence of a Christian Mother

Dean Kirman

What a public blessing, what an instrument of exalted good, is a Christian mother! It would require a pen superior to mine to trace the merits of such a character. How many, perhaps who now hear me, feel that they owe to it all the virtue and piety that adorns them; or may recollect, at this moment, some saint in heaven that brought them into light, to labor for their happiness, temporal and eternal. No one can be ignorant of the irresistible influence which such a mother possesses in forming the hearts of her children, at a season when nature takes in lesson and example at every pore.

Confined by duty and inclination within the walls of her own house, every hour of her life becomes an hour of instructions. Every feature of her conduct a transplanted virtue. Methinks I behold her encircled by her beloved charge, like a being more than human, on whom every mind is bent, and every eye directed—the eager simplicity of infancy inhaling from her lips the sacred truths of religion in adapted phrase and familiar story, the whole rule of, the oral and religious duties simpified for easier infusion, the countenance of this fond and anxious parent all beaming with delight and love, and her eye raised occasionally to heaven in fervent supplication for a blessing on her work. Oh! What a glorious part does such a woman act on the great theatre of humanity, and how much is the mortal to be pitied who is not struck with the image of such excellence. When I look to its consequences, near and remote, I see the plant she has raised and cultivated, spreading through the community with richest increase of fruit. I see her diffusing happiness and virtue through a great portion of the human race. I can fancy generations yet unborn rising to prove and hail her worth, and I adore that God who can destine a single human being to be the stem of such incalculable benefits to the world.

The Mother's Power

Mrs. A. G. Whittelsey

Nearly all have known the depth, and strength, and warmth of a mother's affection. The most unquenchable earthly love is that of a mother to her child, insomuch that God has singled this passion as the emblem of his own affection to his covenant people in Christ. This principle of attachment is as much a part of a mother's nature, as the heart and the blood are parts of the human frame. A child may be wayward and cause much disquietude to a mother's mind, but let that child become sick or diseased, instantly all are forgotten, and sleepless nights without a grudge are spent in the sufferer's chamber. Or let that child grow up to manhood, and become a reckless prodigal, still a mother's affection clings to him. Her half-broken heart feels whole again, even at the hope of his being reclaimed to virtue and to God.

On the other hand, this love is in general reciprocated by the child. That affection, which many waters cannot quench in a mother's heart, is responded to by her offspring often with equal warmth. Even a long course of sin cannot extirpate that attachment; for in some cases, guilty youth have been known to confess, that amid all their wanderings, they never could never could forget, affection or the spell-like charm of their mother. It haunted them in all their ways, and from time to time it loudly protested and reclaimed against their sins.

Now, this reciprocal affection is the great secret of a mother's influence in training. It arms her with tremendous power to ruin her offspring, if she is unconverted, but it may render her also another Lois, or another Eunice, if her heart be influenced by 'unfeigned faith.' Let mothers ponder well on it. In consequence of the strong tie that binds them to their children such is their influence, that under God, they may abundantly promote their offspring's happiness, or misery.

Mother's Vacant Chair

T. De Witt Talmage

I go a little farther on in your house and I find the mother's chair. It is very apt to be a rocking-chair. She had so many cares and troubles to soothe, that it must have rockers. I remember it well. It was an old chair and the rockers were almost worn out, for I was the youngest, and the chair had rocked the whole family. It made a creaking noise as it moved, but there was music in the sound. It was just high enough to allow us children to put our heads into her lap. That was the bank where we deposited all our hurts and worries. Oh, what a chair that was! It was different from the father's chair—it was entirely different. You ask me how? I cannot tell, but we all felt it was different. Perhaps there was about this chair more gentleness, more tenderness, more grief when we had done wrong. When we were wayward, father scolded, but mother cried. It was a very wakeful chair. In the sick day of children, other chairs could not keep awake; that chair always kept awake—kept easily awake. That chair knew all the old lullabies, and all those worldless songs which mothers sing to their sick children—songs in which all pity and compassion and sympathetic influences are combined. That old chair has stopped rocking for a good many years. It may be set up in the loft or the garret, but it holds a queenly power yet. When at midnight you went into the store to get the intoxicating draught, did you not hear a voice that said, "My son, why go in there?" and a louder than the boisterous encore of the theatre, a voice saying, "My son, what are you doing here?" And when you went into the house of sin, a voice saying, "What would your mother do if she knew you were here?" And you were provoked at yourself, and you charged yourself with superstition and fanaticism, and your head got hot with your own thoughts, and you went home and you went to bed, and no sooner had you touched the

42

bed than a voice said, "What a prayerless pillow!" Man! What is the matter? This! You are too near your mother's rocking-chair. "Oh, pshaw!" you say, "there's nothing in that. I'm five hundred miles off from where I was born—and three thousand miles off from the Scotch kirk whose bell was the first music I ever heard." I cannot help that. You are too near your mother's rocking-chair. "Oh!" you say, "there can't be anything in that; that chair has been vacant a great while." I cannot help that. It is all the mightier for that; it is omnipotent, that vacant mother's chair. It whispers. It speaks. It weeps. It carols. It mourns. It prays. It warns. It thunders. A young man went off and broke his mother's heart, and while he was away from home his mother died, and the telegraph brought the son, and he came into the room where she lay, and looked upon her face, and cried out, "O mother, mother, what your life could not do your death shall effect. This moment I give my heart to God." And he kept his promise. Another victory for the vacant chair. With reference to your mother, the words of my text were fulfilled: "Thou shalt be missed because thy seat will be, empty."

Working and Waiting

n this busy world of crowding cares and multiplied labor, is there not danger, amid the general din, of forgetting, or partially ignoring, those aged ones to whom the evening of life is fast approaching? They have borne the noontide toil and heat, and now, at eventide, with tired, folded hands, they are waiting for the summons which shall open unto them a morning of eternal

day. But how often in quiet reverie, with dim eyes gazing out over the hills, does the heart of the watcher go back to the hours of her own youthful days when she, too, joined the busy workers and took no note of time! The bright, girlish days! How golden fair they gleam over the hills of memory! Then there come visions of days and nights of happy toil for her babes—sweet recollections of baby kisses and dimpled fingers. Where are the children now? Some gone into the land above, others toiling in her place in the busy world. Let us come nearer to those bowed with years and worn with life's struggle—the grandmothers left alone in their silent corners. Let us remember that their hearts are young yet, and that they long for a bit of merriment, the sound of youthful voices speaking tender, loving words to them, thrilling their hearts like chords of music. Gather around the old arm-chairs, speak cheerily to the waiting ones; tell them that they are still life's workers and the world is better for their presence. So you will make the gray twilight brighten into a sunset of light and hope, until the angels take their waiting spirits into a realm of eternal peace and rest.—*Anonymous*

Appeal to Mothers

Christian Treasury

re you a mother? Then your position is one of the most favorable on the face of the earth for carrying out this noble principle. Dignity and power are given to you; responsibility is laid upon you; for you are intrusted with dependent little immortals. They will rise up before you in the final judgement and testify either for you or against you in that great and solemn day, according to the use or abuse you now make of the important trust committed to your care.

Do you ever picture to yourself—you and your children meeting in eternity? Will it be a bright and glorious meeting—a whole family in heaven, never to part again—"fullness of joy, and pleasures forevermore? Oh mothers! Many feel that everlasting separation from their beloved children would be too overwhelming to contemplate.

The "voice" is directed at mothers to look at home, and examine themselves. A full conviction that they are naturally blind to self, yet full of self, must accompany a faithful self-examination. The mother of each home must take the hearts of her children into her own. Let your children see that their tears are your tears, and their pleasures are your pleasures.

A KISS from my mother made me a painter.—*Benjamin West*

A Mother's Love

James Mongomery

> A mother's love, how sweet the name!
>> What is a mother's love?
> A noble, pure, and tender flame,
>> Enkindled from above,
> To bless a heart of earthly mould;
>> The warmest love that can grow cold;
> This is a mother's love.

The Mother's Charge

Mrs. Lydia H. Sigourney

> And say to mothers what a holy charge
>> Is theirs; with what a kingly power their love
> Might rule the fountains of the new-born mind.
>> Warn them to wake at early dawn and sow
> Good seed, before the world has sown its tares.

Mother's Empire

H. H. Birkins

The queen that sits upon the throne of home, crowned and sceptered as none other ever can be, is mother. Her enthronement is complete, her reign unrivaled, and the moral issues of her empire are eternal. "Her children rise up, and call her blessed." Rebellious, at times, as the subjects of her government may be, she rules them with marvelous patience, winning tenderness and undying love. She so presents and exemplifies divine truth, that it reproduces itself in the happiest development of childhood—character and life.

Her memory is sacred, and becomes a perpetual inspiration, even when the bright flowers bloom above her sleeping dust. She is an incarnation of goodness to the child, and hence her immense power. Scotland, with her well-known reverence for motherhood, insists that "An ounce of mother is worth more than a pound of clergy."

Napoleon cherished a high conception of a mother's power, and believed that the mothers of the land could shape the destinies of his beloved France. Hence he said in his sententious, laconic style, "The great need of France is mothers."

The ancient orator bestowed a flattering compliment upon the homes of Roman mothers when he said, "The empire is at the fireside." Who can think of the influence that a mother wields in the home, and not be impressed with its far-reaching results? What revolutions would take place in our families and communities if that strange, magnetic power were fully consecrated to the welfare of the child and the glory of God.

There is one vision that never fades from the soul, and that is the vision of mother and of home. No man in all his weary wanderings ever goes out beyond the overshadowing arch of home. Let him stand on the surf-beaten coast of the Atlantic, or roam over western wilds, and every dash of the wave and murmur of the breeze will whisper, home, sweet home.

Set him down amid the glaciers of the North, and even there thoughts of home, too warm to be chilled by the eternal frosts, will float in upon him. Let him rove through the green, waving groves, and over the sunny slopes of the South, and in the smile of the soft skies, and in the kiss of the balmy breeze, home will live again.

John Randolph was once heard to say that only one thing saved him from atheism, and that was the tender remembrance of the hour when a devout mother, kneeling by his side, took his little hand in hers, and taught him to say "Our Father, who art in Heaven."

God hasten the time when our families, everywhere, shall catch the cry of childhood as it swells up over all the land, like the voice of God's own sweet evangel, calling the home—the home to enter the children's temple, and crowd its altars with fine offerings of sympathy and service.

Fathers, mothers, let the home go with your children to Jesus, let it go with them at every step, to cheer them in every struggle, until from the very crest of the cold wave that bears them from you forever, they shout back their joy over a home on earth, that helped them rise to a home in Heaven.

My Mother's Bible

Bishop Gilbert Haven

n one of the shelves in my library, surrounded by volumes of all kinds, on various subjects, and in various languages, stands an old book, in its plain covering of brown paper, unprepossessing to the eye, and apparently out of place among the more pretentious volumes that stand by its side. To the eye of a stranger it has certainly neither beauty nor comeliness. Its covers are worn. Its leaves marred by long use. Its pages, once white, have become yellow with age. Yet, old and worn as it is, to me it is the most beautiful and most valuable book on my shelves. No other awakens such associations, or so appeals to all that is best and noblest within me. It is, or rather it was, my mother's Bible—companion of her best and holiest hours and source of her unspeakable joy and consolation. From

it she derived the principles of a truly Christian life and character. It was the light to her feet and the lamp to her path. It was constantly by her side. As her steps tottered in the advancing pilgrimage of life, and her eyes grew dim with age, more and more precious to her became the well-worn pages.

One morning, just as the stars were fading into the dawn of the coming Sabbath, the aged pilgrim passed on beyond the stars and beyond the morning, and entered into the rest of the eternal Sabbath to look upon the face of Him of whom the law and the prophets had spoken, and whom, not having seen, she had loved. And now, no legacy is to me more precious than that old Bible. Years have passed, but it stands there on its shelf, eloquent as ever, witness of a beautiful life that is finished, and a silent monitor to the living. In hours of trial and sorrow it says, "Be not cast down, my son; for you shall yet praise Him who is the health of your countenance and your God." In moments of weakness and fear it says, "Be strong now, my son, and quit yourself manfully." When sometimes, from the cares and conflicts of external life, I come back to the study, weary of the world and tired of men—of men that are so hard and selfish, and a world that is so unfeeling—and the strings of the soul have become untuned and discordant, I seem to hear that Book saying, as with the well-remembered tones of a voice long silent, "Let not your heart be troubled. For what is your life? It is even as a vapor." Then my troubled spirit becomes calm, and the little world that had grown so great and so formidable sinks into its true place again. I am peaceful, I am strong.

There is no need to take down the volume from the shelf, or open it. A glance of the eye is sufficient. Memory and the law of association supply the rest. Yet there are occasions when it is otherwise; hours in life when some deeper grief has troubled the heart, some darker, heavier cloud is over the spirit and over the dwelling, and when it is a comfort to take down that old Bible and search its pages. Then, for a time, the latest editions, the original languages, the notes and commentaries, and all the critical apparatus which the scholar gathers around him for the study of the Scriptures are laid aside; and the plain old English Bible that was my mother's is taken from the shelf.

Maternal Instruction

John S. C. Abbott

o one else can possibly have the influence which a mother may possess, or the facilities which she enjoys. She knows the various dispositions of her children, their habits of thought, and their moods of mind. Therefore can she adapt instruction to their wants. She alone can improve the numberless occurrences which open the mind for instruction and give it susceptibility to religious impression. She is with them when they are in sickness or pain. She can take advantage of the calm of the morning and of the solemn stillness of the evening. In moments of sadness she can point their minds to brighter worlds and to more satisfying joys. God has conferred upon the mother advantages which no one else can possess. With these advantages he has connected responsibilities which cannot be laid aside or transferred to another. At home, and by the parents, the great duty of religious education must be faithfully performed. The quiet fireside is the most sacred sanctuary. Maternal affection is the most eloquent pleader and an obedient child is the most promising subject of religious impressions. Let mothers feel this as they ought and they will seldom see their children leave the paternal roof unfortified with Christian principles and sincere piety.

Consequences of Neglect

John S. C. Abbott

ou love your child. Your child loves you and cannot dream that you are abusing its confidence, and leading it in the paths of sin and destruction. How would it be shocked in being told that its mother is the cruel betrayer of its eternal happiness! You are wedded to the world. You have not given your heart to God. Not content with being the destroyer of your own soul, you must carry with you to the world of woe, the child who is loving you as its mother and its friend. O there is an aggravation of cruelty in this which cannot be described. One would think that every smile would disturb your peace; that every proof of affection would pierce your heart; that remorse would keep you awake at midnight and embitter every hour.

But here we see a mother leading her child, her own immortal child, far from God and peace, to the rebellion of worldliness and the storms of retribution. That little child following in your footsteps is the heir of eternity. It is to survive the lapse of all coming years; to emerge from the corruptions of the grave; to expand in spiritual existence, soaring in the angel's lofty flight, or groping in the demon's gloom. Thou, O mother, art its guide to immortality; to heaven's green pastures, or to despair's dreary wastes. If you go on in unrepented sin, your child, in all probability, will go with you.

It was not, mother, that I knew thy face:
　　The luminous eclipse that is on it now,
Though it was fair on earth, would have made it strange
Even to one who knew as well as he loved thee;
　　But my heart cried out in me, Mother!—*William Cowper*

Mother's Influence

John B. Gough

know myself the results of my own Sabbath-school instruction, and I remember the teachings of a praying mother. That mother taught me to pray in early life—gave me the habit of praying; the teacher at the Sabbath-school strengthened it; they stored my mind with passages of Scripture, and these things, I tell you, young man, we do not entirely forget. They may be buried, they may be laid away for a time in some obscure corner of the heart, but circumstances will show that we know much more than we thought. After that mother's death I went out into the world, exposed to its manifold temptations. I fell, and acquired bad habits. For seven years of my life I wandered over God's beautiful earth like an unblessed spirit wandering over a barren desert, digging deep wells to quench my thirst and bringing up the dry hot sand.

Bound with the fetters of evil habits, habits like an iron net encircling me in its folds—fascinated with my bondage, and yet with a desire, O how fervent, to stand where I once hoped to stand. "Ah," said one, "what is the effect of a mother's teaching, and a mother's prayers, of the Sunday-school, and of early good habits?"

O! I stood there, I remember it well, feeling my own weakness, and thinking that the way of the transgressor is hard; knowing that the wages of sin is death; feeling in the great depth of my heart all the bitterness that arises from the consciousness of powers wasted and opportunities lost; conscious that I had been chasing mere bubbles and gained nothing. There I stood. That mother had passed to heaven, but her words came back to my mind. I remember, when one night in our garret the candle was failing, that she said: "John, I am growing blind, and I don't mind it much. But you are young, it is hard for you. But never mind, John, where I am going there is no night. There is no need of any candle there. The Savior is the light thereof." She has changed the dark gloomy garret to bask in the sunshine of her Savior's smiles. But her influence was not lost. As I stood feeling my own weakness, knowing that I could not resist temptation, it seemed as if the very light she left as she passed had spanned the dark gap of seven years of sin and dissipation and struck the heart and opened it. I felt utterly my own weakness, and the passages of Scripture that were stored away in my mind came as if whispered again into my ear by the loving lips of that mother. Made strong by the recollection of her teaching and her prayers, I fled from the ways that lead down to death and was saved, saved through the influence of a mother's love.

ALL THAT I AM or hope to be I owe to my mother.—*Abraham Lincoln*

Maternal Influence

Sunday at Home

he mother of the Rev. John Newton, a pious woman of the south of England, died when he was but seven years old, leaving him only the memory of her religious teaching and goodness. At an early age he became a dissipated sailor. The memory of his mother brought him to himself and started a stream of incalculable influence. Through him Claudius Birchman was converted, who went as missionary to India. He wrote "The Star in the East," which led Adoniram Judson to become a missionary to India.

Newton was also the means of converting Thomas Scott, the commentator. Through his influence Cowper was rescued from despondency and his harp tuned to the key of religion. His influence upon the

55

career of Wilberforce is asserted, and the abolition of the slave trade was also one of its remote results. Wilberforce wrote "A Practical View of Christianity," a useful book, and the instrument of converting Leigh Richmond, the author of "The Dairyman's Daughter," which has saved thousands. Behind all this stands the faithful mother of John Newton.

The Mother of John Quincy Adams

Sunday at Home

he mother of John Quincy Adams brought to her routine domestic duties a wealth of love, a breadth of intellect, and a strength of moral purpose, such as has never been displayed by the Elizabeths or Catharines of history. When she died, in 1818, her illustrious son penned the following sketch of her character: "My mother was an angel upon earth. She was a minister of blessing to all human beings within her sphere of action. Her heart was the abode of heavenly purity. She had no feelings except of kindness and beneficence, yet her mind was as firm as her temper was mild and gentle. She had known sorrow, but her sorrow was silent. She had completed within less than a month her seventy-fourth year. Had she lived to the age of the patriarchs, every day of her life would have been filled with clouds of goodness and of love. She had been fifty-four years the delight of my father's heart. If there is existence and retribution beyond the grave, my mother is happy. But if virtue alone is happiness below, never was existence upon earth more blessed than hers. She was married at twenty, and had five children—three sons and two daughters. Two only of the sons have survived her. Her attention to the domestic economy of her family was unrivaled—rising with the dawn and superintending the household concerns with indefatigable and all-foreseeing care. She was an ardent patriot and the earliest lessons of unbounded devotion to the cause of their country that her children received, were from her. She was always cheerful and never frivolous. She had neither gall nor guile."

To a Bereaved Mother

John Quincy Adams

> Sure, to the mansions of the blest
>   When infant innocence ascends,
> Some angel, brighter than the rest,
>   The spotless spirit's flight attends.
>
> On wings of ecstasy they rise,
>   Beyond where worlds material roll,
> 'Till some fair sister of the skies
>   Receives the unpolluted soul.
>
> That inextinguishable beam,
>   With dust united at our birth,
> Sheds a more dim, discolored gleam
>   The more it lingers upon earth.
>
> But when the Lord of mortal breath
>   Decrees his bounty to resume,
> And points the silent shaft of death
>   Which speeds an infant to the tomb,
>
> No passion fierce, nor low desire
>   Has quenched the radiance of the flame

Back to its God, the living fire
    Reverts, unclouded as it came.

Fond mourner, be that solace thine!
    Let Hope her healing charm impart,
And soothe, with melodies divine,
    The anguish of a mother's heart.

Oh think! the darlings of thy love,
    Divested of this earthly clod,
Amid unnumbered saints, above,
    Bask in the bosom of their God.

O'er thee, with looks of love, they bend;
    For thee the Lord of life implore;
And oft from sainted bliss descend
    Thy wounded spirit to restore.

Then dry, henceforth, the bitter tear;
    Their part and thine inverted see;
Thou wert their guardian angel here,
    They guardian angels now to thee!

I BELIEVE I would have been swept away by the flood of infidelity, if it had not been for one thing—the remembrance of the time when my sainted mother used to make me kneel by her side, taking my little hands folded in hers, and caused me to repeat the Lord's Prayer.

        —*John Randolph*

Responsibility of Mothers

T. De Witt Talmage

hristian mother, a good many years ago, sat instructing a child in the knowledge of Christ. She had no idea that that child, young Lanphier, would come forth in time to establish the Fulton Street Prayer Meeting of New York—a meeting that has revolutionized the devotions of the whole earth. That Lanphier would stand in the presence of all nations as a consecrated man, known as the founder of such a prayer-meeting, his example thrilling the eternities. Yet, Lanphier says, his mother brought him to God.

Had his mother any idea that she was leading forth such tremendous destinies? Leading forth that one child, leading forth the eternal salvation of thousands? O that God would impress this upon every mother's soul—that she has in her hands tremendous destinies, whether she understands it or not, and in the great day of eternity will have to give an account of the manner in which she discharged her duty.

Who is that lad at Sutton Pool, Plymouth, England, with bare feet wading into the slime and slush of the village pond, until his foot strikes a piece of glass on the bottom of the pond, and the boy lifts his foot all bleeding and injured for life? That wound of the foot decides that his habits shall be sedentary, and decides that he shall spend his life as a student, and decides that it shall be John Kitto, who is to make one of the most wonderful Bible encyclopedias the world has ever seen, throwing more light on mysterious passages of Scripture than any other man of the century. Had his mother any idea of the great destiny of her boy?

O mother, mother! That little hand that wanders over your face sometimes, may yet hurl thunderbolts of war, drop a benediction on nations, or cry "forward!" to the host's of God as they rush on to their last victory.

Mother's Comfort

Elizabeth Prentiss

We never know, or begin to know, the great Heart that loves us best, till we throw ourselves upon it in the hour of our despair. Friends say and do all they can for us, but they do not know what we suffer or what we need. But Christ who formed, has penetrated the depths of the mother's heart. He pours in the oil that no human hand possesses, and "as one whom his mother comforteth, so will He comfort you."

Recollections of My Mother

Horace Greeley

My mother was a glad and easy learner of Scottish and Scotch-Irish traditions, songs, anecdotes, and shreds of history, which her grandmother freely imparted to her. Her schooling was better than that of most farmer's daughters in her day, and she naturally became a most omnivorous and retentive reader. Doubtless, there were many, whose literary acquisitions were more accurate and more profound than hers, but few can have been better qualified to interest or to stimulate the unfolding mind in its earliest stages of development.

I was for years a feeble, sickly child, often under medical treatment and unable to watch, through a closed window, the falling rain, without incurring an instant and violent attack of illness. Having suddenly lost her two former children, just before my birth, my mother was led to regard me even more fondly and tenderly than she otherwise might have done. I was her companion and confidant about as early as I could talk. Her abundant store of ballads, stories, anecdotes, and traditions was daily poured into my willing ears. I learned to read at her knee,—of course longer ago than I can remember, but I can faintly recollect her sitting spinning at her "little wheel," with the book in her lap when I was taking my daily lesson.

My Mother's Picture

William Cowper

O that those lips had language! Life has pass'd
    With me but roughly since I heard thee last,
Those lips are thine—thy own sweet smile I see,
    The same that oft in childhood solac'd me;
Voice only fails, else how distinct they say,
    "Grieve not, my child, chase all thy fears away!"
"The meek intelligence of those dear eyes,
    (Bless'd be the art that can immortalize,
The art that baffles Time's tyrannic claim
    To quench it,) here shines on me still the same.
Faithful remembrancer of one so dear,
    O welcome guest, though unexpected here!
Who bid'st me honor with an artless song,
    Affectionate, a mother lost so long
I will obey, not willingly alone,
    But gladly, as the precept were her own;

And, while that face renews my filial grief,
    Fancy shall weave a charm for my relief,
"Shall steep me in Elysian reverie,
    A momentary dream, that thou art she."

A Dying Child and Her Departed Mother

Henry Harbaugh

little girl, in the family of a friend, a lovely and precious child, lost her mother at an age too early to fix the loved features in her mind. She was beautiful, and as the bud of her heart unfolded it seemed won by her mother's prayers to turn instinctively heavenward. The sweet, conscientious, and prayer-loving child, was the idol of the bereaved family. But she faded away early. She would lie upon the lap of the friend who took a mother's kind care of her. Winding one wasted arm about her neck, the little girl would say, "Now tell me about my mamma!" And when the oft-told tale had been repeated, she would ask softly, "Take me into the parlor. I want to see my mamma!" The request was never refused, and the affectionate sick child would lie for hours, gazing on her mother's portrait.

Pale and wan she grew, and weakly—
Bearing all her pains so meekly,
That to them she still grew dearer
As the trial hour grew nearer.

That hour came at last, and the weeping neighbors assembled to see the child die. The dew of death was already on the flower, as its life-sun was going down. The little chest heaved faintly and spasmodically.

"Do you know me darling?" sobbed close in her ear, the voice that was dearest; but it awoke no answer. All at once a brightness as if from the upper world, burst over the child's colorless countenance. The eye-lids flashed open and the lips parted. The wan curdling hands flew up, in the little one's last impulsive effort, as she looked piercingly into the far above. "Mother!" she cried, with surprise and transport in her tone-and passed with that breath to her mother's bosom.

Said a distinguished divine who stood by that bed of joyous death, "If I had never believed in the ministration of departed ones before, I could not doubt it now."

"Peace I leave with you," said the wisest spirit that ever passed from earth to heaven. Let us be at "peace" amid the spirit-mysteries and questionings on which His eye soon shed the light of Eternity.

Jesus to His Mother

J. R. Miller

t was on the cross that Jesus paid his last tribute of love and honor to his mother. The nails were in his hands and feet and he hung there in agony. He was dying in deepest shame. The obloquy of the world was pouring its blackest tides upon his head. In the throng below, his eye fell on a little group of loving friends, and among them he saw his mother. Full as his heart was of its own anguish, it was not too full to give thought to her. She would have no protector now. The storms would beat in merciless fury upon her unsheltered head. Besides the bitterness of her bereavement there would be the shame she must endure on his account, the shame of being the mother of one who died on a cross. His heart felt all this, and there, in the midst of his own agony, he made provision for her, prepar-ing a home and shelter for her. Amid the dark scenes of the cross his example shines like a star in the bosom of the blackest clouds, saying to us, "Honor thy father and thy mother."

President Garfield's Mother

J. R. Miller

In all the story of the life of President Garfield there is no one incident that will be longer or more tenderly remembered than that little scene on the day of his inauguration, in which he showed such honor to his aged mother. When the last words were spoken and the ceremony was ended; when he was made President of this great nation, and when the greatest and noblest of the land were pressing forward to speak their applause—he turned away from all the cheers of a nation, from the salutations of the great, from the congratulations of foreign ambassadors who bore messages from kings and queens, to give the first thought of that supreme hour to a little aged and worn woman who sat behind him—encircling her with his strong arm and kissing her. It was she to whom he owed all that he was. In the days of poverty she had toiled and suffered for him. She had been both father and mother to him. She had struggled with adversity and had never spared herself that she might bless his early years. She was plain and poor and wrinkled and unfashionable, but she was his mother, and in that hour his loyal, manly heart honored her above all the world. President Garfield will be honored himself in all the future of our country. Honored for his noble character and his kingly rank among men. Honored for his achievements in the days of war and in the days of peace. Honored for the splendor of soul that shone out from his sick room in those long, weary days of death struggle. But in all the brilliant glory that flashes about his name no one record will shine more imperishably than the sentence that tells how in the moment of his supremest exaltation he bent and printed a kiss of recognition and honor on the wasted face of his mother.

"The Little Mother"

S. B. Shaw

She was a clear-eyed, fresh-cheeked little maiden, living on the banks of the great Mississippi, the oldest of four children, and mother's "little woman" always. They called her so because of her quiet, matronly care of the younger Mayfields—that was the father's name. Her own name was the beautiful one of Elizabeth, but they shortened it to Bess.

She was thirteen when one day Mr. Mayfield and his wife were called to the nearest town, six miles away. "Be mother's little woman, dear," said Mrs. Mayfield, as; she kissed the rosy face. Her husband added: "I leave the children in your care, Bess. Be a little mother to them."

Bess waved her old sun-bonnet vigorously, and held up the baby Rose, that she might watch them to the last. Old Daddy Jim and Mammy had been detailed by Mr. Mayfield to keep an unsuspected watch on the little nestlings, and were to sleep at the house. Thus two days went by, when Daddy Jim and Mammy begged to be allowed to go to their quarters, to see their daughter, Jinnie, who was suffering from a terrible toothache. They declared they would be back by evening, so Bess was willing. She put the little girls to bed, and persuaded Rob to go; then seated herself by the table with her mother's work-basket, in quaint imitation of Mrs. Mayfield's industry in the evening time. But what was this? Her feet touched something cold! She bent down and felt around with her hand. A pool of water was spreading over the floor. She knew what it was; the Mississippi had broken through the levee. What should she do? Mammy's stories of how houses had been washed away and broken in pieces, were in her mind. "Oh, if only I had a boat," she exclaimed, "but there isn't anything of the sort on the place." She ran wildly out to look for Mammy and stumbled over something sitting near the edge of the porch. A sudden inspiration took her. Here was her boat! A very large, old-fashioned, oblong tub. The water was now several inches deep on the porch, and she contrived to half-float, half-roll the tub into the room.

Without frightening the children she got them dressed in the  warmest clothes they had. She lined the oblong tub with a blanket, and made ready bread and cold meat left from supper. With Rob's assistance she dragged the tub upstairs. There was a single large window in the room, and they set the tub directly by it, so that when the water rose the tub would float out. There was no way for the children to reach the roof, which was a very steep, inclined one. It did not seem long before the water had very nearly risen to the top of the stairs leading from below.

Bess flung the window open, and made Rob get into their novel boat; then she lifted in Kate, and finally baby Rose, who began to cry, was given into Rob's arms, and now the little mother, taking the basket of food, made ready to enter too, but lo! There was no room for her with safety to the rest. Bess paused a moment, drew a long breath, and kissed the children quietly. She explained to Rob that he must guard the basket, and that they must sit still. "Goodbye, dears. Say a prayer for sister, Rob. If you ever see father and mother, tell them I took care of you." Then the water seized the insecure vessel, and out into the darkness it floated.

The next day Mr. Mayfield, who, with his neighbors, scoured the broad lake of eddying water that represented the Mississippi, discovered the tub lodged in the branches of a sycamore with the children weeping and chilled, but safe.

And Bess? Ah, where was Bess, the "little mother," who in that brief moment resigned herself to death? They found her later, floating on the water with her brave childish face turned to the sky; and as strong arms lifted her into the boat, the tears from every eye paid worthy tribute to the "little mother."

He Never Forgot His Mother

Mrs. A. G. Whittelsey

When James was ten years old his father died suddenly. His mother was left to provide for the aged mother of her husband, as well as her own little family, of whom the youngest was an infant of a few weeks old. This was a weary and toilsome task. Neither of her sons were old enough to render her any assistance on the farm, and the slender income arising from it would not warrant the expense of hiring needful laborers. She was obliged to lease it to others, and the rent of her little farm, together with the avails of their own industry, became the support of the widow and fatherless. With this she was still able to send her children to school, and to give them all the advantages which her retired dwelling allowed.

It was during these first years of his mother's lonely widowhood that the tenderness and the loveliness of her son's character were brought out to view. All that he could do to relieve her under her burden became his delight. Though but a child, he was ready to make every sacrifice to promote her comfort and happiness, and to gratify

and console his aged grandmother. Attention to his mother's wants from this time entered into all his plans of life. Her interests and welfare were a part of his constant thoughts. It seemed to be his highest earthly delight to increase her happiness and to relieve her trials. He never forgot his mother. He might be called "the boy who always loved his mother." Beautiful trait of character! And God blessed him in his own character and life, according to His promise. After he had gone from his native home to enter upon the business of life, this trait in his character was very constant and very remarkable. At a subsequent period, when his younger brother was about leaving home to learn a trade, James wrote to him, "Mother informs me that you intend learning a trade. I am very glad of it, because I know that it will be advantageous to you. But before you leave home, I hope you will endeavor to leave our dear mother and grandmother, and the rest of the family, as comfortable as possible. The desire of mother that I should come home and in some measure supply your place, I should not hesitate to comply with, had I not been strongly impressed with the idea that I could render more substantial help by remaining here than by coming home. But I hope before you leave home you will do everything you can for mother; and should you be near home, that you will often visit them, and afford them all the assistance in your power. You know, dear brother, that mother has had many hardships for our sakes. Well do I remember how she used to go out in cold, stormy weather, to help us with our work, in order to afford us the opportunity of attending school. May we live to enjoy the pleasure of having it in our power to return in some small degree the debt we owe her, by contributing to her comfort in the decline of life."

Then again he wrote to his sister, referring to his brother's absence: "I scarcely know how you will get along without him, as mother wrote me he was going to learn a trade this fall. You must try to do all you can

70

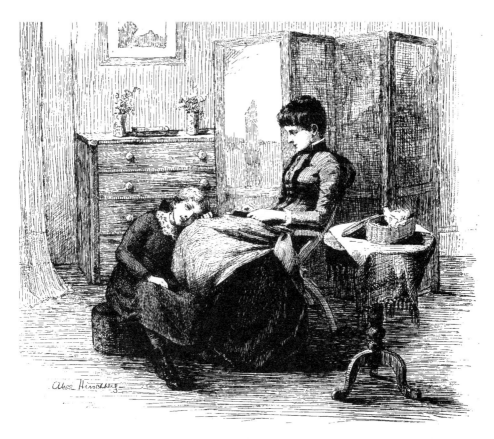

to help along. Think how much trouble and hardship mother has undergone for our sakes. Surely we are old enough to take some of the burden off her hands. I hope you will not neglect these hints. Never suffer mother to undergo any hardship of which you can relieve her. Strive to do all you can to lessen the cares and anxieties which must of necessity come upon her. Be kind, obedient, and cheerful in the performance of every duty. Consider it a pleasure to do anything by which you can render assistance to her."

To another sister he wrote, "I hope you will do all you can to con-

71

tribute to the assistance and comfort of grandmother and mother. You have it in your power to do much for them. Take care not to grieve them by folly or misconduct. If my influence will have any effect on your mind, think how much your brother wishes you to behave well, and to make yourself useful and beloved. But remember above all, that God always sees you, and that you never can be guilty of a fault that is not known to him. Strive when to be dutiful and obedient to our only remaining parent, and to be kind and affectionate to all around you."

These are beautiful exhibitions of his filial love. A remembrance of his mother's wants and sorrows was a constantly growing principle of his youthful heart. It was a spirit, too, which never forsook him through his whole subsequent life. Even while on his bed of death in Africa, his heart still yearned over the sorrows and cares of his widowed mother. Then he gave directions for the sale of his little earthly property that the avails of it might be sent back to America to his mother. Though the sum was small it was enough to contribute much to her comfort for her remaining years. How precious is such a recollection of a boy who never forgot, and never ceased to love his mother. What a beauty does this fact add to the character and conduct of a youth! How valuable is such a tribute to the memory of a youth, "He never forgot his mother!"

The Love of God

Mother's Gift

God is love—full of love. Put your arms about me, my darling child. Look up in my face! Do I not love you? Yes! And God loves my precious little child even better than I do. And everything you love, and everything you have, God gave to you. He gives you your dear papa and mamma, your brothers and sisters, your kind nurse, your food, your clothes. He gave you your life, too, for it was God who made you.

And then he is always watching you, and keeping you from harm. When I and nurse, and everybody are asleep at night, we can't watch you, but God does. And he watches you in the day when your little feet are running across the smooth lawn. And he fills your little heart with joy and gladness, till you laugh, and clap your hands, to hear the birds sing, and see everything about you that God has made, happy too—for "God is love."

Teach Your Children to Love

Jean Paul Richter

ou demonstrate your love to your child less by presents, than by the mother's language of love—by caressing words and looks. Love, in order to appear visibly and undisturbed, should be embodied in nothing but the tender mimicry bestowed by nature itself. A look, a tone of voice, expresses it immediately; but a gift only by the medium of translation.

Parents, teach your children how to love, then you will not find it necessary to enforce any ten commandments. Inculcate love, and your child will have a rich ever-gaining or acquiring life. Teach how to love now, in this cold world, which is the January of time. Teach how to love, so that you yourself, when your sight is old and your eyes are dim, may see around your invalid chair and death-bed, not the cold, greedy looks of your next heirs, but anxious weeping faces, who strive to kindle up the life that is growing cold, and illuminate the darkness of your last hours with gratitude for your former ones. Teach how to love.

To My Mother

Thomas Moore

> They tell us of an Indian tree,
> Which howsoe'er the sun and sky
> May tempt its boughs to wander free,
> And shoot, and blossom, wide and high,
>
> Far better loves to bend its arms
> Downward again to that dear earth,
> From which the life, that fills and warms
> Its grateful being, first had birth.
>
> 'Tis thus, though woo'd by flattering friends,
> And fed with fame (if fame it be),
> This heart, my own dear mother bends,
> With love's true instinct, back to thee.

The Mother's Work

Henry Ward Beecher

mother took alone the burden of life when her husband laid it down; without much property, out of her penury. By her planning and industry night and day, by her willfulness of love, by her fidelity, she brings up her children. Do not read to me the campaigns of Caesar and tell me nothing about Napoleon's wonderful exploits. For I tell you that, as God and the angels look down upon the silent history of that woman's administration, and upon those men-building processes which went on in her heart and mind through a score of years;—nothing exterior, no outward development of kingdoms, no empire-building, can compare with what mother has done. Nothing can compare in beauty, and wonder, and admirableness, and divinity itself, to the silent work in obscure dwellings of faithful women bringing their children to honor and virtue and piety.

My Mother's Bible

George P. Morris

This book is all that's left me now,—
    Tears will unbidden start,
With faltering lip and throbbing brow
    I press it to my heart.
For many generations past
    Here is our family tree;
My mother's hands this Bible clasped,
    She, dying, gave it me.

Ah! Well do I remember those
    Whose names these records bear;
Who round the hearthstone used to close,
    After the evening prayer,
And speak of what these pages said
    In tones my heart would thrill!
Though they are with the silent dead,
    Here are they living still!

My father read this holy book
    To brothers, sisters, dear;

How calm was my poor mother's look,
    Who loved God's Word to hear!
Her angel face,—I see it yet!
    What thronging memories come!
Again that little group is met
    Within the halls of home!

Thou truest friend man ever knew,
    Thy constancy I've tried;
When all were false, I found thee true,
    My counselor and guide.
The mines of earth no treasures give
    That could this volume buy;
In teaching me the way to live,
    It taught me how to die!

A Tender Mother

George Eliot

My childhood, perhaps, seems happier to me than it really was, by contrast with all the years following. For then the curtain of the future was as impenetrable to me as to other children. I had all their delight in the present hour, their sweet, indefinite hopes for the morrow, and I had a tender mother. Even now, after the dreary lapse of long years, a slight trace of sensation accompanies the remembrance of her caress as she held me on her knee—her arms round my little body, her check pressed on mine. I had a complaint of the eyes that made me blind for a little while, and she kept me on her knee from morning 'til night. That unequaled love soon vanished out of my life, and even to my childish consciousness it was as if that life had become more chill. I rode my little white pony with the groom by my side as before, but there was no loving eye looking at me as I mounted, no glad arms opened to me when I came back. Perhaps I missed my mother's love more than most children of seven or eight would have done, to whom the other pleasures of life remained as before; for I was certainly a very sensitive child.

The Young Mother

Mother's Magazine

ew thoughtful girls grow to be seventeen or eighteen years old without forming some theories as to the training of children. In reviewing their own lives they recall what seems to them to be a mistake in their own training—mistakes from which they feel that their characters have suffered; and they say to themselves, "When I have children, I will not make the mistake that my mother made with me. I know better than she does how children feel on this and that point, and I will enter into all my children's sorrows and temptations as no one has ever entered into mine."

Now, if the young girls who have these thoughts utter them to their friends—I do not mean their mothers, to whom, though most mistakenly, they would be rather diffident of speaking thus. They are likely to be met with a laugh of derision and the contemptuous remark, "It will be time enough to think of your children's training when you have them." But this is a great mistake. Your mother would not say so to you, nor would she be offended, as you fear, by hearing that you thought she had sometimes been mistaken in her treatment of you.

Every conscientious mother sees far more faults in her training of her children than the children themselves see. The difference is that she understands the difficulties of her task as the children do not, and she

would tell you, if you spoke with her about it, that you do well to prepare yourself beforehand by all earnest thought for so high and blessed a duty as that of being the mother of children. A teacher, an artist, an author, a dressmaker, prepares herself for her future calling by a long course of study and of thought.

There are few women, though they be not mothers themselves, who have not, sooner or later, some share in the training of a little child. So do not be deterred by any rude jest or want of sympathy, if you choose to train yourself for what, in one shape or another, will probably be the most important business of your life.

There is one consideration which makes it especially fit that you should not delay your preparation until the duty comes to you—this is that it is not what you say—not even what you do—but what you are, that influences others, and most especially children. It is not the beautiful clothes which the young mother may make for her child, nor the stories she may tell her, nor the hymns she may sing, nor the instruction she may give, which will influence this little one at her knee half as much as her tender sympathy in her child's emotions, her interest in her pursuits, her loving patience with her little faults. And all these must come from habits of the heart. They must be thorough—not something put on for the occasion.

A selfish mother may, from very selfishness, so love her child as to be all this to her, but she will not make her child unselfish, patient and sympathetic. It is the mother whose patience and charity for others' weaknesses are as broad as the circle of her influence, whose sympathy fails no human being who needs it, whose interest in others springs from that love to God which makes all whom He loves interesting—it is such a mother as this whose children grow like her in all noble virtues and gentle manners.

It is not an easy thing to be such a mother. You cannot begin too soon to try to be, from your very heart, all that which you would like to help your children, or any children committed to your training, to become.

The Mothers of Two Great Men

Christian Miscellany

enry Clay, the pride and honor of his country, always expressed feelings of profound affection and veneration for his mother. A habitual correspondence and enduring affection subsisted between them to the last hour of life. Mr. Clay ever spoke of her as a model of maternal character and female excellence, and it is said that he never met his constituents in Woodford county, after her death, without some allusion to her, which deeply affected both him and his audience. And nearly the last words uttered by this great statesman, when he came to die, were, "Mother, mother, mother." It is natural for us to feel that she must have been a good mother, that was loved and so dutifully served by such a boy, and that neither could have been wanting in rare virtues.

Benjamin Franklin was accustomed to refer to his mother in the tenderest tone of filial affection. His respect and affection for her were manifested, among other ways, in frequent presents, that contributed to her comfort and solace in her advancing years. In one of his letters to her, for example, he sends her a *moidore*, a gold piece of the value of six dollars, "toward chaise hire," said he, "that you may ride warm to meetings during the winter." In another he gives her an account of the growth and improvement of his son and daughter—topics which, as he well understood, are ever as dear to the grandmother as to the mother.

81

Washington Loved His Mother

Mother's Magazine

mmediately after the organization of the present government, General Washington went to Fredericksburg, to pay his humble duty to his mother, preparatory to his departure for New York. An affecting scene ensued. The son passionately remarked on the ravages which a torturing disease had made upon the aged frame of his mother, and thus addressed her:

"The people, madam, have been pleased, with the most flattering unanimity, to elect me to the chief magistracy of the United States; but before I can assume the functions of my office, I have come to bid you an affectionate farewell. So soon as the public business, which must necessarily be encountered in arranging a new government, can be disposed of, I shall hasten to Virginia, and"—

Here the matron interrupted him. "You will see me no more, my son. My great age, and the disease which is fast approaching my vitals, warn me that I shall not be long of this world. I trust in God, I am somewhat prepared for a better. But go, George, fulfill the high destinies which Heaven appears to have assigned you. Go my son, and may it be that Heaven's and your mother's blessing be with you always."

The president was deeply affected. His head rested upon the shoulder of his parent, whose aged arm feebly, yet fondly, encircled his neck. That brow on which fame had wreathed the purest laurel virtue ever gave to created man, relaxed from its lofty bearing. That look which could have awed a Roman senate in its Fabrician day, was bent in filial tenderness upon the time-worn features of the venerable matron.

The great man wept. A thousand recollections crowded upon his mind, as memory, retracing scenes long past, carried him back to the paternal mansion and the days of his youth, and there the center of attraction was his mother, whose care, instructions and discipline had prepared him to reach the topmost height of laudable ambition. Yet how were his glories forgotten while he gazed upon her, from whom, wasted by time and malady, he must soon part to meet no more!

The matron's predictions came true. The disease which had so long preyed upon her frame completed its triumph, and she expired at the age of eighty-five years, confiding in the promises of immortality to the humble believer.

Advice to Mothers

Celesta

Mothers, do not sacrifice too much for your children. It will have two bad effects. First, it will make them selfish, and then it will cause them to treat you with neglect. Do not be deceived into thinking that if you do a great deal for them, they will be grateful and do a great deal for you after awhile. "Train up a child, and when he is old he will not depart from the training." This is true, whether the training be good or bad. Whatever you train him to be, that he will be.

I knew a mother who denied herself almost every comfort that her son might get through college, and he repaid her by being ashamed of her old-fashioned dress and manners before his fashionable wife and friends, to whom he refused to introduce her. He was doing what he had been taught to do—considering his own feelings. His mother had taught him, by her acts, that hers were not to be taken into account. Now, do not cite Garfield and his mother, for his mother taught him to respect and obey her, and to be strong and deny himself. He was carefully taught not only to help himself, but others.

The woman who does not hold herself too cheap before her children, who requires them to hand her a chair, and get her a drink, and

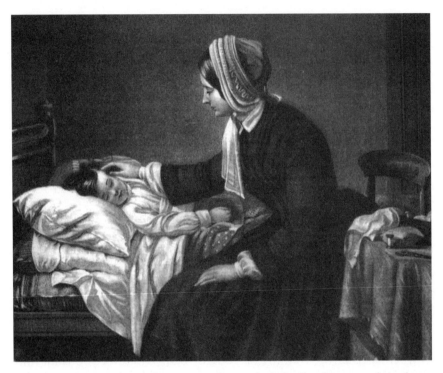

take her wraps when she comes from church, in short, makes them wait upon her, instead of her waiting upon them, is the woman who is treated with loving respect. If a mother is not a queen in her own house, she is to blame, and the chivalry that is in every boy's heart will lead him to pay extravagant devotion elsewhere. Many a mother is pained to see her son give all the loving attention to his wife. She wonders why he never waited upon her so. She does not think that the wife has always expected it, while she did not.

If your sons and daughters are grown, oh, mother, it is almost too late. Still, you might make some change. Work for them less, and get them to do more for on. Do not complain. Why should you? You alone are to blame, and oh, don't scold. Just pleasantly assert yourself. Tell them to take you visiting, ask them to read to you. If they refuse, don't scold or complain; just leave their clothes unironed or unmended, and go to see some friend or read. Now, don't threaten to do this. That would only arouse anger, but just do it. Be brave, and keep this treatment up for six months, and pay no attention to the astonishment and rebellion, you will be almost sure to meet at first, and the result will surprise you; but you must be firm and pleasant, or the plan will fail.

Maternity

Christian Miscellany

oman's charms are certainly many and powerful. The expanding rose, just bursting into beauty, has an irresistible bewitchingness. The blooming bride, led triumphantly to the hymeneal altar, awakens admiration and interest, and the blush of her cheek fills with delight. But the charm of maternity is more sublime than all these. Heaven has imprinted in the mother's face something beyond this world, something which claims kindred with the skies—the angelic smile, the tender look, the waking, watchful eye, which keeps its fond vigil over the slumbering babe.

A Righteous Mother Comforted

The Mother's Journal

t was Saturday night, and the widow of the pine cottage sat by her blazing fireside with her five tattered children at her side, endeavoring, by listening to the artlessness of their juvenile prattle, to dissipate the heavy gloom that pressed upon her mind. For a year her own feeble hands had provided for her helpless family, for she had no supporter. She thought of no friend in all the

85

wide, unfriendly world around. But that mysterious Providence, the wisdom of whose ways are above human comprehension, had visited her with wasting sickness, and her little means had become exhausted. It was now midwinter, and the snow lay heavy and deep through all the surrounding forests, while storms still seemed gathering in the heavens, and the driving wind roared amidst the bending pines, and rocked her puny mansion.

The last herring smoked upon the hearth before her. It was the only article of food she possessed, and no wonder her forlorn desolate state brought up in her lone bosom all the anxieties of a mother, when she looked upon her children. But forlorn as she was, she suffered the heart-swellings of despair to rise. She knew that He whose promise is to the widow and the orphan cannot forget his word. Many years before, her eldest son had left his forest home to try his fortune on the billowy wave. She had heard no note or tidings of him, and in latter times Providence had deprived her of the companion and staff of her worldly pilgrimage, in the person of her husband. Yet to this hour she had been upborne. She had not only been able to provide for her little flock, but had never lost an opportunity of ministering to the wants of the miserable and destitute.

The indolent may well bear with poverty while the ability to gain sustenance remains. The individual who has but his own wants to supply may suffer with fortitude the winter of want. His affections are not wounded, his heart not wrung. The most desolate in populous cities may hope, for charity has not quite closed her hand and heart, and shut her eyes on misery. But the industrious mother of helpless and depending children, far from the reach of human charity, has none of these to console her. And such a one was the widow of the pine cottage. As she bent over the fire and took up the last scanty remnant of food to spread before her children, her spirits seemed to brighten up, as by

some sudden and mysterious impulse, and Cowper's beautiful lines came uncalled across her mind:

Judge not the Lord by feeble sense, but trust him for his grace;
Behind a frowning providence He hides a smiling face.

The smoked herring was scarce laid upon the table, when a gentle rap at the door and loud barking of a dog attracted the attention of the family. The children flew to open it, and a weary traveler, in tattered garments, and apparently indifferent health, entered and begged a lodging and a mouthful of food. "It is now twenty-four hours since I tasted a morsel," he said. The widow's heart bled anew, as under a fresh complication of distress, for her sympathies lingered not round her fireside. She hesitated not, but offered rest and share of all she had to the stranger. "We shall not be forsaken," she said, "or suffer deeper for an act of charity."

The traveler drew near the board, but when he saw the scanty fare, he raised his eyes towards heaven with astonishment. "And this is all your store?" he said, "and a share of this do you offer to one you know not? Then never saw I charity before! But madam," he continued, "do you not wrong your children by giving a part of your last mouthful to a stranger?" "Ah," said the poor widow, with tear-drops gushing from her eyes as she said it, "I have a boy, a darling son, somewhere on the face of the wide world, unless heaven has taken him away, and I only act towards you as I would desire that others should act towards him. God, who sent manna from heaven, can provide for us as he did for Israel, and how should I this night offend Him, if my son should be a wanderer, destitute as you, and should have provided for him a home even poor as this, were, I to turn you unrelieved away!"

The widow ended, and the stranger, springing from his seat,

clasped her in his arms.

"God indeed has provided just such a home for your wandering son, and has given him wealth to reward the goodness of his benefactress. My mother! O my mother!"

It was her long-lost son, returned to her bosom from the Indies. He had chosen that disguise, that he might the more completely surprise his family. Never was surprise more perfect, or followed by a sweeter cup of joy. That humble residence in the forest was exchanged for one comfortable and beautiful in the valley. The widow lived long with her dutiful son in the enjoyment of worldly plenty and in the delightful employments of virtue. At this day, the passer-by is pointed to the luxuriant willow that spreads its branches broad and green above her grave, while he listens to the recital of this simple and homely, but not altogether worthless tale.

A Mother May Forget

Mary Winslow

h, how faintly do we realize the wondrous blessings that await us; the fullness of joy, and the pleasures that are at God's right hand! Would that we lived up to them! This passing world engrosses too much our thoughts and time, that we forget the Lord is caring for us, ordering all our concerns in such a way as that we need be anxious for nothing. All we have to do is to rest upon Him as little helpless children would do upon the tenderest mother. A mother may forget, yet He will never forget us!

I Love My Mother

"Aunt Mary"

I love My mother—oh how sweet!
    To hear her say, "Good night?"
When she has heard my little prayer,
    And fixed the bed-clothes right.
And when she says, "Good morning, dear,"
    And gives my lips a kiss,
With her lov'd hand upon my head,
    Oh! This is happiness.
But, when I think too much of play,
    And do not wash me clean,
And comb my hair without delay,
    No kiss I can obtain,
Or, when I've disobedient been,
    No sweet "good night" can hear,
Unless I'm sorry for my sin,
    In grieving mother dear.

My Grandmother

Mrs. S. B. Phelps

The aged saint lay upon her death-bed. She had passed all through the way of the wilderness and was now arrived at last upon the borders of the promised Canaan. She had been fed with manna during her journey, yet at times even that had almost seemed to fail. Then she would greatly fear that drought and thirst would consume her, and would gaze with failing eye upon the end and barren sands of the desert. Yet her strength quite departed, the hand of faith wielded the rod of prayer, till the water of life gushed into her soul. Sometimes grim phantoms of doubt and terror beset the traveler, striving to assure her that this path through the sterile wild would never terminate in a safe and tranquil passage over the deep Jordan, at its close. Alas for her! These lies were powerfully echoed by a hateful shadow that had haunted her faltering steps every moment of her way. It was a spectre of timid unbelief, slight and untangible to appearance, and yet of gigantic proportions and awful might. It was continually eclipsing the rays of the Sun of Righteousness, that would otherwise have shone upon her chilled spirit with vivifying warmth and cheering light. But this black envious phantom was ever coming between. Alas for her! When she should have smitten this midnight ghoul from her path, she far too often believed and encouraged him.

Yet, though sorely bewildered, her faith never utterly failed for lifting her eye, she beheld amid the thick vapors that overhung the river in the distance, the rainbow of promise in unfading splendor. Now and then a green gourd, whose pleasant shade had refreshed her, perished, yet she pressed on, knowing that on the other side of the river were greener fields and unfailing fountains. Her God had led her all the toilsome way, and now, as a shock of corn fully ripe, was she about to be gathered into the garner of the Lord. She had greatly feared the grim King of Terrors, and the thought of encountering his dark frown, and feeling his icy breath, had ever appalled her shrinking spirit. But this was when she viewed him in the obscure dusk of distance, for now as he approached, his scepter of horror gradually fell from his iron hand, until, as he at length reached her bedside, the fearful messenger of despair was transformed into a mild angel of mercy. She met him with a smile, which remained, after he had exerted all his power, as a sweet witness to her peace.

Yet now, while standing even at the opening gate of the New

Jerusalem, with "joys unutterable and full of glory," all ready to burst upon her redeemed spirit with the thought of beholding in peace Him who had purchased all these blessings for her at an unspeakable price; with the hope of joining the prophets, martyrs, and all the holy ones of old. Amid all this effulgence of light, all this affluence of glory, a soft ray of human affection, a sweet note of earthly music yet lingered around her heart. The child who, radiant in budding hope, had bounded around its fond grandparent, the bright day-gleam of her twilight years had been touched and laid in the earth. She knew that the soul of the infant had returned to its God, and the holy will of her King was done. Still the affections of the submissive saint yet clung to the little clay, and it grieved her to see it laid far away from her sight and care, to know that its sweet carol of joy should ring out no more upon her ear, or its gentle face be uplifted, wondering at her yearning tears. But now she had herself arrived at the brink of that very stream through which the babe had passed, and what lovely thought was busy at her failing heart-strings? "Perhaps the first angel who shall welcome me to Heaven, will be my little seraph, Rosalie."

That cord of natural affection had clustered around her spirit, till she was so near Paradise that its light had touched this love and enwreathed it in this beautiful thought with its own glories.

How charming is household tenderness, thus clinging, chastened, and made holy, around the believer with the bliss of heaven almost dawning on her gaze! What, a beam of light is kindred love, shining athwart the darkness of this chill world! What human heart, however wretched and degraded, that is wholly destitute of some vibrating chord which the tender hand of a dear relative might wake to long-forgotten harmonies! We would, and do even believe that we shall carry this "bliss of Paradise that has survived the fall," cleared of the shadows with which sin has been successful in dimming its luster with us through the portals of heaven, and be welcomed by the "spirits of the just made perfect," among our own kindred.

> *O! when a mother meets on high*
>   *The babe she lost in infancy,*
> *Hath she not then, for pains and fears,*
>   *The day of woe, the watchful night,*
> *For all her sorrow, all her tears,*
>   *An over-payment of delight?*

A MOTHER loses a child. It ever remains her child. It is only she that can be said to have a child, for she remembers it as it was.—*Charles Dickens*

Mother

Elizabeth Prentiss

> As I have seen a mother bend
>   With aching, bleeding heart,
> O'er lifeless limbs and lifeless face
>   So have I had to part
> With the sweet prattler at my knee,
>   The baby from my breast,
> And on the lips so cold in death,
>   Such farewell kisses pressed.
> If I should live a thousand years
>   Time's hand cannot efface,
> The features painted on my heart

95

Of each beloved face.
If I should bathe in endless seas
　　They could not wash away
The memory of these children's forms;
　　How fresh it is today.
Ah, how my grief has taught my heart
　　To feel another's woe!
With what a sympathetic pang
　　I watch the tear-drops flow!
Dear Jesus! Must Thou take our lambs,
　　Our cherished lambs away?
Thou hast so many, we so few
　　Canst Thou not let them stay?
Must the round limbs we love so well,
　　Grow stiff and cold in death?
Must all our loveliest flowerets fall
　　Before his icy breath?
Nay Lord, but it is hard, is hard
　　Oh, give us faith to see,
That grief, not joy, is best for us
　　Since it is sent by Thee.
And oh, by all our mortal pangs
　　Hear Thou the mother's plea—
Be gracious to the darling ones
　　We've given back to Thee.
Let them not miss the mother's love,
　　The mother's fond caress;
Gather them to Thy gentle breast
　　In faithful tenderness.
Oh lead them into pastures green,

And unto living springs;
Gather them in Thine arms, and shield
Beneath Thy blessed wings.
Ah, little reck we that we weep,
And wring our empty hands;
Blessed, thrice blessed are infant feet,
That walk Immanuel's lands!
Bless the souls that ne'er shall know
Of sin the mortal taint,
The hearts that ne'er shall swell with grief
Or utter a complaint!
Brief pangs for us, long joy for them
Thy holy Name we bless,
We could not give them up to Thee,
Lord, if we loved them less!

Sir Isaac Newton's Mother

Jabez Burns

ir Isaac Newton, the great, the learned, and the good; who followed in the track of his illustrious predecessor, Sir Francis Bacon, styled by Walpole, "the prophet of arts which Newton was afterward to reveal," was indebted to maternal solicitude for the development of that genius which has never since been surpassed, nor ever equaled.

Unlike Lord Bacon, however, Newton had no illustrious father to pave the way for his son's celebrity. He had no learned and accomplished mother to direct his infant mind to principles of science, at the time when it was most susceptible of imbibing him. He knew not the blessing even of a father's encouragement, for it was the fate of this

great philosopher to be a posthumous child, and so sickly and diminu-
tive was he at birth, that little hope was entertained of preserving his
life. But Newton, though not blessed with learned parents, possessed a
devout and Christian mother, whose sole aim and study was to sow the
seeds of piety and virtue in his mind, and whose tender care preserved
to us, under God's blessing, one destined to be the glory of his country, and his race.

Sir Isaac Newton was born in 1642, and about the time he attained
his fourth year his mother married, secondly, a clergyman, but she did
not permit this alliance to interfere with her duties to her son.

When the watchful attention of maternal love had strengthened his
feeble constitution, and her judicious instruction had invigorated the
dawning powers of his intellect, she sent him to school to be taught the
classics. But having given him such few scholastic advantages as she
considered sufficient for the inheritor of a small patrimony, she again
withdrew him to his home to be initiated into the management of a
farm, so that, like his ancestors, he might be devoted to a country life.
If not for the retirement thus afforded—a retirement so suited to fos-
ter the reflective powers of his expanding mind—Newton perhaps
might never have been led to those contemplative habits which afterward produced his immortal theory of universal gravitation. At the
insistance of his uncle, he had been previously removed to Cambridge
for mathematical instruction, yet the predisposition of the young
philosopher for metaphysics was encouraged, if not originally induced,
by that previous retirement, which was almost forced upon him by the
prudence and affection of his anxious mother.

Great, indeed, are the obligations of literature to the mother whose
untiring watchfulness in infancy preserved the life of so great a man,
and whose gentle sway allowed him in childhood perfect freedom of
thought and action, except in the one point peculiarly apportioned to

a mother's care, the task of inculcating the truths of our holy religion—a task never more beautifully illustrated than by its result. Sir Isaac Newton was not only a philosopher, but a Christian, and spent much of his time in meditating on the sacred Scriptures; nor could anything discompose his mind so much as light and irreverent expressions on the subject of religion. The illustrious son and the pious mother were equally worthy of each other.

Suzannah Wesley and Her Children

Jabez Burns

Mrs. Wesley was assiduous in teaching her children their duty to God and to their parents. She had nineteen children, most of whom lived to be educated. All these were educated by herself! Their times of going to bed, rising in the morning, dressing, eating, learning, and exercise, she managed by rule, which was never suffered to be broken. From her, Mr. John Wesley derived all that knowledge in the education of children which he has detailed so simply, and so successfully enforced. It has been considered that a man who had no children of his own, could not have known so well how they should be managed and educated—but wonder will at once cease when it is recollected who was his instructress in all things during his infancy and youth.

Mrs. Wesley had little difficulty in breaking the wills of her children. They were early brought, by rational means, under a mild yoke. They were obedient to their parents, and were taught to wait their decision in everything they were to have, and in everything they were to perform. They were taught to ask a blessing upon their food, to behave quietly at family prayers, and to reverence the Sabbath. They were never permitted to command the servants or use any words of author-

100

ity in their addresses to them.

Mrs. Wesley charged the servants to do nothing for any of the children, unless they asked it with humility and respect.

They were never permitted to contend with each other. Whatever difficulties arose, the parents decided, and their decision was never disputed. The consequence was, there were few misunderstandings among them, and no unbrotherly or vindictive passions. As a result, they had the common fame of being the most loving family in the county of Lincoln.

How much evil may be prevented, and how much good may be done, by judicious management in the education of children!

Mrs. Wesley has explained her own views and conduct in a letter, dated July 24th, 1732, part of which is here given. "In order to form the mind of children, the first thing to be done is to conquer their will, and bring them to an obedient temper. To inform the understanding is a work of time, and must, with children, proceed by slow degrees, as they are able to bear it. But the subjecting the will is a thing that must be done at once, and the sooner the better. By neglecting timely correction, they will correct a stubbornness and obstinacy which are hardly ever after conquered, and never without using such severity as would be as painful to me as to the child. In the esteem of the world, they pass for kind and indulgent, whom I call cruel parents; who permit their children to develop habits which they know must be afterward broken. When a child is corrected, it must be conquered, and this will be no hard matter to do, if it be not grown headstrong by too much indulgence. And when the will of a child is totally subdued, and it is brought to revere and stand in awe of its parents, then a great many childish follies and inadvertencies must be passed by—some should be overlooked, and taken no notice of, while others mildly reproved. But no sinful transgression ought ever to be forgiven children, without chastisement less or more, as the nature and circumstances of the offence may require. I insist upon conquering the will of children betimes, because this is the only strong and rational foundation of a religious education. Without this both precept and example will be ineffectual. But when this is thoroughly done, then a child is capable of being governed by the reason and piety of its parents, till its own understanding comes to maturity, and the principles of religion have taken root in the mind. I cannot yet dismiss this subject. As self-will is the root of all sin and misery, so whatever cherishes this in children, insures their after wretchedness and irreligion; whatever checks and mortifies it, promotes their future happiness and piety."

So wise, judicious, and affectionate a mother was worthy of those illustrious sainted sons [John and Charles], the influence of whose learning and piety will bless mankind to the latest posterity.

Richard Knill's Mother

Jabez Burns

have a vivid recollection of the effect of maternal influence. My honored mother was a religious woman who watched over and instructed me, as pious mothers are accustomed to do. Alas! I often forgot her admonitions, but in my most thoughtless days I never lost the impressions which her holy example had made on my mind.

After spending a large portion of my life in foreign lands, I returned again to visit my native village. Both my parents died while I was in Russia, and their house is now occupied by my brother. The furniture remained just the same as when I was a boy, and at night I was accommodated with the same bed in which I had often slept before. But my busy thoughts would not let me sleep. I was thinking how God had led

me through the journey of life. At last, the light of the morning darted through the little window, and then my eye caught sight of the spot where my sainted mother, forty years before, took me by the hand and said, "Come, my dear, kneel down with me, and I will go to prayer."

This completely overcame me. I seemed to hear the very tones of her voice—I recollected some of her expressions, and I burst into tears, and arose from my bed and fell upon my knees, just on the spot where my mother kneeled, and thanked God that I had once a praying mother. And, Oh! if every parent could feel what I felt then, I am sure they would pray with their children, as well as pray for them.

Christian mothers I think of this, and then think of the millions of your own sex who are the mere slaves of men who never pray. Remember, it is only where the Lord Jesus Christ is known and loved that women are exalted to their proper place in society.

The Mother of President Andrew Jackson

Jabez Burns

he deceased ex-president had no half-way character. He was known and read of all. He was a man to secure ardent friends and bitter enemies. He could disguise nothing. Simulation was a thing he abhorred as much by the instinct of his nature, as by the decision of his judgment.

In a conversation with the writer of this article, General Jackson spoke of his mother in a manner that convinced me that his mother never ceased to exert a secret power over him until his heart was brought into reconciliation with God. She had three sons, Hugh, Robert, and Andrew, the youngest, whose father died not long after his birth; and little prescient of the future fame of this poor boy, whom his mother, with the scanty patrimony, could scarcely educate. But he said that she inculcated religious truth upon his mind. The leading doctrines of the Bible were taught to him in the form of question and answer, as contained in the Westminster Catechism. In those truths, he expressed his decided belief. But their saving power does not seem to have been felt for more than half a century afterward. I think he was about seventy when he united with the church. Few of his friends will probably claim for him the possession of piety while he was the occupant of the Presidential chair; however much in such a perilous position its sovereign virtue is needed to guide the judgment, repress the ambition, chasten the language, and subdue the passions of the conspicuous incumbent of that coveted seat. In retirement, it was different. There he could reflect more deeply, feel more tenderly, and choose more deliberately. One can hardly help contrasting the cold and heartless sneers of Jefferson at the religion of Christ, with the full, warm, and enthusiastic expressions of Jackson, in the all-sufficient merits of the atoning Redeemer.

The old man was characteristic to the last. What ever he resolved to do, he was never ashamed of the Bible. He said, "Upon that sacred volume I rest my hope for eternal salvation, through the merits and the blood of our blessed Lord and Savior, Jesus Christ."

Maternal Influence of Philip Henry

Jabez Burns

he eminent servant of God, Philip Henry, was the son of a pious mother who "feared God above any." She looked well to the ways of her household, prayed with them daily, catechised her children and taught them the knowledge of the Lord. He often mentioned, with thankfulness to God, his great happiness in having such a mother, who was to him as Lois and Eunice were to Timothy, acquainting him with the Scriptures in his childhood. There appeared in him early inclinations both to learning and piety, so that his mother devoted him in his tender years to the service of God in the work of the ministry. This excellent mother died before her son was quite fourteen years old, but her influence over him remained throughout life, and was ever prompting him to be faithful unto death, that he might inherit the crown of everlasting life.

Maternal Influence

J. S. Law

Behold the tenderest sight on earth—the mother giving the first bent to the mind that is immortal. O! What lessons of heavenly wisdom may come down through her lips and find their way to a heart not yet in contact with the world! How may she seize on the first indications of intellect, and consecrate it to God. How may the eye of a mother, beaming with affectionate regard, direct the little dependent being to the Savior! A warm-hearted and prudent mother will exert almost an unlimited influence over her children the first six or eight years of their life; a period, above all others, when the heart is susceptible to deep and lasting impressions. Solomon frequently adverts, with great tenderness, to the pious counsels of a mother. Timothy was instructed, when a child, by his mother and grandmother. There are few men eminent for science and religion, who have not expressed deep-felt gratitude for the example, counsels, and prayers of a pious mother. And it would be difficult to find an instance in which children have been brought up in the fear of God, and the love of the Savior, where the mother has showed no marked solicitude to cherish a life of piety in her family.

OH, A MOTHER'S LOVE! It conquers all. It is identified in the mind of a child with its first knowledge of God. She is contemplated with God. Next to divine efficiency, her influence is all-pervading and most powerful.—*Mother's Magazine.*

A Sick Daughter to Her Mother

Mrs. Davidson

bout three weeks before Margaret's death, I found her in the parlor one morning, where she spent a portion of her time in retirement. I saw that she had been much agitated, and seemed weary. I seated myself by her and rested her head on my bosom, while I gently pressed my hand on her throbbing temples to soothe the agitation of her nerves. She kissed me again and again, and seemed as if she feared to trust her voice to speak lest her feelings should overcome her. As I returned her caress, she silently put a folded paper into my hands. I began to open it, when she gently laid her hand on mine, and said in a low, tremulous tone, "not now, dear mother!" I then led her back to her room, placed her upon the sofa, and retired to examine the paper. It contained the following lines:

TO MY MOTHER

O, mother! Would the power were mine
    To wake the strain then lov'st to hear,
And breathe each trembling, new-born thought,
    Within thy fondly listening ear;
As when, in days of health and glee,
    My hopes and fancies wandered free.
But, mother, now a shade has past
    Athwart my brightest visions here

A cloud of darkest gloom has wrapt
    The remnant of my brief career.
No song, no echo can I win,
    The sparkling fount has died within.
The torch of earthly hope burns dim,
    And fancy spreads her wings no more;
And, O, how vain and trivial seem
    The pleasures that I prized before.
My soul, with trembling steps and slow,
    Is struggling on through doubt and strife;
O, may it prove, as time rolls on,
    The pathway to eternal bliss
Then, when my cares and fears are o'er,
    I'll sing thee as in days of yore.
I said that hope had passed from earth;
    It was but to fold her wings in heaven;
To whisper of the soul's new birth,
    Of sinners saved, and sins forgiven.
When mine are washed in tears away,
    Then shall my spirit swell its lay.
When God shall guide my soul above,
    By the soft cords of heavenly love,
When the vain cares of earth depart,
    And tuneful voices swell my heart;
Then shall each word, each note I raise,
    Burst forth in pealing hymns of praise;
And all not offered at his shrine,
    Dear mother, I will place on thine.

It was long before I could regain sufficient composure to return to her.

When I did so I found her sweetly calm, and she greeted me with a smile so full of affection, that I shall cherish the recollection of its brightness until my latest breath. It was the last piece she ever wrote, except a parody of four lines on the hymn, 'I would not live alway,' which was written within the last week of her life.

A Good Daughter

Dr. Palfrey

good daughter! There are other ministers of love more conspicuous than her, but none in which a gentler, lovelier spirit dwells, and none to which her heart's warm requitals more joyfully respond. There is no such thing as a comparative estimate of a parent's love for one or another child. There is little which he needs to covet, to whom the treasure of a good child has been given. But a son's occupation and pleasures carry him abroad, and he resides more among temptations, which hardly permit affection that is following him, perhaps, over half the globe, to be unmingled with anxiety, until the time when he comes to relinquish the shelter of his father's roof for one of his own—while a good daughter is the steady light of her parent's house.

Her ideal is indissolubly connected with that of his happy fireside. She is his morning sunlight and evening star. The grace, vivacity, and tenderness of her sex have their place in the mighty sway which she holds over his spirit. The lessons of recorded wisdom which he reads with her eyes, come to his mind with a new charm, as blended with the beloved melody of her voice. He scarcely knows weariness which her son does not make him forget, or gloom which is proof against the young brightness of her smile. She is the pride and ornament of his hospitality, the gentle nurse of his sickness, and the constant agent in those nameless, numberless acts of kindness which one chiefly cares to have rendered because they are unpretending but expressive proofs of love. And then what a cheerful sharer she is and what an able lightener of her mother's cares! What an ever-present delight and triumph to a mother's affection.

Ah! How little do those daughters know of the powers God has committed to them, and the happiness God would have them enjoy, who do not, every time a parent's eye rests upon them, bring a rapture to a parent's heart. A true love will almost certainly always greet their approaching footsteps with expressions of delight. But their ambition should be not to have it a love merely which feelings implanted by nature excite, but one made intense and overflowing by approbation of worthy conduct. She is strangely blind to her own happiness, as well as undutiful to them to whom she owes most, in whom the perpetual appeals of parental disinterestedness do not call forth the prompt and fond echo of filial devotion.

HOME

"As for me and my house, we will serve the Lord."—Joshua 24:15

*"And these words which I command thee this day, shall be in
thine heart. And thou shalt teach them diligently unto thy children,
and thou shalt talk of them when thou sittest in thine house,
and when thou walkest by the way, and when thou liest down,
and when thou risest up."—Deuteronomy 6:6,7*

*"Children, obey your parents in the Lord: for this is right.
Honor your father and mother; which is the first commandment
with promise; that it may be well with thee, and thou mayest live
long on the earth. And, ye fathers, provoke not your children to wrath,
but bring them up in the nurture and admonition
of the Lord."—Ephesians 6:1-4*

*"The curse of the Lord is in the home of the wicked, but He blesseth
the habitation of the just."—Proverbs 3:33*

*"As arrows are in the hand of a mighty man; so are children of thy youth.
Happy is the man who has his quiver full of them."—Psalm 127:4-5*

*"Thy wife shall be as a fruitful vine by the sides of thine house:
thy children like olive plants round about thy table."—Psalm 128:3*

*"But if any widow has children or grandchildren, let them first
learn to show piety at home and to repay their parents:
for that is good and acceptable to the Lord."—1 Timothy 5:4*

*"Children's, children are the crown of old men: and the glory of
children are their fathers."—Proverbs 17:6*

*"The heart of her husband safely trusts her; so he will have no lack of gain.
She does him good and not evil all the days of her life."—Proverbs 31:11-12*

111

HAPPY FAMILY IN THE LORD

HOME?

BY FANNY J. CROSBY

'Tis whispered in the ear of God,
    'Tis murmured through our tears
'Tis linked with happy childhood days,
    And blessed in riper years.

That hallowed word is ne'er forgot,
    No matter where we roam,
The purest feelings of the heart,
    Still cluster round our home.

Dear resting-place, where weary thought,
    May dream away its care,
Love's gentle star unveils her light,
    And shines in beauty there.

Family Worship

Rev. V. A. Boardman

s it possible to conceive of a service better adapted than this to repress all jealousies and envies, to drive away the gloomy air of moroseness, to restore serenity to every clouded brow, refurnish the chain of affection, and diffuse an air of cheerfulness throughout the house? If there is a transient interruption of conjugal cordiality, can the coolness survive the family-prayer? If there are heart-burnings among the children, will they not dissolve like snow in the sun as the petition goes up, "Forgive us our trespasses as we forgive those who trespass against us?" If misfortune has come down upon them, will they not cling the more closely to each other as they pour their common sorrows into the ear of their common heavenly Father? If they are enriched with unlooked-for blessings, will they not feel them to be the more precious as they present their united thank-offering to the Giver of all good?

But I must not detain you with this animating theme. Let me rather invite you to prove for yourselves the efficacy of family worship as a help to domestic happiness. Let it be your first care to rear an altar to God, if your house is without one—to repair your altar, if it has fallen into misuse or decay.

And by this and every other means which God has placed within your reach, strive to prepare yourselves and those who are dearest to you for a better world. Give the Bible the place in your families to which it is entitled, and then, through the unsearchable riches of Christ, many a household among you may hereafter realize that most blessed consummation, and appear a whole family in heaven!—The Bible in the Family.

Parental Authority

Mother's Treasury

The very height of human wickedness is described in the Holy Book as "lawlessness." Subjection to the holy, just, and good law of the Most High God is the essential condition of well-being here, and the essential element of glory hereafter. In keeping with this, human beings come into this world in a state of dependence and subjection, and for about one-half of the average term of human life that is their proper and natural state.

I cannot doubt that the great idea of the long pupilage of man is just that the principle and habit of obedience, of submission to authority, may be wrought into his inmost nature. Being taught to obey an earthly parent, even from infancy, he may pass from subjection to the earthly father to subjection to the heavenly one. Reverent obedience of the child to parents is the preparation for reverent obedience of the man to God. The one is the steppingstone to the other. It is asked in the Epistle of John, "If a man love not his brother whom he hath seen, how can he love God whom he hath not seen?" In the same spirit and with at least equal emphasis it may be asked, "If a child honor not the father whom he hath seen, how shall he honor his Father whom he hath not seen?" There is rebellion against God in our inmost nature. Well, train up a child in willfulness and insubordination, and what must you expect as the result of nature's tendencies and such a training.

Law is everywhere. There is law in the Bible. There is law in our souls. There are laws written with a pen of iron upon our bodily frames. There are laws upon earth and sky—and to send forth from your home a lawless creature is to send forth a blind man to walk among pitfalls and precipices, to offer up an immortal nature to the god of misrule.

In a religious point of view it seems to me just of the last importance that the parent should exercise over his children a sovereign authority. There must be no permitted resistance to his will. Obedience must be the primary law of the family. Does this have a sound of harshness? But it is the Bible way! The confidence in regard to Abraham was that he would command his children after him. Children are bidden by the apostle to obey their parents. It is the essential requisite of a ruler in God's house that he should be able to rule in his own house, having his children in subjection. And authority is not tyranny. As the authority of God is not tyranny, neither is the authority of a parent, rightly used. If it is rightly used, it will be used under the feeling of tender love and affectionate interest. The children themselves will more and more come to feel that; and feeling it, to render willing and cheerful obedience to it. We parents should rule in love—in Christian love—*but we should rule!*

Parental authority, like all authority, needs a wise hand to wield it. There is needed especially great wisdom in the exercise of it, when the boy is passing into the man. At that stage of human life when you have the feeling of independence beginning to come—when you have so often the passions of manhood to deal with without manhood's checks and sense—no one can tell what the blessing is of having, say, a father to whom a son has been in the habit of looking with submissive reverence and who has the wisdom to use his influence aright.

But altogether, we may depend on it that there is nothing more ruinous than disobedience allowed in our little ones. I may even venture to say, that it is great cruelty and great sin in us to permit it, out of an indolent easiness of mind or an unwise softness of disposition. The parent is to rule in home, the world of childhood, as the Great Parent rules in the world, the home of manhood.

Care for the Soul

John Bunyan

implore you to take care of your soul. Mistrust your own strength; get down on your knees in prayer to the Lord, for the Spirit of truth; search His Word for direction; flee seducer's company; keep company with the soundest Christians that have the most experience in the things of Christ. Only, you must take care of two things: 1. Rely not on the outward obedience to any of God's commands, or of thinking you are better in the sight of God because of that. 2. Beware of searching for peace for your soul from any inherent righteousness. Believe that you are a sinner, so you are freely justified by the love of God, through the redemption that is in Christ Jesus; and that He has forgiven you of your transgressions—not because He saw anything done, or to be done, in or by you. This is the right way. Lord put you into it, and keep you in it!

The Family Gathering

William Sprague

We are all here!
Father, Mother, Sister, Brother,
All who hold each other dear.
Each chair is filled—we're all at home:
Tonight let no cold stranger come:
Our old familiar hearth we're found;
Bless, then, the gathering, the spot;
For once be every care forgot;
Let gentle Peace assert her power,
And kind affection rule the hour;
We're all—all here.

We are all here!
E'en they the dead—though dead, so dear;
    Fond memory, to her duty true,
Brings back their faded forms to view.
    How life-like, through the mist of
        years,
Each well-remembered face appears!
    We see them as in times long past,
From each to each kind looks are
        cast;
    We hear their words, their smiles
        behold,
They're round us as they were of old;
        We are all here!

We are all here!
Father, Mother, Sister, Brother,
    You that I love with love so dear,
This may not long of us be said;
    Soon must we join the gathered
        dead;
And by the hearth we now sit round,
    Some other circle will be found.
O! then, that wisdom may we know,
    Which yields a life of peace below;
So, in the world to follow this,
    May each repeat, in words of bliss,
        We're all—all here!

Increasing Love for Christ

Edward Payson

hristians seem to expect that their views of Christ and love to Him will increase without their using the proper means. They should select some scene in His life, and meditate long upon it, and strive to bring the circumstances before their minds, and imagine how he thought and felt at the time. At first, all will appear confused and indistinct; but let them continue to look steadily, and the mists will disappear, and their hearts will begin to burn with love to their Savior. At least one scene in Christ's life should be thus reviewed every day, if the Christian hopes to find his love to his Redeemer increase.

Hints to a Happy Home and Virtuous Family

V. T. Moore

1. Learn to govern yourselves, and to be gentle and patient.

2. Guard your tempers, especially in seasons of ill-health, irritation and trouble, and soften them by prayer, penitence, and a sense of your own short-comings and errors.

3. Never speak or act in anger, until you have prayed over your words or acts, and concluded that Christ would have done so in your place.

4. Remember that valuable as is the gift of speech, the gift of silence is often much more so.

5. Do not expect too much from others, but remember that all have an evil nature, whose development we must expect, and which we should forbear and forgive, as we often desire forbearance and forgiveness ourselves.

6. Never retort a sharp or angry word. It is the second word that

119

makes the quarrel.

7. Beware of the first disagreement.

8. Learn to speak in a gentle tone of voice.

9. Learn to say kind and pleasant things whenever an opportunity offers.

10. Study the character of each one, and sympathize with them in their troubles, however small.

11. Do not neglect little things, if they can affect the comfort of others in the smallest degree.

12. Avoid moods and pets, and fits of sulkiness.

13. Learn to deny yourself and to prefer others.

14. Beware of meddlers and tale-bearers.

15. Never charge a bad motive, if a good one is conceivable.

16. Be gentle, but firm, with children.

17. Do not allow your children to be away from home at night, without knowing where they are.

18. Do not allow them to go where they please on the Sabbath.

19. Do not furnish them much spending money.

20. Remember the grave, the judgment seat, and the scenes of eternity, and so order your home on earth that you shall have a home in heaven.

Comfort Out of Trouble

John Willison

While sorrows are afloat, turn them into a godly channel. It will be easier at such a time to employ them in mourning for sin. This brings comfort out of trouble; and makes sorrow, otherwise fruitless and hurtful, to be of use and service. Perhaps this is one intention of the providence. At least, it will be a wise and happy improvement of it. "Since I am so ready to burst into tears, I will weep part of them over a sinful life." This will make it a healing wound and a comforting sorrow, and at the same time give vent to nature and exercise to grace.

Masters of Families
William Jay

You ought to be concerned for your spiritual welfare. You ought to value that which has a tendency to restrain you from sin, and to excite you to holiness. Can he who is going to prayer with his family swear or be obscene? He will be on his guard, if it be only to preserve himself from the charge of hypocrisy.

If family worship was duly attended to, the public preaching of the Word would not long be the common method of conversion. We may observe that there is certainly enough to encourage the heads of families to exert themselves to this duty, and to condemn them if they do not.

Heart Religion
J. C. Ryle

We live in an age of peculiar spiritual danger. Never perhaps since the world began was there such an immense amount of mere outward profession of religion as there is in the present day. A painfully large proportion of all the congregations in the land consists of unconverted people, who know nothing if heart-religion, and never confess Christ in their daily lives. Myriads of those who are following preachers and crowding to hear sermons, are nothing better than empty tubs, and tinkling cymbals, without a jot of real

Christianity at home.

The lives of many professing believers, I fear, is nothing better than a continual course of spiritual drunkenness. They are often craving fresh excitement; and seem to care little what it is if they only get it. All preaching seems to come alike to them; and they appear unable to see differences, so long as they hear what is clever and have their ears tickled. Too many of these professors, alas, behave like young recruits who show how little deep root they have, and how little knowledge of their own hearts—by noise, forwardness, readiness to contradict and rebuke old Christians, and over-weaning trust in their own fancied soundness and new-found wisdom. Surely in times like these there is great need of self-examination.

Let me ask if you are trying to satisfy your conscience with a mere formal religion? There are myriads who are making shipwreck on this rock. Like the Pharisees of old, they make much of the outward Christianity, while the inward and spiritual part is totally neglected. They are careful to attend all the services of their place of worship. and are regular in using its forms and ordinances. They are often keen partisans of their own Church or congregation, and ready to contend with any who do not agree with them. Yet all this time there is no heart in their religion. Anyone who knows them intimately can see with half an eye that their affections are set on things below, not on things above; and they are trying to make up for the lack of inward Christianity by an excessive emphasis on the outward form. This formal religion does them no real good. They are not truly satisfied. Beginning at the wrong end, by making the outward things first, they know nothing of inward joy and peace, and pass their lives in a constant struggle, secretly conscious that there is something wrong, yet not knowing why. When professing Christians of this kind are so painfully numerous, no one need wonder if I press upon him the paramount importance of close self-examination. If you love life and Lord, do not be content with the husk, and shell of religion. Means of grace and forms of religion are useful in their ways, and God seldom does anything for His Church without them. But let us beware of making shipwreck on the very lighthouse which helps to show the channel into the harbor.

Let me ask, "do you know anything by experience of conversion to God? Without conversion there is no salvation. We are all by nature so weak, so worldly, so earthly-minded, so inclined to sin, that without a thorough change we cannot serve God in life, or enjoy Him after death. Sense of sin and deep hatred of it, faith in Christ and love to Him, delight in holiness and longing after more of it, love to God's people and distaste for the things of the world,—these are the signs and evidences which always accompany conversion.

Education of Children

Cotton Mather

otton Mather poured out continual prayers to God for his children, especially for spiritual blessings. It was his usual way to pray for each of them by name.

He entertained them at times with delightful stories, chiefly out of Scripture history, from which he would always draw some lessons of piety—where he endeavored to fix it upon their minds the meaning of the story. This was one part of the stated entertainment of his family table every day.

He endeavored to engage his children, very early, in exercises of piety and devotion; especially in secret prayer, for which he gave them plain directions. He often reminded them of this their duty, "Child, don't you forget everyday to go alone and pray, as I have directed you."

He endeavored also to form their tender minds into a temper of

123

kindness and beneficence, by putting them on doing kind services for one another and for other children, and he encouraged them and delighted in them when he saw them doing it. He made them to see that a backwardness of such acts of kindness and love was highly displeasing to him. He earnestly cautioned them against all manner of revenging injuries, and instructed them to return good for evil, showing them that they would become more holy and Christ-like. Therefore, he labored to form his children to sweetness of temper and an affectionate, gentle, obliging behavior.

As soon as his children had learned to write, he employed them in writing short lessons of piety and morals, to fix those lessons deeper in their memories.

At the same time, he endeavored to assure them of his love, and taught them to pay a becoming deference to his judgement. He labored also to convince them of the baseness and hatefulness of all sin, and the amiableness of virtue and goodness.

His usual method of correcting his children for their faults was very tender, and yet not less effectual. The first correction generally was to let the child see him in a perfect astonishment at its being guilty of such a thing, hardly believing it could be true—hoping, with this, the child would never do so again. For the child to be banished from its father's presence for some time, was ordinarily the heaviest punishment of all. And so his children were taught to consider their actions, and the joys or consequences which followed.

He endeavored, with all possible kind insinuations, to bring his children to a love of learning, and to make them consider it one of the noblest things in the world. He would have them think it a privilege to be taught; therefore, his refusing to teach them was the punishment which he sometimes inflicted for a fault. On the other hand, he led them to expect, as a reward for their doing well, that their father would teach them something that was curious and entertaining.

Above all other instructions, he labored most earnestly and diligently to acquaint his children with the sacred truths of religion, and deeply to impress a sense of it upon their minds. He often called them to remember their Creator, telling them that the eye of the great God was always upon them. He endeavored to recommend Christ to their love, and his example to their imitation, as a proper expression of their love to the blessed Jesus. He would particularly recommend to them the pattern of Christ's obedience to his Father's will in all things, which they should follow, in doing whatever their parents required of them. He often told them of the world to come, of judgement, heaven and hell, and the consequences of their good and bad behavior here. And when his children became capable of superior and advanced methods of instruction, he took them alone, one by one, and after many affectionate and solemn charges to fear God, to love Christ, and to hate sin, he would pray with them in his study, and make them witnesses of his strong cries and earnest wrestling with God on their behalf.

The Sabbath School

Asa Bullard

he happy results and extensive influence of Sabbath Schools can never be fully described, but enough is unfolded by recent history to commend them to the hearty approbation of every parent and to the redoubled efforts of all who would advance the interests of the rising generation.

Sabbath schools impart to the children and youth many useful hints upon the subjects of piety and good manners, which will be of great advantage to them as they pass along through the journey of life.

Sabbath schools materially aid children in their education. Often parents have acknowledged that their children have learned more to read by attending the Sabbath school.

Sabbath schools tend to make children more obedient to their parents, and aid in maintaining family government, for which parents often express their gratitude.

Sabbath schools are, through the power of Christ, raising up ministers of the Gospel and missionaries of the cross.

Sabbath schools are preparing many children and youth for heaven's eternal Sabbath school, where Jesus is the Teacher, and where He will unfold the mysteries of providence, the mysteries of redemption, and the glories of His perfections forever and ever.

The Happy Family

William Jay

pity the family where there is no one beloved of Jesus; no friend to attract the Savior's regard; no protector to stand in the breach and keep back invading judgements; no intercessor to draw down the blessing of heaven; no good example to reprove, encourage, and stimulate. What does an angel think when he passes by such an irreligious dwelling! It is a mercy to find even one pious individual in a house. And whoever that distinguished character be, I would say to him—Be thankful; be circumspect; remember every eye observes you; and every tongue is asking, "what do you more than others?" Labor to be the happy instrument of conversion of the rest.

SORROWS are often like clouds, which, though black when they are passing over us, when they are past become as if they were the garments of God, thrown off in purple and gold along the sky. —*H. W. Beecher.*

Not One Child to Spare

Mrs. Ethel L. Beers

A father and mother in straitened circumstances, with seven children, were offered by a wealthy, but childless neighbor, a comfortable provision, on condition that they would give him one of their children. This beautiful poem tells the result.

"Which shall it be? Which shall it be?"
    I looked at John—John looked at me,
(Dear, patient John, who loves me yet,
    As well as though my locks were jet),
And when I found that I must speak,
    My voice seemed strangely low and weak:
"Tell me again what Robert said!"
    And then I listening bent my head.
"This is his letter:— 'I will give
    A house and land where you shall live,
If, in return, from out your seven,
    One child to me for aye is given.'"
I looked at John's old garments worn,
    I thought of all that John bad borne
Of poverty, and work, and care,
    Which I, though willing, could not share;
I thought of seven mouths to feed,
    Of seven little children's need,
And then of this. "Come, John," said I,
    "We'll choose among them as they lie
Asleep;" so, walking hand in hand,
    Dear John and I surveyed our band—
First to the cradle lightly stepped,
    Where Lilian the baby slept.

A glory 'gainst the pillow white;
    Softly the father stooped to lay
His rough hand down in loving way,
    When dream or whisper made her stir,
And huskily he said: "Not her, not her."
    We stooped beside the trundle-bed,
And one long ray of lamplight shed
    Athwart the boyish faces there,
In sleep so pitiful and fair;
    I saw on Jamie's rough, red check,
A tear undried. Ere John could speak,
    "He's but a baby, too," said I,
And kissed him as we hurried by.
    Pale patient Robbie's angel face
Still in his sleep bore suffering's trace.
    "No, for a thousand crowns, not him,"
He whispered, while our eyes were dim.
    Poor Dick! Bad Dick! our wayward son,
Turbulent, reckless, idle one—
    Could be be spared? "Nay, He who gave
Bid us befriend him to his grave;
    Only a mother's heart can be
Patient enough for such as he;
    "And so," said John, "I would not dare
To send him from her bedside prayer."
    Then stole we softly up above
And knelt by Mary, child of love.
    "Perhaps for her 'twould better be,"
I said to John. Quite silently,
    He lifted up a curl that lay

Across her cheek in willful way,
> And shook his head, "Nay, love, not thee,"
The while my heart beat audibly.
> Only one more, our eldest lad,
Trusty and truthful, good and glad—
> So like his father. "No, John, no—
I can not, will not, let him go."
> And so we wrote, in courteous way,
We could not drive one child away;
> And afterward toil lighter seemed,
Thinking of that of which we dreamed.
> Happy in truth that not one face
Was missed from its accustomed place;
> Thankful to work for all the seven,
Trusting the rest to One in heaven!

Babies and Their Rights

Margaret E. Sangster

Baby has a right, too frequently denied it, to be left alone. It ought to be a rule in the nursery never to disturb the infant when it is happy and quiet. Older children as well—two, three, and four years of age, who are amusing themselves in a peaceful, contented way, ought not to be wantonly interfered with. I have often seen a little creature lying in its crib cooing and laughing to itself in the sweetest baby fashion, without a care in the world to vex its composure. Then in would come mamma, or nurse, seize it, cover it with endearments, and effectually break up its tranquillity. Then, the next

time, when these thoughtless people wanted it to be quiet, they were surprised that it refused to be so. It is habit and training which make little children restless and fretful, rather than natural disposition, in a multitude of cases. A healthy babe, coolly and loosely dressed, judiciously fed, and frequently bathed, will be good and comfortable if it does not have too much attention. But when it is liable a dozen times a day to be caught wildly up, bounced and jumped about, smothered with kisses, poked by facetious fingers, and petted till it is thoroughly out of sorts, what can be expected of it? How would fathers and mothers endure the martyrdom to which they allow the babies to be subjected?

Family Prayer

When the Rev. William Jay, of Bath, was but a boy, having heard a minister preach on the duty of family prayer, he told his father that if he did not lead the family in prayer, he must do it himself. He began this duty and then at sixteen commenced the ministry which was blessed by God for more than forty years.

Courtesies to Parents

Sunday School Times

arents lean upon their children, and especially their sons, much earlier than either of them imagine. Their love is a constant inspiration, a perennial fountain of delight, from which other lips may quiver and be comforted thereby. It may be that the mother has been left a widow, depending on her only son for support. He gives her a comfortable home, sees that she is well clad, and allows no debts to accumulate and that is all. It is considerable,

132

more even than many sons do, but there is a lack. He seldom thinks it worth while to give her a caress. He has forgotten all those affectionate ways that kept the wrinkles from her face, and make her look so much younger than her years. He is ready to put his hand in his pocket to gratify her slightest request, but to give of the abundance of his heart is another thing entirely. He loves his mother? Of course he does! Are there not proofs enough of his filial regard? Is he not continually making sacrifices for her benefit? What more could any reasonable woman ask?

Ah, but it is the mother's heart that craves an occasional kiss, the support of your youthful arm, the little attentions and kindly courtesies of life that smooth down so many of its asperities, and make the journey less wearisome. Material aid is good so far as it goes, but it has not that sustaining power which the loving, sympathetic heart bestows upon its object. You think she has out-grown these "weaknesses and follies," and is content with the crust that is left, but you are mistaken. Every little offer of attention, your escort to church or concert, or for a quiet walk, brings back the youth of her heart—her cheeks glow and her eyes sparkle with pleasure, and oh! how proud she is of her son!

Even the father, occupied and absorbed as he may be, is not wholly indifferent to these filial expressions of devoted love. He may pretend to care very little for them, but having faith in their sincerity, it would give him serious pain if they were entirely withheld. Fathers need their sons quite as much as the sons need their fathers, but in how many deplorable instances do they fail to find in them a staff for their declining years!

My son, are you a sweetener of life? You may disappoint the ambition of your parents; may be unable to distinguish yourself as they fondly hoped; may find your intellectual strength inadequate to your own desires, but let none of these things move you from a determination to be a son of whose moral character they need never be ashamed. Begin early to cultivate a habit of thoughtfulness and consideration for others, especially for those whom you are commanded to honor. Can you begrudge a few extra steps for the mother who never stopped to number those you demanded during your helpless infancy? Have you the heart to slight her requests, or treat her remarks with indifference, when you cannot begin to measure the patient devotion with which she bore with your peculiarities?

Anticipate her wants, invite her confidence, be prompt to offer assistance, express your affections as heartily as you did when a child, that the mother may never grieve in secret for the son she has lost.

Family Government

V. T. Moore

he oldest form of government on earth is that of the family, It existed before all others and was the source from which they originally sprung. The father became the patriarch, the chief or sheik, and thus the earliest governments had their origin. But the existence of other forms of government does not obviate the necessity for this one. It rather increases it; for without the proper government of the family, there can never be the proper government of the State. The tree of liberty has roots that twine themselves around every hearth stone, and according to the stability of the one, will be the permanence of the other.

The governing power of the family is lodged in the parents. "Honor thy father and mother," is the Divine law, and the duty to obey implies the right to command. The supreme, controlling authority, however, is vested in the husband and father. God has expressly vested the ultimate, supreme authority, where he has placed the physical strength to enforce it. "Thy desire shall be unto thy husband, and he shall rule over thee," was the original charter of this government. And the inspired comment upon it is, that "the husband is the head of the wife, even as Christ is head of the Church." This is the law of the relation, and they who dislike the law, should avoid the relation.

It is true that the wife may often be more capable of ruling than the husband, just as the private citizen may often be more capable of ruling than the civil magistrate, but to refuse obedience for this reason, in either case, would be absurd.

The authority of the husband is of course not unlimited, but restricted to the sphere of conjugal rights and duties. Should he require the wife or child to do what is morally wrong, he would be invading the sphere of God's authority, and those over whom he would attempt such an act, would be under no obligation to obey him. Hence there is nothing in this investiture of authority that is in the slightest, conflicting with right reason, or the best interests of society.

Although the authority of husband and wife is not co-equal, yet it should always be co-incident, and especially in the enactment and execution of the laws of the family. Every family should have rules, or it is an anarchy or a tyranny. These rules should be formed with care and consultation. As there may be too much legislation in the State, so there may be in the family; but in both, the greatest danger consists, not in undue so much as unsteady legislation. A few plain rules steadily enforced, will do more to secure order, than the most minute attention to trivial details. These rules should be the expression of the united will of the parents. If any discussion of them is demanded, it should never be in the presence of the children, for nothing will more certainly teach them to disregard and disobey, than to see a difference of opinion about the duties required of them. These rules should, as far as possible, be such as would commend themselves to the moral sense of the child, and convince him that they are based on principle rather than convenience.

The moment a child suspects selfishness in the heart of a parent in his government of him, the authority of the parent is weakened, and the respect and love of the child impaired. It is not necessary, or indeed wise, that in every case the child should understand the reason for the rules of the family, for he should be taught to regard the will of the parent as a sufficient reason. But this confidence in the decisions of the parental will must be greatly strengthened, by perceiving the propriety of these decisions, and hence as far as possible, the reasons for these family laws should be explained to the child. This will enlist both reason and conscience on the side of authority, and tend to secure more certain obedience.

It is here that failures in family government are most frequent and disastrous. The causes of these failures will be more fully presented, when we come to speak of the mistakes usually committed in family government. The laws of the family should be enforced, gently and kindly, and yet with inflexible firmness.

The grand agent in executing family laws, is love. This should manifest itself in words, looks, and tones, to be properly effective. The parent whose cold and repulsive manner represses all confiding familiarity in the child, is building a wall of ice between himself and his offspring, which even the warmth of love cannot penetrate. The child should be early taught to confide his feelings freely to his parents, by the open and loving manner of the parent, or he will seek companions elsewhere.

This executive love of the parental government should manifest itself in rewards and punishments. The honest, though mistaken, effort of the child to do right should be greeted with a smile and a kind word, and his faithful obedience to parental authority should be duly and

properly rewarded. It is not necessary nor proper to buy his obedience by rewards, but simply to enable him to feel that the path of duty is a path of pleasure, and this can be done only by a judicious system of rewards, highest among which he should learn to feel is the approving smile of his father and mother. The kindly glances of a parent has, in many other cases, determined the destiny of life.

But as long as the nature of man and the word of God remain what they are, it will likewise be true that the parent must also use punishment for disobedience and wrongdoing. There is a growing disposition to regard all punishment, and especially all corporeal punishment, as cruel, the relic of a barbaric age, and inconsistent with the benign era in which we live. It is true that some parents err on the side of harshness, that there are unwise and even cruel parents, and that the rod is often used because it is the easiest mode of punishment. But it is also true that God himself has said, that "foolishness is bound up in the heart of a child, and that the rod of correction will drive it far from him;" and that "the parent that spares the rod hates the child;" and we believe that the foolishness of God is wiser than man. It is not necessary that punishment should always be of the same kind, or that it should be administered for every offense; but to lay it aside entirely, and attempt to govern children by moral persuasion entirely, is a thing as futile and foolish in a family, as it would be in the State; and in the end will bring a far heavier punishment on both parent and child. The parent who lays aside the rod entirely, only puts it into the hand of the child, and will usually pay the penalty of his perilous experiment in the ingratitude and disobedience of those who have been ruined by a fond and foolish indulgence.

The want of proper family government is one of the most serious evils of our land. The growing amount of juvenile depravity in our towns and cities is owing, in great measure, to the want of family discipline and control.

No parent governs their family aright, who allow their children to be absent from home at night or on the Sabbath without knowing where they are, and with what companions. To do this, however, implies previous control and discipline in the early stages of childhood, without which the task will be hopeless. Obedience is the fundamental and primary virtue of childhood; for if a child be obedient, the parent can fashion it (so far as human power goes) to any mold he chooses, as the potter fashions the clay. But obedience is the effect only of family government.

We urge this matter of family government, because the evils of its neglect are manifold and spreading. Why are there so many complaints about the education of children, and difficulty in securing certain improvement? Chiefly because of the neglect of family government. Children that are never taught to obey at home, will not be likely to obey at school; and a disobedient child cannot be a successful scholar.

Unless the parent requires the child to respect his commands when young, he will fail to respect his opinion when older; and if allowed to do as he pleases in childhood, he is not likely to please his parents in later life. But the perception of the evil may be more easy than discovery or application of the remedy. That remedy will be found in correcting the errors into which parents fall in family government, and training their children first to obedience in general, and then to obedience to what is right.

There are many parents who cannot punish their children, except when angry, and hence who never punish them properly. Even a heathen master would not correct his servant when he was angry, how much more then should a Christian parent avoid such an error? It is much less painful to the parent to chastise in anger, but it is much more likely to sour and provoke the child. Anger rises to meet anger, and the conquest is one of physical force merely. The child is subdued, not softened; punished, but not profited. One chastisement of calm deliberate duty, though in tears of pain to the parent, will do more good than a dozen outbursts of angry excitement.

Many choose the easiest mode of punishment, rather than that most adapted to the nature of the offense, or the nature of the child. This error leads many to resort to the rod as the quickest and easiest mode of punishing, instead of reserving it for an ultimate appeal, and using other modes of punishment, more troublesome, but often more effectual. Susceptibility to bodily pain, is not the only susceptibility to which punishment can appeal.

Many parents think it cruel to restrain a young child, deeming it too young to control, until it can be reasoned with. But this is a cruelty far more refined for it lays up a thousand pangs for the little offender, when one at the proper time would have sufficed. A single touch would break off the budding of evil, which, if allowed to grow, will demand many a stroke and wrench for its removal. As soon as a child can understand the meaning of a refusal, it is old enough to learn the first and last lesson of family discipline—submission to parents. And this occurs in all that are not hopelessly stupid, long before they can speak. A quiet, gentle, but firm restraint of the little struggler in the arms of his mother, will save many a painful scene in later life. Character begins to form as soon as the will begins to act, and the will should be controlled as soon as the child can understand a refusal, which with children of ordinary good sense, will be within the first nine months of life.

There are many minor faults in childhood that are like the branches and sprays from a large bough, all of which will be removed by the removal of the main stem. To be continually fretting and harping at these secondary faults, while the primary causes of heedlessness, waywardness or wilfulness are neglected, is like dipping out the stream and neglecting the fountain. It is an error to use too many words in governing. Instruction demands many words, government few; and these few connected closely with prompt, decisive acts, or they will be mere empty air. A fussy, scolding parent will usually have a careless, disobedient family.

It is difficult for any parent, but especially for those of variable temperament and health, to preserve that uniform bearing toward their children that is requisite. But special effort should be made to do so, for to allow a child today to do and say things, or to overcome us by pleading, when tomorrow, because of a change of humor, we will punish and rebuke such liberties, is to injure all good government.

There are but two courses for every parent to take. One with Abraham of whom it was said that he would command his children and his household after him, and that for this reason he should be peculiarly favored; the other, with Eli, whose sons made themselves vile, and he restrained them not, and that for this reason his household should be judged forever, and his descendants should die before they had reached the flower of their age, or live only to beg bread. And as surely as the duty to obey involves the duty to command, so surely the curse (implied in the blessing appended to the first commandment with promise) shall recoil on those parents who allow their children to break this command, by neglecting to control and govern them. To fail in family government is to be accessory to a breach of the fifth commandment, and this command cannot be broken by either parent or child with impunity. If juvenile depravity is to be thoroughly corrected, we must begin the task by restoring family government.

The Husband's Part

J. R. Miller

ach member of the household has a part in the family life, and the fullest happiness and blessedness of the home can be attained only when each one's part is faithfully fulfilled. If any one member of the family fails in love or duty, the failure affects the whole household life, just as one discordant voice in a company of singers spoils the music.

The husband has a part all his own, which no other can do. How does the Word of God define his duties? What is involved in his part in the marriage relation? What does he owe his wife? One word covers it all—LOVE. "Husbands, love your wives," comes the command with all divine authority. This counsel is short, but becomes exceedingly long when it is fully accepted and observed.

What are some of the things embraced in a husband's love?

One is *fondness, affectionate regard*. When a man offers his hand in marriage to a woman he says by his act that his heart has made a choice of her among all women, that he has for her a deeper affection than for any other. At the marriage altar he solemnly pledges to her a continuance of that love until death. When the beauty has faded from her face and the luster from her eyes; when old age has brought wrinkles, or when sickness or sorrow has left its marks; the faithful husband's love is to remain deep and true as ever. His heart is still to find its truest delight in her.

But the Word implies more than mere emotional fondness. The Scriptures give the measure of the love which husbands are to bear to their wives; "Husbands, love your wives even as Christ loved the Church and gave Himself for it." In the true husband who realizes all that this divine command involves, selfishness dies at the marriage altar. He thinks no longer of his own comfort, but of his wife's. He

143

denies himself that he may bring new pleasures and comforts to her. He counts no sacrifice too great to be made which will bring benefit to her.

The wife yields all up to the husband, gives herself in the fullest sense. Will he be faithful in the holy trust reposed in his hands? Will he cherish her happiness as a precious jewel, bearing all things, enduring all things, for her sake. Will he seek her highest good, help her to build up in herself the noblest womanhood? Is he worthy to receive into his keeping all that her confiding love lays at his feet?

Every husband should understand that when a woman, the woman of his own free and deliberate choice, places her hand in his and thus becomes his wife, she has taken her life, with all its hopes and fears, all its possibilities of joy or sorrow, all its capacity for development, all its tender and sacred interests, and placed it in his hand. He is then under the most solemn obligation to do all in his power to make her life happy, noble and blessed. To do this he must be ready to make any personal sacrifice. Nothing less can be implied in "loving as Christ loved the Church and gave Himself for it."

This love implies the utmost gentleness in manner. One may be very faithful and true and yet lack that affectionateness in speech and act which has such power to satisfy the heart. Scripture admonishes husbands to love their wives and be not bitter against them. The teaching is that all bitterness should be suppressed in the very workings of the heart and changed into sweetness.

The spirit of love requires a husband to honor his wife. He honored her before she was his wife. He saw in her his ideal of all that was noble, lovely and queenly. He showed her every mark of honor of which his soul was capable. Now that he has lifted her up to the throne of his heart, will he honor her less? Not less, but more and ever more, if he be a true husband and a manly man. He has taken her now into the closest and holiest relation on earth. He has linked her life with his own, so that henceforward whatever affects one affects both. If one is exalted, the other is exalted; if one is dishonored the other is debased. There is definitely more reason why he should honor her now than before she was his wife.

The ways in which he should show her honor are countless. He will do it by providing for her wants on as generous a scale as his position and his means will justify. He will do it by making her the sharer of all his life. He will counsel with her about his business, advise with her concerning every new plan and confide to her at every point the results of his undertakings. A wife to him is not a child. When he chose her to be his wife he believed her to be worthy.

When a man has taken a woman to be his wife, he has linked her life with his own in the closest of all earthly relations. Whatever concerns him also concerns her. He has no interests which are not hers as well as his. He should, therefore, make her the sharer of all his life. She should know of all his successes and triumphs and to be permitted to rejoice with him in his gladness. If trials come, she should know also of these, that she may sympathize with him, encourage and help him in his struggles and stand close beside him when the shadows rest upon him. They have linked their lives together, "for better or for worse," and they should share the pains as well as the pleasures that come to either of them. A true wife is not a child; she is a woman, and should be treated as a woman.

Every true-hearted husband should seek to be worthy of the wife he has already won. For her sake he should reach out after the noblest achievements and strive to attain the loftiest heights of character. To her he is the ideal of all that is manly, and he should seek to become every day more worthy of the homage she pays to him. Every possibility in his soul should be developed. Every latent power and energy of his life should be brought out. His hand should be trained under love's inspiration to do its most skillful work. Every fault in his character should be eradicated, every evil habit conquered, and every hidden beauty of soul should burst into fragrant bloom for her sake. She looks to him as her ideal of manhood, and he must see to it that the ideal is not marred—that he never falls by any unworthy act of his own from the high pedestal in her heart to which she has raised him.

Every husband of a Christian wife should walk with her in common love for Christ. There are some husbands, however, who fail in this. They love their wives very sincerely, and make sacrifices for their sake. They carefully shelter them from life's rude blasts. They bless them with all tenderness and affection. They honor them very highly, bringing many noble achievements to lay at their feet, and show them all homage and respect. They do everything that love can suggest to make their earthly happiness full and complete. They share every burden and walk close beside them in every trial. But when these husbands come to the matter of personal religion and eternal realities, they draw back and leave them to go on alone. While the wife goes on in the sanctuary to worship, the husband waits without. At the very point where his interest in her life should be the deepest it fails altogether.

Surely, it is a great wrong to a woman, tender and dependent, to leave her to walk alone through this world in her deepest life, receiving no sympathy, no companionship, no support, from him who is her dearest friend. She must leave him outside of the most sacred part of her life. She must be silent to him concerning the experiences of her soul in its spiritual struggles, aspirations, yearnings, and hopes. She must bear alone the responsibility of the children's religious nurture and training. Alone she must bow to God in prayer.

It cannot be right that a husband should leave his wife to live such

146

a large part of her life without his companionship and sympathy. His love should seek to enter with her into every sacred experience. In no other way could he give her such joy as by taking his place beside her as a fellow heir of the same grace. It would lighten every burden, since he would now share it with her. It would bring new radiance to her face, new peace to her heart, new zest to all life for her. It would make their marriage more perfect and unite their hearts in a closer union, since it is only those who realize the full sweetness of wedded life who are one at every point and in every feeling, purpose and hope, and whose souls blend in their higher, spiritual part as well as in their lower nature and experiences. Then it would also introduce the husband himself to sources of blessing and strength of which he has never known before; for the religion of Christ is a reality and brings the soul into communication with God and with infinite springs of comfort, help and blessing. In sharing her life of faith and prayer and devotion to Christ, he would find his own life linked to heaven.

United, then, on earth in a common faith in Christ, their mutual love mingling and blending in the love of God, they shall be united also in heaven in eternal fellowship! Why should hearts spend years on earth in growing into one, knitting life to life, blending soul in soul, for a union that is not to reach beyond the valley of shadows? Why not weave for all eternity?

The Wife's Part

J. R. Miller

It is a high honor for a woman to be chosen from among all womankind to be the wife of a good and true man. She is lifted up to be a crowned queen. Her husband's manly love laid at her feet exalts her to the throne of his life. Great power is placed in her hands. Sacred destinies are reposed in her keeping. Will she wear her crown beneficently? Will she fill her realm with beauty and with blessing? Or will she fail in her holy trust? Only her married life can be the answer.

A woman may well pause before she gives her hand in marriage, and inquire whether he is worthy to whom she is asked to surrender so much; whether he can bring true happiness to her life; whether he can meet the cravings of her nature for love and for companionship; whether he is worthy to be lifted to the highest place in her heart and honored as a husband should be honored.

But the question should be turned and asked from the other side. Can she be a true wife to him who asks for her hand? Is she worthy of the love that is laid at her feet? Can she be a blessing to the life of him who would lift her to the throne of his heart? Will he find in her all the beauty, all the tender loveliness, all the rich qualities of nature, all the deep sympathy and companionship, all the strengthful, uplifting love, all the sources of joy and help, which he seems now to see in her? Is there any possible future for him which she could not share? Are there

needs in his soul, or hungers, which she cannot answer? Are there chords in his life which her fingers cannot wake?

The true wife needs to be no mere poet's dream, no artist's picture, no ethereal lady too fine for use, but a woman healthful, strong, practical, industrious, with a hand for life's common duties, yet crowned with that beauty which a high and noble purpose gives to a soul.

One of the first essential elements in a wife is faithfulness, too, in the largest sense. "The heart of her husband doth safely trust in her." Perfect confidence is the basis of all true affection. A shadow of doubt destroys the peace of married life. A true wife by her character and by her conduct proves herself worthy of her husband's trust. He has confidence in her affection; he knows that her heart is unalterably true to him. He has confidence in her management, and he confides to her the care of his household. He knows that she is true to all his interests—that she is prudent and wise, not wasteful nor extravagant. It is one of the essential things in a true wife that her husband shall be able to leave in her hands the management of all domestic affairs, and know that they are safe. Wifely thriftlessness and extravagance have destroyed the happiness of many a household and wrecked many a home. On the other hand, many a man owes his prosperity to his wife's prudence and her wise administration of household affairs.

A true wife makes a man's life nobler, stronger, grander, by the omnipotence of her love, "turning all the forces of manhood upward and heavenward." She inspires him with courage and earnestness. She beautifies his life. She softens whatever is rude and harsh in his habits or his spirit. She clothes him with the gentler graces of refined and cultured manhood. While she yields to him and never disregards his lightest wish, she is really his queen, ruling his whole life and leading him onward and upward in every proper path.

The true wife clings and leans, but she also helps and inspires. Her husband feels the mighty inspiration of her love in all his life. Toil is easier, burdens are lighter, battles are less fierce, because of the face that waits in the quiet of the home, because of the heart that beats in loving sympathy whatever the experience, because of the voice that speaks its words of cheer and encouragement when the day's work is done. No wife knows how much she can do to make her husband honored among men, and his life a power and a success, by her loyal faithfulness, by the active inspiration of her own sweet life.

The good wife is a good housekeeper. I know well how unromantic this remark will appear to those whose dreams of married life are woven of the fancies of youthful sentiment; but these frail dreams of sentiment will not last long amid the stern realities of life, and then that which will prove one of the rarest elements of happiness and blessing in the household will be housewifely industry and diligence.

The newly married are not long within their own doors before they find that something more than tender sentiment is needed to make their home life a success. They come down from the clouds when the daily routine begins and touch the common soil on which the feet of other mortals walk. There certainly have been cases in which very tender love has lost its tenderness and when the cause lay in the disorder and mismanagement of the housewifery. There is no doubt that many a heart-estrangement begins at the table where meals are unpunctual and food is poorly prepared or served. Bad housekeeping will soon drive the last vestige of romance out of any home. The illusion which love weaves about an idolized bride will soon vanish if she proves incompetent in her domestic management. The wife who will keep the charm of early love unbroken through the years, and in whose home the dreams of the wedding day will come true, must be a good housekeeper.

The good wife is generous and warm-hearted. She does not grow grasping and selfish. In her desire to economize and add to her stores she does not forget those about her who suffer or want. While she gives her wisest and most earnest thought and her best and most skillful work to her own home, her heart does not grow cold toward those outside who need sympathy. I cannot conceive of true womanhood ripened into mellow richness, yet wanting the qualities of gentleness

and unselfishness. A woman whose heart is not touched by the sight of sorrow, and whose hands do not go out in relief where it is in her power to help, lacks one of the elements which make the glory of womanhood.

It is in her own home that this warmth of heart and this openness of hand are first to be shown. It is as wife and mother that her gentleness performs its most sacred ministry. Her hand wipes away the teardrops when there is sorrow. In sickness she is the tender nurse. She bears upon her own heart every burden that weighs upon her husband. No matter how the world goes with him during the day, when he enters his own door he meets the fragrant atmosphere of love.

In sickness, how thoughtful, how skillful, how gentle a nurse is the true wife! In struggle with temptation or adversity or difficulty, what an inspirer she is! In misfortune or disaster, what lofty heroism does she exhibit and what courage does her bravery kindle in her husband's heart! Instead of being crushed by the unexpected loss, she only then rises to her full grandeur of soul. She turns away from luxury and ease to the plainer home, the simpler life, the humbler surroundings, without a murmur. It is in such circumstances and experiences that the heroism of a woman's soul is manifested. Many a man is carried victoriously through misfortune and enabled to rise again, because of the strong inspiring sympathy and the self-forgetting help of his wife.

But a wife's ministry of mercy reaches outside her own doors. Every true home is an influence of blessing in the community where it stands. Its lights shine out. Its songs ring out. Its spirit breathes out. Its doors stand ever open with a welcome to everyone who comes seeking shelter from the storm, or sympathy in sorrow, or help in trial. It is a place where one who is in trouble may go confident ever of sympathy and comfort. It is a place where the young people love to go, because they know they are welcome and because they find there inspiration and help.

A true wife is universally beloved. She is recognized as one of God's angels scattering blessings as far as her hand can reach. Her neighbors are all blessed by her ministrations. When sickness or sorrow touches any other household, some token of sympathy finds its way from her hand into the shadowed home. To the old she is gentle and patient. To

153

the young she is inciting and helpful. To the poor she is God's hand reached out. To the sufferer she brings strength. To the sorrowing she is a consoler. There is trouble nowhere near but her face appears at the door and her hand brings its benediction.

A true wife gives her husband her fullest confidence. She hides nothing from him. She gives no pledge of secrecy which will seal her lips in his presence. She listens to no words of admiration from others which she may not repeat to him. She expresses to him every feeling, every hope, every desire and yearning, every joy or pain. Then while she utters every confidence in his ear she is most careful to speak in no other ear any word concerning the sacred inner life of her home.

It has been said that "the wife should always leave something to be revealed only to her husband, some modest charm, some secret grace, reserved solely for his delight and inspiration, like those flowers which give of their sweetness only to the hand that lovingly gathers them." She should always care more to please him than any other person in the world. She should prize more highly a compliment from his lips than from any other human lips. Therefore she should reserve for him the sweetest charms; she should seek to bring ever to him some new surprise of loveliness; she should plan pleasures and delights for him. Instead of not caring how she looks or whether she is agreeable or not when no one but her husband is present, she should always be at her best for him. Instead of being bright and lovely when there is company, then relapsing into languor and silence when the company is gone, she should seek always to be brightest and loveliest when only he and she sit together in the quiet of the home. Both husband and wife should ever bring their best things to each other.

So it all comes back to a question of character. She can be a good wife only by being a good woman. And she can be a good woman in the true sense only by being a Christian woman. Nowhere except in

154

Christ can she find the wisdom and strength she needs to meet the solemn responsibilities of wifehood. Only in Christ can she find that rich beauty of soul, that gemming and impearling of the character, which shall make her lovely in her husband's sight when the bloom of youth is gone, when the brilliance has faded out of her eyes and the roses have fled from her cheeks. Only Christ can teach her how to live so as to be blessed and a blessing in her married life.

155

The Parent's Part

J. R. Miller

t is a new marriage when the first-born enters the home. It draws the wedded lives together in a closeness they have never known before.

It touches chords in their hearts that have lain silent until now. It calls out powers that have never been exercised before. Hitherto unsuspected beauties of character appear. The laughing, heedless girl of a year ago is transformed into a thoughtful woman. The careless, unsettled youth leaps into manly strength and into fixedness of character when he looks into the face of his own child and takes it in his bosom. New aims rise up before the young parents, new impulses begin to stir in their hearts. Life takes on at once a new and deeper meaning. The glimpse they have had into its solemn mystery sobers them. The laying in their hands of a new and sacred burden, an immortal life, to be guided and trained by them, brings to them a sense of responsibility that makes them thoughtful. Self is no longer the center. There is a new object to live for, an object great enough to fill all their life and engross their highest powers. It is only when the children come that life becomes real, and that parents begin to learn to live. We talk about training our children, but they train us first, teaching us many a sacred lesson, stirring up in us many a slumbering gift and possibility, calling out many a hidden grace and disciplining our wayward powers into strong and harmonious character.

"Children are God's apostles, day by day, sent forth to preach of love, of hope, and of peace."

Our homes would be very cold and dreary without the children. Sometimes we weary of their noise. They certainly bring us a great deal of care and solicitude. They cost us no end of toil. When they are very young they break our rest many a weary night with their colics and teethings, and when they grow older they well nigh break our hearts many a time with their waywardness. After they come to us we may as well bid farewell to living for self and to personal ease and independence, if we mean to do faithful duty as parents. There are some who therefore look upon the coming of children as a misfortune. They talk about them lightly as "responsibilities." They regard them as in the way of their pleasure. They see no blessing in them. But it is cold selfishness that looks upon children in this way. Instead of being hindrances to true and noble living, they are helps. They bring benedictions from heaven when they come, and while they stay they are perpetual benedictions.

It is a great thing to take these young and tender lives, rich with so many possibilities of beauty, of joy, of power, all of which may be wrecked, and to become responsible for their shaping and training and for the upbuilding of their character. This is what must be thought of in the making of a home. It must be a home in which children will grow up for true and noble life, for God and for heaven. Upon the parents the chief responsibility rests. They are the builders of the home.

This responsibility rests upon both the parents. There are some fathers who seem to forget that any share of the burden and duty of making the home life belongs to them. They leave it all to the mothers. They come and go as if they were scarcely more than boarders in their own house, with no active interest in the welfare of their children. They plead the demands of business as the excuse for their neglect. But what is so important as to justify a man's evasion of the sacred duties which he owes to his own family? There cannot be any other work in this world which a man can do that will excuse him at God's bar for having neglected the care of his own home and the training of his own children. No success in any department of the world's work can possibly atone for failure here. No piling up of this world's treasures can compensate a man for the loss of those incomparable jewels, his own children. The fathers should awake to the fact that they have something to do in making the life of their own homes besides providing food and clothing and paying taxes and bills. They owe to their homes the best influences of their lives. Whatever other duties press upon them, they should always find time to plan for the good of their own households. The very center of every man's life should be his home. Instead of being to him a mere boardinghouse where he eats and sleeps, and from which he starts out in the mornings to his work, it ought to be the place where his heart is anchored, where his hopes gather, to which his thoughts turn a thousand times a day, for which he toils and struggles, and into which he brings always the richest and best things of his life. He should realize that he is responsible for the character and the influence of his home life, and that if it should fail to be what it ought to be, the blame and guilt must lie upon his soul.

The true idea of a home is that it is a place for growth. It is a place for the parents themselves to grow—to grow into beauty of character, to grow in refinement, in knowledge, in strength, in wisdom, in patience, gentleness, kindliness, and all the Christian graces and virtues. It is a place for children to grow—to grow into physical vigor and health and to be trained in all that shall make them true and noble men and women.

If this be the true object and design in setting up a home, the question arises, What sort of home culture and home-education will produce these results? What influences will best fashion human infancy and childhood into strong, noble manhood and lovely, queenly womanhood?

For one thing, the house itself in which we live, with its surroundings and adornments, is important. Every home influence, even the very smallest, works itself into the heart of childhood and then reap-

pears in the opening character. Homes are the real schools in which men and women are trained, and fathers and mothers are the real teachers and builders of life. The poet's song that charms the world is but the sweetness of a mother's love flowing out in rhythmic measure through the soul of her child. The lovely things which men make in their days of strength are but the reproductions in embodied forms of the lovely thoughts that were whispered in their hearts in tender youth. The artist's picture is but a touch of a mother's beauty wrought out on the canvas.

In the choosing and preparation of a home the educating power of beauty must not be forgotten. The surroundings should be cheerful and attractive. The house itself, whether large or small, should be neat and tasteful. Its ornaments and decorations should be simple yet chaste and pleasing to the eye. The rooms in which our children are to sleep and play and live we should make just as bright and lovely as our means can make them.

The home life itself is more important than the house and its adornments. By the home life is meant all the intercourse of the members of the family. It is a happy art, the art of living together in tender love. It must begin with the parents themselves. Unless their life together is loving and true it will be impossible for them to make their home life so. They give the keynote to the music. If their intercourse is marked by bickerings and quarrelings they must expect their children to imitate them. If gentleness and affectionateness characterize their bearing toward each other the same spirit will rule in the family life. For their children's sake, parents should cultivate their own lives and train themselves to live together in the most Christlike way.

We enter some homes, and they are full of sweetness as summer fields are of fragrance. All is order, beauty, gentleness and peace. We enter other homes, where we find jarring, selfishness, harshness and disorder. This difference is not accidental. There are influences at work in each home which yield just the result we see in each. Every home takes its color and tone from its makers. A refined spirit puts refinement into a home, though it be only one plain room without an ornament or a luxury; a coarse nature makes the home coarse, though it be a palace filled with all the elegances that wealth can buy. No home life can ever be better than the life of those who make it. It is nothing less nor more than the spirit of the parents like an atmosphere filling all the house.

What should this home-spirit be? First of all, I would name the law of unselfishness as one of its essential elements.

As love grows, selfishness dies out in the heart. Love is always ready to deny itself, to give, to sacrifice, just in the measure of its sincerity and intensity. Perfect love is perfect self-forgetfulness. Hence, where there is love in a home, unselfishness is the law. Each forgets self and lives for the others. But when there is selfishness it mars the joy. One selfish soul will destroy the sweetness of the life of any home. It is like an ugly thorn-bush in the midst of a garden of flowers.

The home life should also be made bright and full of sunshine. The courtesy of the true home is not stiff and formal, but sincere, simple and natural. Children need an atmosphere of gladness. Law should not make its restraints hang like chains upon them. Sternness and coldness should have no place in home life or in family government. No child can ever grow up into its richest and best development in a home which is gloomy and unhappy. No more do plants need sunshine and air than children need joy and gladness. Unhappiness stunts them, so that their sweetest graces never come out.

Whatever parents may do for their children, they should at least make their childhood sunny and tender. Their young lives are so delicate that harshness may mar their beauty forever, and so sensitive that

every influence that falls upon them leaves its trace which grows into the character either as a grace or a blemish. A happy childhood stores away sunshine in the chambers of the heart which brightens the life to its close. An unhappy childhood may so fill the life's fountains with bitterness as to sadden all the after years.

Something must be said concerning the training of children. It is to be kept in mind that the object of the home is to build up manhood and womanhood. This work of training belongs to the parents and cannot be transferred. It is a most delicate and responsible duty, one from which a thoughtful soul would shrink with awe and fear were it not for the assurance of divine help. Yet there are many parents who do not stop to think of the responsibility which is laid upon them when a little child enters their home.

The parents are to take this infant and nurse it into manhood or womanhood, to draw out these slumbering powers and teach it to use them. That is, God wants a man trained for a great mission in the world, mother a little babe, and bids them nurse it and train it for him until the man is ready for his mission; or at least to have sole charge of his earliest years when the first impressions must be made, which shall mold and shape his whole career.

What we want to do with our children is not merely to control them and keep them in order, but to implant true principles deep in their hearts which shall rule their whole lives; to shape their character from within into Christlike beauty, and to make of them noble men and women, strong for battle and for duty. They are to be trained rather than governed. Growth of character, not merely good behavior, is the object of all home governing and teaching. Therefore the home-influence is far more important than the home laws, and the parents' lives are of more moment than their teachings.

When I think of the sacredness and the responsibility of parents, I do not see how any father and mother can look upon the little child that has been given to them and consider their duty to it, and not be driven to God by the very weight of the burden that rests upon them, to cry to him for help and wisdom. When an impenitent man bends over the cradle of his first-born, when he begins to realize that here is a soul which he must train, teach, fashion and guide through this world to God's bar, how can he no longer stay away from God? Let him, as he bends over his child's crib to kiss its sweet lips, ask himself, "Am I true to my child while I shut God out of my own life?"

Let parents be faithful. Let them do their best. The work may seem too great for them, and they may faint under its burdens and seem to fail. But what they cannot do the angels will come and finish while they sleep. Night by night they will come and correct the day's mistakes, and if need be do all the poor, faulty work over again. Then at last when the parents sleep in death, dropping out of their hands the sacred work they have been doing for their children, again God's angels will come, take up the unfinished work and carry it on to completeness.

The Children's Part

J. R. Miller

hat should the child-life be that would perfectly fulfill its part in the home? We have a model. Once there was a home on earth in which a Child lived whose life was spotless and faultless, and who realized all that is lovely, tender and true in child-life. If we only knew how Jesus lived as a child in that Nazareth home it would help other children to live aright. We know that he helped to make the home happy. He never caused his parents one anxiety, one pang, one moment of shame. He never failed in a duty. We know that he did his part well in the making of that home, and if we only had a memoir of his years of childhood telling us what he did, every other child could study it and imitate his example.

We see, for thirty years, from infancy to full manhood, this holy Child exhibiting toward his parents the most perfect dutifulness, obedience, honor and helpfulness. He obeyed them, not by constraint but

cheerfully, all these years. He did his part well in the making of that home.

This example is the answer to the question here, that the great duty of childhood in the home life is to obey? He was subject unto them. Although he was the Son of God, yet he learned obedience to human parents. He did their will and not his own. That was the work which was given him to do for that time. He had come to the earth on a great mission, the greatest ever undertaken or performed in the universe, yet the place in which he was prepared for that mission was not in any of the fine schools of the world, but in a lowly home; not at the feet of rabbis and philosophers, but with his own mother for his teacher. What an honor does this fact put upon home! What a dignity upon motherhood!

It would seem that no argument after that was needed to prove to children the duty and the dignity of obedience to parents.

Does some evil spirit suggest that such subjection to parents keeps one down, puts chains on his freedom, keeps him under restraint and hinders him from rising into grandeur and nobleness of character? Did it have such effect on Jesus? Did the thirty years of submission in his home cramp and fetter his manhood? Did his subjection break his power, repress the glorious aspiration of his soul, stunt and hinder the development of his life and make his career a failure in the end? We know well that it did not. There was a preparation for his mission which, as a man, he could have gotten in no other way but by the discipline he obtained in his own home. No human powers were ever yet cramped or stunted or repressed by taking the place of subjection in a true home. Rather, that life will always be more or less a failure which in its earlier years does not learn to submit and be ruled. No one is fitted for ruling others who has not first learned in his place to obey.

Such, in general, is the central feature of the children's part in the home life—to recognize their parents as the head and to yield to them in all things. This is not meant to make them slaves. The home life I am depicting is ruled by love. The parental authority is exercised in love. It seeks only the highest good of each child. It asks nothing unreasonable or unjust. If it withholds things that a child desires, it is either because it is not able to grant them or because the granting of them would work injury rather than benefit. If it seeks to guide the tender feet in a way that is not the chosen way, nor the most easy and pleasant way, it is because a riper wisdom sees that it is the best way. True parental guidance is love grown wise. It is an imitation of God's government. He is our Father and we are his children. We are to obey him absolutely and without question. True human parenthood is a faint copy of the divine, and to its direction and guidance children are to submit.

This subjection implies obedience to the commands of parents. Thus Paul interprets it, "Children, obey your parents in the Lord; for this is right," and again, "Children, obey your parents in all things; for this is well-pleasing unto the Lord." It is right on moral grounds, and this ought to settle the matter. True manliness never wants to know more than that a thing is right, is duty. Devotion to duty, at whatever cost, is one of the first elements of heroism. It is right that children should obey their parents, and no further question need be asked, no further reason for obeying need be sought.

This obedience is to extend to "all things," the things that are agreeable and the things that are disagreeable. Though he may be unjustly treated the child is not to rebel. He may know that his parent is unkind or oppressive, or even cruel, but his duty is not thereby changed. Wrong on the parent's part will never justify wrong on the part of the child. There is only one qualification: children are to obey their parents "in the Lord." (If the parent commands the child to commit a sin of course it is not to obey.) It is such obedience that pleases God, while it

ensures harmony and peace in the home. The parents are the divinely constituted head of the family, and it is the children's part to obey.

This requirement implies also honor and respect. "Honor thy father and thy mother," says the command. Honor is a larger word than obey. We may obey a person whom we do not respect. We are to honor our parents—that is, reverence them—as well as obey them.

There is no need for any argument to prove that every child should honor his parents. Yet it is idle to deny that there is on every hand a lack of filial respect. There are many children who show by their words or acts that their parents are not sacredly enshrined in their hearts.

I heard a bright young girl, well dressed, with good manners and good face, say that her mother looked so old-fashioned that she was ashamed to have her in the parlor or to walk with her on the street. I chanced to know a little about that mother and that daughter. I knew that one reason why the mother looked so old-fashioned, and probably lacked something of refinement of manner was because of her devotion to the interests of her daughter. She had made a sacrifice of herself for her daughter's sake. She had denied herself in dress and ornament that her daughter might appear well and be admired.

Some young people may read these pages who at times feel as this young girl did. Have you ever sat down quietly to think over and sum up the debt you owe to your old-fashioned mother? Look at the matter for a few moments. Begin with the time when you were a very little baby, as you certainly were once, however great you are now, and think what she had to do for you then. She had to nurse you hour after hour and lie awake many a night to take care of you. Sometimes you were very cross, though you are so gentle now; yet, no matter how cross you were, she was as patient as an angel with you. She wore herself out for you then.

As you grew older she taught you. Did you ever think how little you knew when you came into this world? You had hands and feet and eyes and tongue and brain, but you did not know what they were for or how to use them. It was your loving, patient mother who taught you to walk and to talk and to look and to think.

You have been a great deal of trouble to your mother in your time, but she has borne it all cheerfully for you. She has gone without many things herself that you might have what you wanted. She has worked very hard that you might receive an education and be fitted to shine in society among your friends and be ready for an honored and useful place in this world.

Sometimes you think she looks very plain and old-fashioned.

Perhaps she does, perhaps she is more than a little faded and worn, but did you ever think that it is because she has given so much of the best power and energy of her life to caring for you? If she had not chosen to toil and suffer and deny herself for your sake, if she had thought more of herself and less of you, she might have been very much fairer and fresher now.

Look at your father too. He is not so fresh and youthful as once he was. Perhaps he does not dress so finely as some of the young people you see about you or as their fathers dress. There are marks of hard toil upon him, marks of care and anxiety, which in your eye seem to disfigure his beauty. It may be that you blush a little sometimes when your young friends meet you walking with him or when he comes into the parlor when you have company, and wish he would take more pains to appear well. Do not forget that he is toiling these days for you and that his hard hands and his bronzed face are really tokens of his love for you. If he does not appear quite so fresh and handsome as some other men, very likely it is because he has to work harder to give you your pleasant home, your good clothes, your daily food and many comforts, and to send you to school. When you look at him and feel tempted to be ashamed of his appearance just remember this.

You look at your father and see signs of toil, of pain, of self-denial, of care. Do you know what they reveal? They tell the story of his life. He has passed through struggles and conflicts. Do you know how much of this story, if rightly interpreted, concerns you? Is there nothing in the bent form, the faded hands, the lines of care, that tells you of his deep love for you and of sufferings endured, sacrifices made and toils and anxieties for your sake?

When you think thus of what you owe your parents and of what they have borne and wrought for you, can you ever again be ashamed of them? Will not the shame rather be for yourself that you could ever have been so ungrateful as to blush at their homeliness? All the reverence of your soul will be kindled into deepest, purest admiration as you look upon these marks of love and sacrifice for your sake. You will honor them all the more, the more they are worn and wasted, the more they are broken and their grace and beauty shattered. These tokens of self-neglect and self-sacrifice are the jewels in the crown of love.

This honor is not to be shown only by the young child living yet as a child in the old home, but by those who are grown up to full manhood and womanhood. While parents live there never comes a time when a child is no longer a child, owing love and honor. Few things in this world are so beautiful as the sight of a middle-aged man or woman showing true devotion to an aged father or mother.

If true honor for parents has its seat in the heart, there is little need for rules or detailed suggestions. Yet a few particular ways may be mentioned in which children can add to the happiness and blessedness of the home life. They should show their love for their parents by confiding in them, not simply by believing in them and trusting their love and their wisdom, but by making them the recipients of all their confidences. A wise parent teaches his child from the very beginning to conceal nothing from him, to tell him everything, and there is no part of the child's life in which he takes no interest. True filial love maintains this openness of heart and life toward a parent, even into the years of maturity.

Children must learn self-denial if they would faithfully do their part. They cannot have everything they desire. They must learn to give up their own wishes for the sake of others. They must learn to do without things that they would like to have. In no other way can home life be made what it should be. Every member of the family must practice self-denial. The parents make many sacrifices for the children, and it is certainly right that the children early learn to practice self-denial to relieve their parents, to help them and to minister to their comfort.

They should also learn thoughtfulness. A home is like a garden of tender plants which are easily broken or bruised. A thoughtless person is forever causing injury or pain, not through intention, but heedlessly. Many, also, who outside are thoughtful, careful of the feelings of others and quick to speak the gentle word that heals and blesses, at home are thoughtless. But surely there is no place in the world where we ought to be so studiously thoughtful as in our own homes. It does not seem unreasonable to expect that even quite young children shall learn to be thoughtful, for those who are older there certainly cannot be a shadow of excuse for rudeness and thoughtlessness. There are in every home abundant opportunities for the culture and display of a thoughtful spirit.

Children should early learn to bear some little share in the home work. Instead of being always and only a burden to the loving ones who live and toil and sacrifice for them, they should seek in every way they can to give help.

Home is the school in which we are first to learn and practice the lessons of life. Children should learn there to be useful to their parents and to one another. They can do much in this direction by not requiring unnecessary attendance, by not making trouble and work for others on their account. There are some spoiled children who are such selfish tyrants at home that all the other members of the family are taxed to wait upon them. As soon as possible children should learn to wait upon themselves and in a measure be independent of the help of others, so as to become self-reliant and strong. What more painful picture do we see than that of sons and daughters growing up idle and selfish in their own homes, too indolent to put forth an exertion, too proud to soil their dainty hands with any kind of work, but not too proud to let delicate or already overwrought parents slave to keep them in dainty food or showy array of dress! Nothing good or noble can ever come out of such home life.

Children should make themselves worthy of their parents. They should seek to be all that the father and mother in their most ardent dreams hoped for them. It is a sad thing to disappoint love's brilliant expectations.

In the heart of every true Christian parent there glows an ideal of very fair beauty of character and nobleness of soul, which he wants to see his child attain. It is a vision of the most exalted life, lovelier than that which fills the thought of any sculptor as he stands before his marble and begins to hew at the block; fairer than that which rises in the poet's soul as he bows in ecstatic fervor over his page and seeks to describe his dream. Every true, godly parent dreams of the most perfect manhood and womanhood for his children. He wants to see them grow

up into Christlikeness, spotless in purity, rich in all the graces, with character fully developed and rounded out in symmetrical beauty, shining in this world, but shining more and more unto the perfect day.

If children would do their part well in return for all the love that has blessed their helpless years and surrounded them in their youth, and that lingers still unwasted in the days of manhood and womanhood, they must seek to realize in their own lives all the sacred hopes of their parents' hearts. A wrecked and debauched manhood or a frivolous and purposeless womanhood is a poor return for parental love, fidelity and sacrifice. But a noble life, a character strong, true, earnest and Christ-like, brings blessed and satisfying reward to a parent for the most toilsome and painful years of self-forgetting love. Parents live in their children, and children hold in their hands the happiness of their parents. Let them never be untrue to their sacred trust. Let them never bring down the gray hairs of father or mother with sorrow to the grave. Let them be worthy of the love, almost divine, that holds them in its deathless grasp. Let them so live as to be a crown of honor to their parents in their old age. Let them fill their declining years with sweetness and tenderness. Let them make a pillow of peace for their heads when death comes.

The Aim and Object of Life

Charles Haddon Spurgeon

hat we could wake men up to exercise the faculty of thinking, and then to direct, to regulate, and to control their thoughts! But thinking is an occupation that a great many persons altogether dislike. They are frivolous. We cannot get them to think about anything. Many minds never get on the wing at all. Not a few men work so hard with their hands, and suffer such fatigue from bodily labor, that they are scarcely able to think much; while there are others who dissipate their time and consume their lives in idleness, till they are utterly disqualified for any vigorous thought. They are lazy and sluggish. They have the dry rot in their very souls. Their brains do not work. They seem to live in one everlasting lethargy and day-dream. O that men were wise, that they were thoughtful.

Ask many a man whom you meet with, "Sir, what are you living for?" He would, perhaps, tell you what his trade or what his profession might be; but if you pressed him with the question, "What is the main object of life?" he would not like to say that he was living only to enjoy himself-seeking his own pleasure. He would hardly like to say that he was living to grasp and grab and get a fortune. He would hardly know how to answer you. Many young men are in this condition, they have not a definite object. Now, you will not make a good captain if you do not know the port you are sailing for. You will make a poor life of it, young man, if you go out as an apprentice, and then afterwards out as a master, with no definite aim and end. Say to yourself, "I can only live for two things. I can live for God, or I can live for the devil; which, now, am I going to do?" Get your mind well fixed and firmly resolved as to which it shall be. I will put it to you as boldly and badly as even Elijah did when he said, "If Baal be God, serve Him; and if Jehovah be God, serve Him." If the world, if the flesh, if the devil, be worth serving, go follow out the career of a sensualist, and say so. Let yourself know what you are at; but if God be worth serving, and your soul worth the saving, go in for that; but do not sneak through this world really seeking yourself, and yet not having the courage to say to yourself, "Self, you are living for yourself." Do have a definite and distinct object, or else your vital energies will be wasted, and your most industrious days will be recklessly squandered.

Making the Most of Each Day

Philip Doddridge

he orderly distribution of our time is a matter of great consequence. It is a commodity so precious, that God, who gives everything else liberally, imparts this with a sparing hand. There is only one moment in the world at once, and that is taken away before the next is bestowed.

To make the most of a day we must:

1. *Rise early and begin it with God.* Time waits upon each of us when we awake, and says, What wilt thou have me do today? Our answer to this inquiry is of no trivial importance.

2. *We must have a plan, general and subordinate.* Our great moralist, Johnson, remarks, "I believe it is best to throw life into a method, that every hour may bring its employment and every employment have its hour." If everything be kept in a certain place, when anything is worn out or consumed, the vacuity which it leaves will show what is wanting; so if every part of time has its appropriate duty, the hour will call into remembrance its engagement.

3. *We must undertake no more than we can reasonably expect to perform,* and do one thing at a time.

4. *While we should avoid voluntary hindrances; if interruptions occur, instead of wasting our time in fruitless regret, we should endeavor to improve passing circumstances.*

5. *We must carefully gather up fragments.* Betwixt the more earnest employments and important occurrences of life, there are several intervals, which, though in one day they may be inconsiderable, yet in the whole time of a man's life they amount to a great deal of it. These uncertain intervals are often lost; either as not valued by most people, or neglected, though not despised, by good men, for want of skill to make use of them. As goldsmiths and refiners preserve the very sweep-

ings of their shop, to save the filings of gold and silver, so a Christian ought to be very careful of those small portions of time which are more precious than metals.

6. We should aim at strict punctuality in engagements. A man who is not punctual, not only wastes his own time, but often intrudes upon that of others, which may be still more valuable.

7. We must guard against a spirit of procrastination. The sacrifices under the Law were offered, "as the duty of every day required;" "whatsoever thy hand findeth to do, do it with thy might." We must also be watchful over ourselves, lest a habit of unprofitable anxiety, as to the future, rob us of our time. Many hours are consumed in wild and groundless anticipations of evil.

8. To recall at night the transactions of the day, and endeavor to make the following a practical comment on the past, would be highly advantageous. To inquire, What has the day done for me? Has it set me nearer heaven? Has it brought an increase of knowledge and virtue? Has it been devoted to the service of God and man? Or has it been spent in sloth, sensuality, or self-pleasing?

9. Should our active powers be suspended, and a season of languor and sickness intervene, there are still duties to be performed. Days of affliction are not idle days. "They who sow in tears shall reap in joy." He who goes forth weeping, bearing "the precious seed" of faith, patience, prayer, submission, penitence, and hope, shall doubtless come again rejoicing, bringing his sheaves with him. All who have diligently improved the talents committed to them, shall serve God when "time shall be no longer," without imperfection, without weariness, and without end.

The Happiest Home

There is the happiest home on earth?
　　Tis not 'mid scenes of noisy mirth;
But where God's favor, sought aright,
　　Fills every breast with joy and light.

The richest home? It is not found
　　Where wealth and splendor most abound;
But wheresoe'er, in hall or cot,
　　Men live contented with their lot.

The fairest home? It is not placed
　　In scenes with outward beauty graced;
But where kind words and smiles impart
　　A constant sunshine to the heart.

On such a home of peace and love
　　God showers his blessing from above;
And angels, watching o'er it, cry,
　　"Lo! this is like our home on high!"

179

Home

James Montgomery

There is a land of every land the pride,
    Beloved by heaven o'er all the world beside;
Where brighter suns dispense serener light,
    And milder moons emparadise the night;
A land of beauty, virtue, valor, truth,
    Time-tortured age, and love-exalted youth.
The wandering mariner, whose eye explores
    The wealthiest isles, the most enchanting shores,
Views not a realm so bountiful and fair,
    Nor breathes the spirit of a purer air;
In every clime the magnet of his soul,
    Touched by remembrance, trembles to that pole;
For in this land of heaven's peculiar grace,
    The heritage of nature's noblest race,
There is a spot of earth supremely blest.
    A dearer, sweeter spot than all the rest,
Where man, creation's tyrant, casts aside
    His sword and scepter, pageantry and pride,
While in his softened looks benignly blend
    The sire, the son, the husband, brother, friend.
Here woman reigns; the mother, daughter, wife,
    Strew with fresh flowers the narrow way of life!
In the clear heaven of her delightful eye
    An angel-guard of loves and graces lie;
Around her knees domestic duties meet,
    And fireside pleasures gambol at her feet.
Where shall that land, that spot of earth be found

Art thou a man?—a patriot?—look around;
Oh, thou shalt find, howe'er thy footsteps roam,
That land *thy* country, and that spot *thy* home.

True Godliness

William Jay

What is godliness? It is the desire and tendency of the mind towards God. It is exercised in believing in Him, loving and fearing Him, holding communion with Him, resembling His perfections, and employing ourselves in His service. It is the introduction of God into all our concerns, our acknowledging Him in all our ways, our doing all we do in His name, and with a reverence to His authority and glory, through the mediation of the Savior, and by the influences of the Holy Spirit.

Design of the Family

V. T. Moore

As God has provided a fountain of nutriment in the body, that is softly unsealed at the time it is needed, without any agency of man, so has he treasured in the human heart a deep fountain of affection, that is ready to meet the claims of this helpless feebleness; and the more absolute the helplessness, the more exhaustless and untiring the love by which it is enfolded.

Within the protecting walls of the family circle, there has been provided the warm pressure of a mother's love, and the strong activities of a father's affection. And as the cares of life thicken around both, there grows up around the little pillow, and twines about the little form, the rejoicing affections of brotherly and sisterly kindness; so that each new necessity finds ready a new supply for its wants.

The Old Folks

The Congregationalist

f you would make the aged happy, lead them to feel that there is still a place for them where they can be useful.

When you see their powers failing, do not notice it. It is enough for them to feel it, without a reminder. Do not humiliate them by doing things after them. Accept their offered services, and do not let them see you taking off the dust their poor eye-sight has left undisturbed, or wiping up the liquid their trembling hands have spilled; rather let the dust remain, and the liquid stain the carpet, than rob them of their self-respect by seeing you cover their deficiencies. You may give them the best room in your house, you may garnish it with pictures and flowers, you may yield them the best seat in your church-pew, the easiest chair in your parlor, the highest seat of honor at your table; but if you lead, or leave them to feel that they have passed their usefulness, you plant a thorn in their bosom that will rankle there while life lasts. If they are capable of doing nothing but preparing your kindlings, or darning your stockings, indulge them in those things, but never let them feel that it is because they can do nothing else; rather that they do this so well.

Do not ignore their taste and judgment. It may be that in their early days, and in the circle where they moved, they were as much sought and honored as you are now; and until you arrive at that place, you can ill imagine your feelings should you be considered entirely void of these qualities, be regarded as essential to no one, and your opinions be unsought, or discarded if given. They may have been active and successful in the training of children and youth in the way they should go; and will they not feel it keenly, if no attempt is made to draw from this rich experience?

Indulge them as far as possible in their old habits. The various

forms of society in which they were educated may be as dear to them as yours are now to you. And can they see them slighted or disowned without a pang? If they relish their meals better by turning their tea into the saucer, having their butter on the same plate with their food, or eating with both knife and fork, do not in word or deed imply to them that the customs of their days are obnoxious in good society; and that they are stepping down from respectability as they descend the hillside of life. Always bear in mind that the customs of which you are now so tenacious may be equally repugnant to the next generation.

In this connection I would say, do not notice the pronunciation of the aged. They speak as they were taught, and yours may be just as uncourtly to the generations following. I was once taught a lesson on this subject, which I shall never forget while memory holds its sway. I was dining when a father brought his son to take charge of a literary institution. He was intelligent, but had not received the early advantages which he had labored hard to procure for his son, and his language was quite a contrast to that of the cultivated youth. But the attention and deference he gave to his father's quaint though wise remarks, placed him on a higher pinnacle in my mind, than he was ever placed by his world-wide reputation as a scholar and writer.

The Home of Childhood

Samuel D. Burchard

he most impressive series of pictures I have ever seen are by Thomas Cole, an American artist, and termed "The Voyage of Life."

The first represents a child seated in a boat surrounded by varied and beautiful flowers, and his guardian angel standing by to guard and protect the little voyager.

The second represents the youth, still on his voyage, guiding his own boat down the stream, his finger pointing upward to a beautiful castle painted in the clouds.

The third represents the man, still in the boat, going down the rapids; the water rough, the sky threatening, and the guardian angel looking on from a distance, anxiously.

The fourth represents an old man, still in his boat, the sun going down amid floating clouds tinged with gold, purple, and vermillion. The castle or House Beautiful in full view, and the guardian angel with an escort of shining celestials waiting to attend him to his home in glory.

The pictures have suggested to me a series of articles on Life's Great Mission and work for the grander life beyond. And on this sublime voyage to the land of immortals, to the Palace Beautiful in the skies, let us start from the dear old home of childhood, that home which, though it may be desolate, is still imperishable in memory.

Home of my childhood, thou shalt ever be dear
 To the heart that so fondly revisits thee now ;
Though thy beauty be gone, thy leaf in the sere,
 The wreaths of the past still cling to thy brow.

Spirit of mine, why linger ye here;
 Why cling to those hopes so futile and vain?
Go, seek ye a home in that radiant sphere,
 Which through change and time thou shalt ever retain.

Let our destined port be the home of the blessed—the city which hath foundations, whose builder and maker is God!

"And thou shalt bring thy father, and thy mother, and thy brethren, and thy father's household home unto thee."—Joshua 2:18.

The Christian home, implying marriage, mutual affection, piety, gentleness, refinement, meekness, forbearance, is our ideal of earthly happiness—a beautiful and impressive type of heaven.

It is more than a residence, a place of abode, however attractive in its surroundings, however richly adorned with art and beauty. It is where the heart is, where the loved ones are—husband, wife, father, mother, brothers, sisters, all united in sympathy, fellowship and worship. It may be humble, unpretentious, exhibiting no signs of material wealth; but there is the wealth of mutual affection, which fire cannot consume, and no commercial disaster alienate or destroy. This is home—the home of the heart, the home of childhood, the comfort of riper years, the refuge of age.

That we may better appreciate the Christian homes that God has given us—the homes of comfort and refinement, that rocked the cradle of our infancy—let us consider, first, the vast multitudes of our fallen race that really have no home; none in the Christian sense, none that antedate heaven in peace, refinement and mutual love. How many children are born to the heritage of vice, poverty and crime, left to drift upon the tide of circumstances, to be buffeted in the wild and angry storm, to be chilled on the desolate moor of life—to wander amid the voids of human sympathy, the solitude and estrangement of human society, the children of dire misfortune, victims of vice and crime, polluted and polluting from the first.

How many fall, like blossoms prematurely blown, nipped by the lingering frosts of winter and sinking into the shadowed stream, or the sobbing soil of earth to be seen no more.

Think of the dwellings of hard-handed, wearied, ill-requited labor, where ignorance and discontent reign supreme—where there is no recognition of God, who in his all-wise Sovereignty, raises up one and

casts down another. Such homes exist all over the land, all over the dark and wide realm of heathendom.

Look now to the other extreme of society, to the habitations of the millionaires, adorned with all the luxuries of wealth, the appliances of art, taste, beauty, whose children are trained up to worship at the shrine of Mammon, to exclude from their minds all thoughts of God and the hereafter, to live only for this world. They feel that there is no society worth cultivating except that of the rich, the elite, the would-be fashionable. They believe that all enjoyments are material, sensuous, worldly, and that the chief end of man is to eat, drink, and be merry. Such households do not furnish the best schools in which to educate children to wrestle with misfortune and to do the great work of life. They are liable to grow up effeminate, lacking executive strength—cold, proud, misanthropic, and alienated in sympathy from the toiling masses.

There can be no well-regulated home without piety, without the fear and love of God. And such homes are usually found in the middle walks of life, not among the extreme poor, nor the proudly affluent, but among the mutually loving—the reverently worshipful.

It is to such homes that the world owes its highest interests. The old patriarchs understood the secret, even under the former dispensation, long before the dawn of the Christian era. God testified of Abraham, of Moses, of Samuel, and Job how truly they comprehended the nature of that family institution, around which cluster all the associations of the first period of human life.

And it has only been in the line and in the light of the Christian revelation, that the highest type of the household has been produced and preserved. And it is upon the application of Christian principles alone, that the structure of the Christian family and the Christian home can stand.

The family in its origin is divine, and God has instituted laws for its regulation and perpetuity, and these laws must be scrupulously observed and obeyed or it ceases to be an ornament and a blessing—the great training-school for the Church and the State—the safeguard of society and a type of heaven.

Home Training of Children

D. L. Moody

I have no doubt some parents have become discouraged and disheartened that they have not seen their children brought to the Savior as early as they expected. I do not know anything that has encouraged me more in laboring for children than my experience in the inquiry room. In working there I have found that those who had religious training, whose parents strove early to lead them to Christ, have been the easiest to lead toward Him. I always feel as if I had a lever to work with when I know that a man has been taught by a godly father and mother; even if his parents died when he was young, the impression that they died praying for him has always a great effect through life. I find that such men are always so much easier reached, and though we may not live to see all our prayers answered, and all our children brought into the fold, yet we should teach them diligently, and do it in love. There is where a good many make a mistake, by not teaching their children in love—by doing it coldly or harshly. Many send them off to read the Bible by themselves for punishment. Why, I would put my hand in the fire before I would try to teach them in that way. If we teach our children as we ought to do, instead of Sunday being the dreariest, dullest, weary day of the week to them, it will be the brightest and happiest day of the whole seven. What we want to do is to put religious truths before our children in such an attractive form that the Bible will be the most attractive of books to

189

them. Children want the same kind of food and truth that we do, only we must cut it up a little finer, so that they can eat it. I have great respect for a father and mother who have brought up a large family and trained them so that they have come out on the Lord's side. Sometimes mothers are discouraged and do not think they have so large a sphere to do good in as we have, but a mother who has brought up a large family to Christ need not consider her life a failure. I know one who has brought up ten sons, who are all Christians. Do you think her life has been a failure? Let us teach our children diligently, in season and out of season. We might train them that they shall be converted so early they can't tell when they were converted. I do not believe, as some people seem to think, that they have got to wander off into sin first, so that they may be brought back to Christ. Those who have been brought up in that way from their earliest childhood, do not have to spend their whole life in forgetting some old habit. Let us be encouraged in bringing our children to Christ.

HOME is the grandest of all institutions.—*C. H. Spurgeon.*

Knowing Christ

Octavius Winslow

et the chief object of your study be to know the Lord Jesus. It may be in the region of your sinfulness, emptiness, weakness, and foolishness that you learn Him. Nevertheless, however humiliating the school, slow the progress, and limited the attainment, count every fresh step you make in a personal acquaintance with the Lord Jesus as a nobler triumph, and as bringing you into

191

the possession of more real wealth than were the whole sphere of human knowledge and science mastered, and its untold treasures poured at your feet. When adversity comes—when death approaches—when eternity unveils—oh! How indescribably valuable, how inconceivably precious will then be one faith's touch, one faith's glimpse of a crucified and risen Savior! All other attainments then vanish and the only knowledge that abides, soothes, and comforts, is a heart-felt acquaintance with the sublimest fact of the Gospel, that "Christ Jesus came into the world to save sinners." Oh! Whatever other studies may engage your thoughts, forget not, as you value your eternal destiny to study the Lord Jesus Christ.

The Beautiful Home

Oliver Wendell Holmes

never saw a garment too fine for a man or maid. There never was a chair too good for a cobbler or cooper or a king to sit in, and never a house too fine to shelter the human head. Elegance fits man. But do we not value these tools a little more than they are worth and sometimes mortgage a house for the mahogany we bring into it? I had rather eat my dinner off the head of a barrel, or dress after the fashion of John the Baptist in the wilderness, or sit on a block all my life, than consume all myself before I got to a home, and take so much pains with the outside that the inside was as hollow as an empty nut. Beauty is a great thing, but beauty of garment, house, and furniture are tawdry ornaments compared with domestic love. All the elegance in the world will not make a home, and I would give more for a spoonful of real hearty love than for whole shiploads of furniture and all the gorgeous things the world can gather.

Study Christ's Life

Elizabeth Prentiss

oliness is not a mere abstraction. It is praying and loving and being consecrate; but it is also the doing kind deeds, speaking friendly words, being in a crowd when we thirst to be alone; and so on, and so on. The study of Christ's life on earth reveals Him to us as incessantly busy, yet taking special seasons for prayer. It seems to me that we should imitate Him in this respect, and when we find ourselves particularly pressed by outward cares and duties, break short off, and withdraw from them till a spiritual tone returns. For we can do nothing well unless we do it consciously for Christ.

Home Happiness

Rev. F. S. Cassady

> *"Mid pleasures and palaces tho' we may roam,*
> *Be it ever so humble, there is no place like home."*

ome! What a world of interest and happiness is crowded into that talismanic word! How the bosom swells with deepest feeling and profoundest emotion at its very mention! What hallowed memories and soul-inspiring associations cluster around that sacred shrine—our childhood's happy home! Never do our minds live in busy thought, over the scenes and remembrances of this sanctuary of our heart's purest and holiest affections. Its cheerful spirits, sunny faces, and revered forms-whatever changes time may have wrought since our severance from the old homestead are all vividly before us, and we again seem to be living over the tranquil days of the eventful past.

We can never—no, never—forget that happy family group, made up of father, mother, brothers, and sisters, of which in other years we formed a member. Although long years have circled away since that peaceful domestic circle gathered around that familiar hearth-stone, yet the whole scene, in all its interest and naturalness, is indelibly imprinted on our minds and hearts. 'Tis mournfully true that some of the members of that household, perchance that devoted father, or pious mother, or brother, or sister, have gone down to the land of shadows and of death, but still there is a sanctity and sacredness lingering around that precious spot of earth that will ever endear it to our hearts. And why should it not be so? It was there we were born; there we spent the days of our childhood; and there for the first time, around that family altar, celestial influences operated upon our hearts, and sought to win them to the skies. With such holy and hallowing memories attaching to that sacred place, why should we not love and venerate it? Why should not mellowing and soul-touching influences play around our hearts, when:

Fond memory brings the light
Of other days around us?

Even the old man who has long had a home of his own sheds the briny tear as he talks about the home and associations of his own childhood. The fountain of tears is unsealed every time that in memory he revisits those old and familiar scene. Heaven intended that home should be a cherished spot, and man would be untrue to all the higher and nobler instincts of his being if it were not so. The love for home and kindred is the last passion that grows cold in the human breast. Even the savage, dead to sympathy as is his heart for the white man, cherishes an almost idolatrous reverence for his hunting-grounds and the graves of his forefathers. This sacred principle of veneration for home and its cherished objects, runs all through the lower and higher grades of humanity. It obtains as much in the humble cottage of the poor and unlettered, as in the splendid mansions of the opulent and the great.

The sentiment is universally received, that "there is no place like home." How sweet and beautiful are the touches of an anonymous verse upon this subject:

I've wandered on through many a clime where flowers of beauty grew
Where all was blissful to the heart, and lovely to the view;
I've seen them in their twilight pride, and in their dress of morn,
But none appeared so sweet to me as the spot where I was born.

195

My Heart Shall Be Glad

J. R. Miller

very true father is affectionately interested in the lives of his children. His own joy, in later years, depends largely upon the way they live. He is made very happy by seeing them make something noble and worthy of their lives, and living honorably and righteously among men.

We are never better than our own heart. If our heart be evil, full of wrong thoughts, dispositions, and tempers, our character cannot be lovely and winning. "Beautiful thoughts make a beautiful soul." As we think in our heart so we are.

If parents would have happiness in seeing their children live beautiful lives, they must do more than give them good and wise counsels. Solomon was splendid at advising. His words are full of wisdom. If followed faithfully they will build into a life whatsoever things are true, whatsoever things are pure, whatsoever things are lovely. But we know how Solomon lived. It is little wonder that his son did not turn out well. Other parents need to guard against the same fatal mistake. No matter how well they may advise, if they do not themselves live godly lives, they will probably draw their children with them to ruin. They cannot by good advice overcome the force of bad example.

Happiness in the Home

Christian Parlor Magazine

he happiness of life, the happiness of the family especially, is made up of minute fractions. The little, soon-forgotten charities of a kiss, a smile, a kind look, a gentle word, a heartfelt compliment in the disguise of playful raillery,—these, and the thousand other little kindnesses of genial feelings, make a perpet-

196

ual summer in the household where they prevail. And if there be a spot on earth which angels might long to visit, and where they might fondly linger, it is the loving Christian family, where parents and children, husband and wife, brothers and sisters, bound together in the blessed compact of love, and moving in harmonious spheres of duty and affection, fulfill the holy and beautiful purposes of the Family Institution.

The Old Home

Alfred Tennyson

> We love the well-beloved place
>> Where first we gazed upon the sky;
>> The roofs that heard our earliest cry,
> Will shelter one of stranger race.

> We go, but ere we go from home,
>> As down the garden-walks I move,
>> Two spirits of a diverse love
> Contend for loving masterdom.

> One whispers, "Here thy boyhood sung
>> Long since, its matin song, and heard
>> The low love-language of the bird,
> In native hazels tassel-hung."

> The other answers, "Yea, but here
>> Thy feet have strayed in after hours,
>> With thy best friend among the bowers,
> And this hath made them trebly dear."

These two have striven half a day;
 And each prefers his separate claim,
 Poor rivals in a losing game,
That will not yield each other way.

I turn to go: my feet have set
 To leave the pleasant fields and forms:
 They mix in one another's arms
To one pure image of regret.

Home Shadows

Robert Collyer

riends, I wonder whether we have any deep consciousness of the shadows we are weaving about our children in the home; whether we ever ask ourselves if, in the far future, when we are dead and gone, the shadow our home casts now will stretch over them for curse or blessing. It is possible we are full of anxiety to do our best, and to make our homes sacred to the children. We want them to grow up right, to turn out good men and women, to be an honor and praise to the home out of which they sprang. But this is the pity and the danger, that while we may not come short in any real duty of father and mother, we may yet cast no healing and sacramental shadow over the child. Believe me, friends, it was not in the words he said, in the pressure of the hand, in the kiss, that the blessing came when Jesus took the little ones in his arms. So it is not in these, but in the shadow of my innermost, holiest self; in that which is to us what the perfume is to the flower, a soul within the soul. It is that which, to the child in the home, is more than the tongue of men or angels, or

prophecy or knowledge, or faith that will move mountains, or devotion that will give the body to be burned. I look back with wonder on that old time, and ask myself how it is that most of the things I suppose that what my father and mother built on especially to mold me to a right manhood are forgotten and lost out of my life. But the thing they hardly ever thought of—the shadow of blessing cast by the home—the tender, unspoken love; the sacrifice made, and never thought of, was so natural to make them. Ten thousand little things, so simple as to attract no notice, and yet so sublime as I look back at them, they fill my heart still and always with tenderness, and my eyes with tears. All these things, and all that belong to them, still come over me, and cast the shadow that forty years, many of them lived in a new world, cannot destroy.

I fear few parents know what a supreme and holy thing is this shadow cast by the home, especially over the first seven years of the life of a child. I think the influence that comes in this way is the very breath and bread of life. I may do other things for duty or principle or religious training; they are all, by comparison, as when I cut and trim and train a vine; and when I let the sun shine and the rain fall on it, the one may aid the life, the other is the life. Steel and string are each good in their place, but what are they compared to sunshine?

Let the Little Children Come

J. R. Miller

hen the disciples wanted to know who was greatest, Jesus called a little child, and took him on his knee. The disciples were clustered around him, and saw what he did. A little child in the midst is often used to teach great lessons to older people. When a new baby comes into a home, God sets it in the midst of a family as a teacher. Parents suppose they are training their children, but the children are also teaching and training them.

I learned more of the meaning of the fatherhood of God, and of the way he feels toward his children, in one week after the first baby came into my home, than I had learned from teachers and books, even from the Bible, in all the preceding years of my life. Every child's life is a book, a new page of which is turned over each day.

Children are not angels, and yet they bring from heaven to earth many fragments of loveliness. Their influence in a home is a benediction. They soften hearts and change the whole thought of life in their parents. It is no more of self. They begin to live for their children. The children open love's chambers. They train their parents in patience, gentleness, thoughtfulness. While a young child is in a home a school of heaven is set up there. Sad is it for those within, if they miss the chance of learning such blessed lessons.

Religion in the Family

Ladies' Repository

t is a happy day in the history of a family when Jesus takes up his abode with it and is entertained with the affection and reverence with which Martha, Mary, and Lazarus received him. That earthly home, where all are loved by Jesus, and all love him in return, is a type of heaven. There nothing will be retained or practiced which is contrary to Christ, and which is known to be offensive to him. All will serve him, all will sit at his feet, all will love him. And what moral spectacle is there in this world more lovely than that of a family, enlightened, hallowed, and made happy by the presence of Christ dwelling in their midst? And to make all our families happy in this way is the great purpose of the Savior's mission to our world. It was Jehovah's promise respecting Him, that in Him all the families of the earth should be blessed—blessed with His presence, His truth, His precepts, and His rule— blessed with life on earth and immortality in heaven.

A truly Christian family is one in which the doctrines, precepts, and hopes which the Gospel reveals, bear sway, exercising a practical influence daily over the spirit and conduct of its members. And it is only over such family circles that Jesus will himself preside. He will not dwell in the midst of those who reject his truth, for he regards dishonor done to that as done to himself. Then if those families which profess religion would have Christ in the midst of them, protecting guiding, and blessing them, they must purge themselves from everything which is offensive to him, and allow nothing to be practiced which would provoke his displeasure, and cause him in displeasure to depart. And when, from any family in which Jesus has dwelt, he is forced to depart, how terrible are the words which he pronounces as He retires, "Your house is left unto you desolate!" and truly that house is desolate from which Jesus has withdrawn.

Home Affection

H. C. Dane

ffection does not beget weakness, nor is it effeminate for a brother to be tenderly attached to his sisters. That boy will make the noblest, the bravest man. On the battlefield, in many terrible battles during our late horrible war, I always noticed that those boys who had been reared under the tenderest home culture always made the best soldiers. They were always brave, always endured the severe hardships of camp, the march, or on the bloody field most silently, and were most dutiful at every call. More, much more, they resisted the frightful temptations that so often surrounded them, and seldom returned to their loved ones stained with the sins incident to war. Another point, they were always kind and polite to those whom they met in the enemy's country. Under their protection, woman was always safe. How often I have heard one regiment compared with another, when the cause of the difference was not comprehended by those who drew the comparison! I knew the cause—it was the home education.

We see the same every day in the busy life of the city. Call together one hundred young men in our city and spend an evening with them, and we will tell you their home education. Watch them as they approach young ladies, and converse with them, and we will show you who have been trained under the influence of home affection and politeness, and those who have not.

That young man who was accustomed to kiss his sweet, innocent, loving sister night and morning as they met, shows its influence upon him, and he will never forget it. When he takes someone to his heart as his wife, she shall reap the golden fruit of it. The young man who was in the habit of giving his arm to his sister as they walked to and from church, will never leave his wife to find her way as best she can. The young man who has been taught to see that his sister had a seat before he sought his, will never mortify a neglected wife in the presence of strangers. And that young man who always handed his sister to her chair at the table, will never have cause to blush as he sees some gentleman extend to his wife the courtesy she knows is due from him.

Mothers and daughters, wives and sisters, remember that; and remember that you have the making of the future of this great country, and rise at once to your high and holy duty. Remember that you must make that future, whether you will or not. We are all what you make us. Ah! Throw away your weakening follies of fashion, and soul-

famine, and rise to the level where God intended you should be, and make every one of your homes, from this day, schools of true politeness and tender affection. Take those little curly-headed boys, and teach them all you would have men to be, and my word for it, they will be just such men, and will go forth to bless the world, and crown you with a glory such as queens and empresses never dreamed of. Wield your power now and you shall reap the fruit in your ripe age.

IN PROPORTION to your devotion to the Savior will be the blessedness of your life.—*Elizabeth Prentiss*

Home Instruction

Hon. Schuyler Colfax

bove all things, teach children what their life is. It is not simply breathing, moving, playing, or sleeping. Life is a battle. All thoughtful people see it so. A battle between good and evil from childhood. Good influences, drawing us up toward the divine; bad influences, drawing us down to the brute. Midway we stand, between the divine and the brute. How to cultivate the good side of the nature is the greatest lesson of life to teach. Teach children that they lead these two lives: the life without, and the life within. Teach them that the inside must be pure in the sight of God, as well as the outside in the sight of men. There are five means of learning. These are: Observation, reading, conversation, memory, and reflection.

Educators sometimes, in their anxiety to secure a wide range of studies, do not sufficiently impress upon their scholars the value of memory. Now, our memory is one of the most wonderful gifts God has bestowed upon us; and one of the most mysterious. Take a pitcher and pour water into it. When you can pour nor more, it is full. It is not so with the mind. You cannot fill it full of knowledge in a whole life-time. Pour in all you please, and it still thirsts for more.

Remember this:

• Knowledge is not what you learn, but what you remember.

• It is not what you eat, but what you digest, that makes you grow.

• It is not the money you handle, but that you keep, that which makes you rich.

• It is not what you study, but what you remember and reflect upon, that makes you learned.

One more suggestion:

Above all things else, strive to fit the children in your charge to be useful men and women—men and women you may be proud of in after-life. While they are young, teach them that far above physical courage, which will lead them to face the cannon's mouth—above wealth, which would give them farms and houses, and bank stocks and gold, is *moral courage*. That courage by which they will stand fearlessly, frankly, firmly, for the right. Every man or woman who dares to stand for the right when evil has its legions, is the true moral victor in this life and in the land beyond the stars.

WHEREVER we have a home, God should have a church.

—*Matthew Henry*

Home Sweet Home

Saturday Evening Post

here is music in the word home. To the old it brings a bewitching strain from the harp of memory. To the young it is a reminder of all that is near and dear to them. Among the many songs we are apt to listen to, there is not one more cherished than the touching melody of "Home, Sweet Home."

Will you go back with me a few years, dear reader, in the history of the past, and traverse in imagination the happy streets and gilded saloons of Paris, that once bright center of the world's follies and pleasures? Passing through its splendid thoroughfares is one (an Englishman) who has left his home and native land to view the splendors and enjoy the pleasures of a foreign country. He has beheld with delight its paintings, its sculpture, and the grand yet graceful proportions of its buildings, and has yielded to the spell of the sweetest muse.

Yet, in the midst of his keenest happiness, when he was rejoicing most over the privileges he possessed, temptations assailed him. Sin was presented to him in one of its most bewitching garbs. He drank wildly and deeply of the intoxicating cup, and his draught brought madness. Reason was overwhelmed, and he rushed out, all his scruples overcome, careless of what he did or how deeply he became immersed in the hitherto unknown sea of guilt.

The cool night air lifted the damp locks from his heated brow, and swept with soothing touch over his flushed cheeks. Walking on, calmer, but no less determined, strains of music from a distance met his ear. Following in the direction of the sound, he distinguished the words from and air. The song was well-remembered. It was "Home, Sweet Home." Clear and sweet the voice of some English singer rose and fell on the air, in the soft cadences of that beloved melody.

Motionless, the wanderer listened till the last note floated away and he could hear nothing but the ceaseless murmur of a great city. Then he turned slowly, with no feeling that his manhood was shamed by the tear which fell as a bright evidence of the power of song.

The demon had fled, and reason once more asserted her right to control. As the soft strains of "Sweet Home" had floated to his ear, memory brought up before him his own "sweet home." He saw his gentle mother, and heard her speak, while honest pride beamed from her eye of her son, in whose noble and honor she could always trust; and his heart smote him as he thought how little he deserved such confidence. He remembered her last words of love and counsel, and the tearful farewell of all those dear ones who gladdened that far-away home with their presence. Well he knew their pride in his integrity, and the tide of remorse swept over his spirit as he felt what their sorrow would be could they have seen him an hour before. Subdued and repentant, he retraced his steps, and with this vow never to taste of the terrible draught that could so excite him to madness was mingled a deep sense of thankfulness for his escape from further degradation. The influence of home had protected him though the sea rolled between.

None can tell how often the commission of crime is prevented by such memories. If the spell of home is so powerful, how important it is to make it pleasant and lovable! Many a time a cheerful home and smiling face does more to make good men and women, than all the learning and eloquence that can be used. It has been said that the sweetest words in our language are "Mother, Home and Heaven;" and one might almost say the word home included them all; for who can think of home without remembering the gentle mother who sanctified it by her presence? And is not home the dearest name for heaven? We think of that better land as a home where brightness will never end in night. Oh, then, may our homes on earth be the centers of all our joys. May they be as green spots in the desert, to which we can retire when weary of the cares and perplexities of life, and drink the clear waters of a love which we know to be sincere and always unfailing.

Family Religion

Mother's Magazine

he true divine origin of the domestic economy is to train children, by, habits of virtue, obedience, and piety in the family, to become useful members of society at large and good subjects of the State, and above all to be fellow-citizens with the saints and of the household of faith. In order to do this, the strict maintenance of family religion is absolutely essential. It is therefore laid down as an axiom that no State can be prosperous where family order and religion are generally neglected.

I was a Wandering Sheep

Horatius Bonar

I was a wandering sheep, I did not love the fold;
I did not love my Shepherd's voice, I would not be controlled.
I was a wayward child, I did not love my home;
I did not love my father's voice, I loved afar to roam.

The Shepherd sought His sheep, the father sought his child;
they followed me o'er vale and hill, o'er deserts waste and wild.
they found me nigh to death, famished and faint and lone;
they bound me with the bands of love, 'tis He that still doth keep.

Jesus my Shepherd is; 'twas He that loved my soul,
'twas He that washed me in His blood, 'twas He that made me whole;
'twas He that sought the lost, that found the wandering sheep,
'twas He that bought me to the fold, 'tis He that still doth keep.

I was a wand'ring sheep, I would not be controlled,
but now I love my Shepherd's voice, I love, I love the fold.
I was a wayward child, I once preferred to roam;
but now I love my Father's voice, I love, I love his home.

THERE IS NOTHING in this world which is so venerable as the character of parents; nothing so intimate and endearing as the relation of husband and wife; nothing so tender as that of children, nothing so lovely as those of brothers and sisters. The little circle is made one by a single interest, and by a singular union of the affections.—*Timothy Dwight*

The Power of Home

R. S. Storrs

he power of human attachment is as strong in American society today as it has ever been in the past. As long as a boy is anchored to a happy Christian home, to the experience of it in his youth and the remembrance of it in his manhood, he is reasonably safe for this life and the next. As long as a nation is anchored to its homes, that nation is reasonably secure of a continuing, developing, and constantly more powerful spiritual force.

EVERY CHRISTIAN FAMILY ought to be a little church consecrated to Christ, wholly influenced and governed by His rules.—*Jonathan Edwards*

The New Song

Elizabeth Prentiss

There is a song I want to sing—
Or want to learn to sing;
It is a song of praise to Thee,
Jesus, my Lord and King.

Oh, teach me all its varied notes,
Its hidden melody,
Till I have learned to sing by heart
This song of praise to Thee.

I want to sing, while yet on earth,
The tender, thankful strain

210

Of saints, who gladly near thy throne,
   Make Thee their song's refrain.

For though I am not yet a saint,
   And though my praises ring
From an encumbered, earthly soul,
   I love the strains they sing.

And well I love, I know I love,
   Though truly not as they,
Thee, blessed Jesus, whom I praise
   Feebly on earth today.

While there's a song I want to sing—
   Or want to learn to sing;
A blessed song of love to Thee,
   Jesus, my Lord and King.

PRAYER DRAWS ALL the Christian graces into her focus. It draws Charity, followed by her lovely train—her forbearance with faults—her forgiveness of injuries—her pity for errors—her compassion for want. It draws Repentance, with her holy sorrows—her pious resolutions—her self-distrust. It attracts Truth, with her elevated eyes; Hope, with her gospel anchor; Beneficence, with her open hand; Zeal, looking far and wide; Humility, with introverted eye, looking at home.—*Hannah More*

The Light of Home

Sarah J. Hale

My boy, you will dream the world is fair,
    And your Spirit will sigh to roam;
And you must go; but never, when there,
    Forget the light of home.
Though pleasure may smile with a ray more bright,
    It dazzles to lead astray;
Like the meteor's flash, it will deepen the night
    When you tread the lonely way.
But the hearth of home has a constant flame,
    And pure as vestal fire:
'T will burn, 't will burn, forever the same,
    For nature feeds the pyre.
The sea of ambition is tempest-tossed,
    And your hopes may vanish like foam;
But when sails are shivered, and rudder lost,
    Then look to the light of home;—
And there, like a star through the midnight cloud,
    You will see the beacon bright;
For never, till shining on your shroud,
    Can be quenched its holy light.

Sweet Ties of Home

Magaret Sangster

Home hath many sweet ties that bind us earthward. Every year that goes over our heads makes dearer, by a thousand acts and words, the gray-haired father, the tender mother, the gentle wife, the loving hus-

212

band, the dutiful child. Ambition, pleasure, love, science, travel every new achievement, every new delight, every new acquirement, are so many ties, that, unsanctified, may bind us here and help us to forget the sweet hereafter.

Home Religion
Mother's Treasury

house may be full of persons who are very dear to each other, very kind to each other; full of precious things, affections, hopes, and living interests. But if God is not there as the Ruler and Father of the house, the original and true idea of home will not be realized. Vacancy and need will still be at the heart of all. Good things will grow feebly and uncertainly, like flowers in winter, trying to peep out into sunshine, yet shrinking from the blast. Evil things will grow with strange persistency, notwithstanding protests of the affections and efforts of the will. Mysterious gulfs will open at times where it was thought strong foundations had been laid. Little things will produce great distress. Great things, when attained, will shrink to littleness. Flickerings of uncertainty and fear will run along the days. Joys will not satisfy. Sorrow will surprise. In the very heart of the godless home there will be sickness, arising from need unsatisfied and "hope deferred." It will be as when a man of ingenuity tries in vain to put together the separated parts of a complicated piece of mechanism. He tries in this way and that, puts the pieces into every conceivable mode of arrangement, then at last stops, and says, "There must be a piece missing."

Home without Divine presence is at best a moral structure without the central element. The other elements may be arranged and re-arranged; they will never exactly fit, nor be "compact together," until it

213

is obtained. We have heard of haunted houses. That house will be haunted with the ghost of an unrealized idea. It will seem to its most thoughtful inmates at best "the shadow of some good thing to come;" and the longing for the substance will be the more intense, because the shadow, as a providential prophecy, is always there.

In many a house there is going on, by means of those quick spiritual sighs by which one above can read, what we may call a dialogue of souls, composed chiefly of unspoken questions, which might be something like the following, "How is it that we cannot be to each other as we wish, that we cannot do for each other what we try, even when it seems to be quite within the range of possibility? Why is there such a sorrow in our affection? Such a trembling in our joys? So great a fear of change, and so profound a sense of incompleteness in connection with the very best we can do and be?"

And what is the answer to such mute yet eager questionings? And who can speak that answer? That One above who hears the dialogue must take part in it. All must listen while He speaks, and tells of another fatherhood, under which the parents must become little children. He tells of another brotherhood which, when attained, will make the circle complete. When the members of such a houschold, who have been looking so much to each other, shall agree to give one earnest look above, and say, "Our Father, which art in heaven!" "our elder Brother, and Advocate with the Father!" then will come back, sweet as music, into the heart of that house, with these fulfilling words from the everlasting Father, "Ye shall be my sons and daughters;" from the eternal Son, "Behold my mother and sister and brother!" Then the one thing that was lacking will be present. The missing element will be in its place, and all the other elements will be assembled around it. It is a haunted house no more. The ghost has been chased away. The house is wholesome. Mornings are welcome. Nights are restful. The aching sorrow has passed away now from the heart of that home. The long-sought secret is revealed. Soul whispers to soul, "Emmanuel, God with us." Home is home at last.

Family Prayers

Christian at Work

e are far from thinking that the good old custom of having family prayers is being dropped from Christian households. It is a custom held in honor wherever there is real Christian life, and it is the one thing which, more than any other, knits together the loose threads of a home and unites its various members before God. The short religious service in which parents, children, and friends daily join in praise and prayer, is at once an acknowledgment of dependence on the heavenly Father and a renewal of consecration to his work in the world. The Bible is read, the hymn is sung, the petition is offered, and unless all has been done not as a mere formality and with hearty assent, those who have gathered at the family altar leave it helped, soothed, strengthened, and armored, as they were not before they met there. The sick and the absent are remembered. The tempted and the tried are commended to God, and as the Israelites in the desert were attended by the pillar and the cloud, so in life's wilderness the family who inquires of the Lord is constantly overshadowed by his presence and love.

There are many reasons which are allowed to interfere with and thrust aside the privilege of family prayer in homes where father and mother mean to have it daily. Whatever comes in the way of a plain duty ought, however, to be set aside. If there be any among our readers who recognize the need there is in their house to have a daily open worship of God, let them begin it at once. They must find the time, choose the place, and appoint the way. The actual time spent in worship may only be a few minutes. A brief service which cannot tire the youngest child, if held unvaryingly as the sun, in the morning when the day begins, and in the evening when its active labors close, is far more useful and edifying than a long one which fatigues attention.

It is possible to have a daily worship which shall be earnest, vivifying, tender and reverential, and yet a weariness to nobody. Only let the one who conducts it mean toward the Father the sweet obedience of the grateful child, and maintain the attitude of one who goes about earthly affairs with a soul looking beyond and above them to the rest that remains in heaven. It is not every one who is able to pray in the hearing of others with ease. The timid tongue falters, and the thoughts struggle in vain for utterance. But who is there who cannot read a Psalm, or a chapter, or a cluster of verses, and while kneeling, repeat in accents of tender trust the Lord's prayer? When we think of it, that includes everything.

Home and its Queen
Scribner's Monthly

here is probably not a righteous man or woman living, who does not feel that the sweetest consolations and best rewards of life are found in the loves and delights of home. There are very few who do not feel themselves indebted to the influences that clustered around their cradles for whatever good there may be in their characters and condition. Home, based upon Christian marriage, is so evident an institution of God, that a man must become profane before he can deny it. Wherever it is pure and true to the Christian idea, there lives an institution conservative of all the nobler instincts of society.

Of this realm woman is the queen. It takes the cue and hue from her. If she is in the best sense womanly—if she is true and tender, loving and heroic, patient and self-devoted—she consciously and unconsciously organizes and puts in operation a set of influences that do more to mould the destiny of the nation than any man, uncrowned by power of eloquence, can possibly effect. The men of the nation are what mothers make them, as a rule; and the voice that those men speak in the expression of power, is the voice of the woman who bore and bred them. There can be no substitute for this. There is no other possible way in which the women of the nation can organize their influence and power that will tell so beneficially upon society and the state.

A Cheerful Home

Friend's Intelligencer

single bitter word may disquiet an entire family for a whole day. One surly glance casts a gloom over the household, while a smile, like a gleam of sunshine, may light up the darkest and weariest hours. Like unexpected flowers, which spring up along our path, full of freshness, fragrance and beauty, do kind words and gentle acts and sweet dispositions make glad the home where peace and blessing dwell. No matter how humble the abode, if it be thus garnished with grace and sweetened with kindness and smiles, the heart will turn lovingly toward it from all the tumult of the world and will be the dearest spot beneath the circuit of the sun.

And the influences of home perpetuate themselves. The gentle grace of the mother lives in the daughter long after her head is pillowed in the dust of death. The fatherly kindness finds its echo in the nobility and courtesy of sons, who come to wear his mantle and to fill his place. While, on the other hand, from an unhappy, misgoverned, and disordered home, go forth persons who shall make other homes miserable, and perpetuate the sourness and sadness, the contentions and strifes and railings which have made their own early lives so wretched and distorted.

Toward the cheerful home, the children gather "as clouds and as doves to their windows," while from the home, which is the abode of discontent and strife and trouble, they fly forth as vultures to rend their prey. The class of men who disturb and distress the world, are not those born and nurtured within the hallowed influences of Christian homes, but rather those whose early life has been a scene of trouble and vexation—who have started wrong in the pilgrimage, and whose course is one of disaster to themselves, and trouble to those around.

Conversation in the Home

Churchman Magazine

mong home amusements the best is the good old habit of conversation, the talking over the events of the day, in bright and quick play of wit or fancy, the story which brings the laugh, and speaking the good, kind and true things, which all have in their hearts. It is not so much by dwelling upon what members of the family have in common, as bringing each to the other something interesting and amusing, that home life is to be made cheerful and joyous. Each one must do his part to make conversation genial and happy. We are ready to converse with newspapers and books, to seek some companion at the store, hotel, or club-room, and to forget that home is anything more than a place to sleep and eat in. The revival of conversation, the entertainment of one another, as a roomful of people will entertain themselves, is one secret of a happy home. Wherever it is wanting, disease has struck into the root of the tree. There is a want which is felt with increasing force as time goes on. Conversation, in many cases, is just what prevents many people from relapsing into utter selfishness at their firesides. This conversation should not simply occupy husband and wife, and other older members of the family, but extend itself to the children. Parents should be careful to talk with them, to enter into their life, to share their trifles, to assist in their studies, to meet them in the thoughts and feelings of their childhood. It is a great step in education, when around the evening lamp are gathered the different members of a family, sharing their occupation with one another—the older assisting the younger, each one contributing to the entertainment of the other, and all feeling that the evening has passed only too rapidly away. This is the truest and best amusement. It is the healthy education of great and noble characters. There is the freedom, the breadth, the joyousness of natural life. The time spent in this way by parents in the higher entertainment of their children, bears a harvest of eternal blessings, and these long evenings, furnish just the time.

Speak Cheerful Words

Ladies Repository

hy is it that so many people keep all their pleasant thoughts and kind words about a man bottled and sealed until he is dead, when they come and break the bottle over his coffin and bathe his shroud in fragrance? Many a man goes through life with scarcely one bright, cheerful, encouraging, hopeful word. He toils hard and in lowly obscurity. He gives out his life freely and unstintedly for others. I remember such a man. He was not brilliant. He was not great. But he was faithful. He had many things to discourage him. Troubles thickened about his life. He was misrepresented and misunderstood. Everybody believed that he was a good man, but no one ever said a kindly word or pleasant thing to him. He never heard a compliment, scarcely ever a good wish. No one ever took any pains to encourage him, to strengthen his feeble knees, to lighten his burdens, or to lift up his heart by a gentle deed of love, or by a cheerful word. He was neglected. Unkind things were often said of him.

I stood at his coffin, and then there were many tongues to speak his praise. There was not a breath of aspersion in the air. Men spoke of self-denial—of his work among the poor, of his quietness, modesty, his humility, his pureness of heart, his faith and prayer.

There were many who spoke indignantly of the charges that falsehood had forged against him in past years, and of the treatment he had received. There were enough kind things said during the two or three days that he lay in his coffin, and while the company stood around his open grave, to have blessed him and made him happy all his fifty years, and to have thrown sweetness and joy about his soul during all his painful and weary journey. There was enough sunshine wasted about the black, coffin and dark grave to have made his whole life-path bright as the clearest day.

But his ears were closed then, and could not hear a word that was spoken. His heart was still then, and could not be thrilled by the grateful sounds. He cared nothing then for the sweet flowers that were piled upon his coffin. The love blossomed out too late. The kindness came when the life could not receive its blessings.

LET US take our lot in life just as it comes, courageously, patiently, and faithfully, never wondering at anything the Master does.—*Elizabeth Prentiss*

A Happy Home Defined

James Hamilton

ix things are requisite to create a happy home. Integrity must be the architect, and tidiness the upholsterer. It must be warmed by affection, and lightened up with cheerfulness, and industry must be the ventilator, renewing the atmosphere and bringing in refreshment day by day; while over all, as a protecting canopy and glory, nothing will suffice except the blessings of God.

The Family

Bayard Taylor

Dear love, whatever fate
    The flying years unfold,
There's none can dissipate
    The happiness we hold.
Whatever cloud may rise,
    The very storms grow mild
When bend the blissful skies
    O'er husband, wife, and child.
The errant dreams that failed,
    The promises that fled,
The roseate hopes that paled,
    The loves that now are dead,
The treason of the past,—
    All, all are reconciled:
Life's glory shines at last
    On father, mother, child!
To meet the days and years,

With hands that never part;
To shed no secret tears,
    To bide no lonely heart;
To know our longing stilled,
    To feel that God has smiled:
These are the dreams fulfilled
    In Husband, Wife, and Child,
        In Father, Mother, Child!

Make Home Life Beautiful

B. G. Northrop

et me say to parents: Make the home-life beautiful, without and within, and you will sow the seeds of gentleness, true kindness, honesty and fidelity, in the hearts of your children, from which the children reap a harvest of happiness and virtue. The memory of the beautiful and happy home of childhood is the richest legacy any man can leave to his children. The heart will never forget its hallowed influences. It will be an evening enjoyment, to which the lapse of years will only add new sweetness. Such a home is a constant inspiration for good, and as constant a restraint from evil.

If by taste and culture we adorn our homes and grounds and add to their charms, our children will find the quiet pleasures of rural homes more attractive than the whirl of city life. Such attractions and enjoyments will invest home-life, school-life, the whole future of life with new interests and with new dignity and joyousness, for life is just what we make it. We may by our blindness live in a world of darkness and gloom, or in a world full of sunlight and beauty and joy; for the world without only reflects the world within. Also, the tasteful improvement of grounds and home exerts a good influence not only upon the children, but upon the community. An elegant dwelling, surrounded by pleasant attractions, is a contribution to the refinement, the good order, the taste and prosperity of every community, improving the public taste and ministering to every enjoyment.

Building a Home

T. De Witt Talmage

hen a man builds his home, he builds for eternity. Is it not amazing that affiancing in life is so often a matter of merriment and of joke, when it decides so much for this world and the world to come? Oh! build not your home on earth upon the sparkle of a bright eye or the color of a fair cheek. The time will come in your history when you will want in your home not a pet or a toy, but a heroine, and you will find that life is not a gay romance, but a tremendous reality; and coming home from your store, or office, or shop, or factory, or studio, you will need some one in your home with a face both cheerful and sympathetic.

There is an aged man who looks back to a crisis in life when his fortune went away and reason almost left the throne. He knew not what to do. He remembers a particular evening when he came home from the store. He hardly dared break the news to his wife. He could not bear to tell her he had suspended in business and that he had stopped payment and his fortune was gone. He went into the house, he closed the door upon the world, and in domestic peace found a foretaste of that heaven where panics never come. Ah! If it had not been for that help that you had, what would have been the result when you told her of your financial embarrassment and misfortune? She was cheerful, she was sympathetic, she was helpful, she helped you all through those dark days of trial, and after the piano went, she could sing without the

accompaniment just as well as she ever sang with it.

A Christian minister in England called upon a house of great destitution. There were the husband, the wife, and there were the children.

Everything was indicative of want and struggle. The minister of the Gospel said to this young man; "Your mistake was in marrying so early. Do you not think that was the mistake of your life?" The man had been told that that was the mistake of his life before. The minister said; "It would have been better for you to have gone on and got something of a property before you entered into the marriage state. Don't you think it would have been better?" And the man looked around, his eyes filled with tears, and he looked at his poorly clad wife and said; "No, sir! She's been the same to me through it all."

Ah! There are some who would never have known what their homes were worth if trouble had not come. Perhaps your companion in life may have been too fond of the world and its pleasures, but one touch of misfortune turned her into a Miriam, shouting the triumph on the banks of the Red Sea. If you have spoken of frivolity and fondness of display as the chief characteristics of woman, you may have to correct your mistake in some bitter pass of life, when all other resources having failed, you are upheld by a wife's hand suddenly armed for the emergency. Oh! In this tremendous pass of your earthly existence, cry unto God and ask His direction. Make a mistake here, and you make it forever.

Blessed be that home in which the newly-married couple dedicate their souls to Christ. Blessed is the family Bible in which their names have just been written. Blessed is the hour of morning and evening prayer. Blessed are the angels of God who join wing-tip to wing-tip over that home, making a canopy of light and love and blessedness. It may be only yesterday that they clasped hands, but they have clasped hands forever. The orange blossoms may fade, and the fragrance may die on the air, but they who marry in Christ shall walk together on that day when the Church, the Lamb's wife, shall take the hand of her Lord and King amid the swinging of the golden censers.

Joys of Home

Sir John Bowring

Sweet are the joys of home,
    And pure as sweet; for they
Like dews of morn and evening come,
    To make and close the day.
The world hath Its delights,
    And its delusions, too;
But home to calmer bliss invites,
    More tranquil and more true.
The mountain flood is strong,
    But fearful in its pride;
While gently rolls the stream along
    The peaceful valley's side.
Life's charities, like light,
    Spread smilingly afar;
But stars approached, become more bright,
    And home is life's own star.
The pilgrim's step in vain
    Seeks Eden's sacred ground!
But in home's holy joys again
    An Eden may be found.
A glance of heaven to see,
    To none on earth is given;
And yet a happy family
    Is but an earlier heaven.

The Children's Bedtime

Jane Ellis Hopkins

The clock strikes seven in the hall,
    The curfew of the children's day,
That calls each little pattering foot
    From dance and song and lively play;
Their day that in a wider light
    Floats like a silver day-moon white,
Nor in our darkness sinks to rest,
    But sets within a golden west.

Ah, tender hour that sends a drift
    Of children's kisses through the house,
And cuckoo notes of sweet "Good night,"
    That thoughts of heaven and home arouse
And a soft stir to sense and heart,
    As when the bee and blossom part;
And little feet that patter slower,
    Like the last droppings of a shower.

And in the children's room aloft,
    What blossom shapes do gaily slip
Their daily sheaths, and rosy run
    From clasping hand and kissing lip,
A naked sweetness to the eye
    Blossom and babe and butterfly
In witching one, so dear a sight!
    An ecstasy of life and light.

Then lily-dressed in angel white,
    To mother's knee they trooping come.
The soft palms fold like kissing shells,
    And they and we go singing home
Their bright heads bowed and worshipping,
    As though some glory of the spring,
Some daffodil that mocks the day,
    Should fold his golden palms and pray.

The gates of Paradise swing wide
    A moment's space in soft accord,
And those dread angels, Life and Death,
    A moment veil the flaming sword,
As o'er this weary world forlorn
    From Eden's secret heart is borne
That breath of Paradise most fair,
    Which mothers call "the children's prayer."

Then kissed, on beds we lay them down,
    As fragrant white as clover'd sod.
And all the upper floors grow hushed
    With children's sleep, and dews of God
And as our stars their beams do hide,
    The stars of twilight, opening wide,
Take up the heavenly tale at ev'ning,
    And light us on to God and heaven.

Man's Earthly Love and Joy

Donald Mitchell

he heart of a man with whom affection is not a name, and love a mere passion of the hour, yearns toward the quiet of a home as toward the goal of his earthly joy and hope. And as you fasten there your thought, an indulgent, yet dreamy fancy paints the loved image of a wife that is to adorn it, and make it sacred.

She is there to bid you Godspeed! And an adieu that hangs like music on your ear as you go out to the everyday labor of life. At evening she is there to greet you as you come back wearied with a day's toil; and her look, so full of gladness, relieves you of your fatigue. She runs her arm around you with a source of welcome that beams like sunshine on her brow, and that fills your eye with tears of a twin gratitude, to her and Heaven.

She is not unmindful of those old-fashioned virtues of cleanliness and order which give an air of quiet and which secure content. Your wants are all anticipated, the fire is burning brightly, the clean hearth flashes under the joyous blaze, and the old elbow-chair is in its place. Your very unworthiness of all this haunts you like an accusing spirit, and yet penetrates your heart with a new devotion toward your loving wife who is thus watchful of your every comfort.

She is gentle, keeping your love, as she has won it, by a thousand nameless and modest virtues which radiate from her whole life and action. She moves upon your affections like a summer wind breathing softly over sleeping valleys. She gains a mastery over your sterner nature by very contrast, and wins you, unwittingly, to her lightest wish. And yet her wishes are guided by that delicate tact which avoids conflict with your manly pride, which she subdues by seeming to yield. By a single soft word of appeal she robs your vexation of its anger, and with a slight touch of that fair hand and one pleading look of that earnest eye, she disarms your sternest pride.

She is kind, shedding her kindness as heaven sheds dew. Who, indeed, could doubt it? Least of all you, who are living on her kindness, day by day, as flowers live on light. There is none of that officious parade which blunts the point of benevolence, but it tempers every action with a blessing.

If trouble has come upon you, she knows that her voice beguiling you into cheerfulness, will lay aside your fears. As she draws her chair beside you, she knows that the tender and confiding way with which she takes your hand and looks up into your earnest face, will drive away from your annoyance all its weight. As she lingers, leading off your thought with pleasant words, she knows well that she is redeeming you from care and soothing you to that sweet calm which such home and such wife can alone bestow.

And in sickness—sickness that you almost covet for the sympathy it brings—that hand of hers resting on your fevered forehead, or those fingers playing with the scattered locks, are more full of kindness than the loudest vaunt of friends. When your failing strength will permit no more, you grasp that cherished hand with a fullness of joy, of thankfulness, and of love, which your tears only can tell.

She is good—her hopes live where the angels live. Her kindness and gentleness are sweetly tempered with that meekness and forbearance which are born of faith. Trust comes into her heart as rivers come to the sea. And in the dark hours of doubt and foreboding, you rest fondly upon her buoyant faith as the treasure of your common life; and in your holier reckonings you look to that frail hand and that gentle spirit to lead you away from the vanities of ambition to the fullness of that joy which the good inherit.

Home Truths

Thomas Guthrie

"Home is the resort of love, of joy, of peace and plenty, where, supporting and supported, polished friends and dear relations mingle into bliss."

ome! That word touches every fiber of the soul, and strikes every chord of the human heart with its angelic fingers. Nothing but death can break its spell. What tender associations are linked with home! What pleasing images and deep emotions it awakens! It calls up the fondest memories of life and opens in our nature the purest, deepest, richest gush of consecrated thought and feeling.

To the little child, home is his world—he knows no other. The father's love, the mother's smile, the sister's embrace, the brother's welcome, throw about his home a heavenly halo and make it as attractive to him as the home of angels. Home is the spot where the child pours out all his complaint and it is the grave of all his sorrows. Childhood has its sorrows and its grievances, but home is the place where these are soothed and banished by the sweet lullaby of a fond mother's voice.

Ask the man of mature years, whose brow is furrowed by care, whose mind is engrossed in business, ask him what is home. He will tell you that it is a place of rest, a haven of content, where loved ones relieve him of the burden of every-day life, too heavy to be continuously borne, from where he is refreshed and invigorated and goes forth to do battle again.

Ask the lone wanderer as he plods his weary way, bent with the weight of years and white with the frosts of age—ask him what is home. He will tell you that it is a green spot in memory, an oasis in the desert, a center about which the fondest recollection of his grief-oppressed heart clings with all the tenacity of youth's first love. It was once a glorious, a happy reality, but now it rests only as an image of the mind.

Wherever the heart wanders it carries the thought of home with it. Wherever by the rivers of Babylon the heart feels its loss and loneliness, it hangs its harp upon the willows, and weeps. It prefers home to its chief joy. It will never forget it, for there swelled its first throb, there were developed its first affections. There a mother's eye looked into it, there a father's prayer blessed it, there the love of parents and brothers and sisters gave it precious entertainment. There bubbled up from unseen fountains life's first effervescing hopes. There life took form and consistence. From that center went out all its young ambition. Towards that focus return its concentrating memories. There it took form and fitted itself to loving natures, and it will carry that impress wherever it may go, unless it becomes polluted by sin or makes to itself another home sanctified by a new and more precious affection.

If you wanted to gather up all tender memories, all lights and shadows of the heart, all banquetings and reunions, all filial, fraternal, paternal, conjugal affections, and had only just four letters to spell out all height and depth, and length and breadth, and magnitude and eternity of meaning, you would write it all out with the four letters that spell Home.

What beautiful and tender associations cluster thick around that word! Compared with it, wealth, mansion, palace, are cold, heartless terms. But home, that word quickens every pulse, warms the heart, stirs the soul to its depths, makes age feel young again, rouses apathy into energy, sustains the sailor in his midnight watch, inspires the soldier with courage on the field of battle, and imparts patient endurance to the worn-out sons of toil.

Sweet Home

Golden Gems of Life

THE HOME IS THE FOUNTAIN of civilization. Our laws are made in the home. The things said there give bias to character far more than do sermons and lectures, newspapers and books. No other audience are so susceptible and receptive as those gathered about the table and fireside; no other teachers have the acknowledged and divine right to instruct that is granted without challenge to parents. The foundation of our national life is under their hand. They can make it send forth waters bitter or sweet, for the death or the healing of the people.

THE INFLUENCES OF HOME perpetuate themselves. The gentle graces of the mother live in the daughter long after her head is pillowed in the dust of death, and the fatherly kindness finds its echoes in the nobility and character of sons who come to wear his mantle and fill his place. While, on the other hand, from an unhappy, misgoverned, and ill-ordered home, go forth persons who shall make other homes miserable and perpetuate the sorrows and sadness, the contentions and strifes, which have made their own early lives miserable. In every proper sense in which home can be considered, it is a powerful stimulant to noble actions and a high and pure morality. So valuable is this love of home that every man should cherish it as the apple of his eye. As he values his own moral worth, as he prizes his country, the peace and happiness of the world; yea, more, as he values the immortal interests of man, he should cherish and cultivate a strong and abiding love of home.

HOME HAS VOICES of experience and hearts of genuine holy love, to instruct you in the way of life, and to save you from a sense of loneliness as you gradually discover the selfishness of mankind. Home has its trials, in which are imaged forth the stern struggles of your after years, that your character may gain strength and manifestation, for which purpose they are necessary. They open the portals of his heart that the jewels otherwise concealed in its hidden depths may shine forth and shed their luster on the world. Home has its duties to teach you how to act on your own responsibilities. Home gradually and greatly increases its burdens, so that you may acquire strength to endure without being overtasked. Home is a little world in which the duties of the great world are daily rehearsed.

IF WE WOULD HAVE a true home, we must guard well our thoughts and actions. A single bitter word may disquiet the home for a whole day; but, like unexpected flowers which spring up along our path full of freshness, fragrance, and beauty, so do kind words and gentle acts and sweet disposition make glad the home where peace and blessing dwell. No matter how humble the abode, if it be thus garnished with grace and sweetened by kindness and smiles, the heart will turn lovingly towards it from all the tumults of the world, and home, "be it ever so humble," will be the dearest spot under the sun.

EVERY HOME SHOULD BE as a city set on a hill that cannot be hid. Into it should flock friends and friendship, bringing the light of the world, the stimulus and the modifying power of contact with various natures, the fresh flowers of feeling gathered from wide fields. Out of it should flow benign charities, pleasant amenities, and all those influences which are the natural offspring of a high and harmonious home-life.

CHARACTER, good or bad, has a tendency to perpetuate itself.

—A. A. Hodge.

Children in the Home

S. C. Ferguson

hildren are the pride and ornament of the family circle. They create sport and amusement and dissipate all sense of loneliness from the household. When intelligent and well trained they afford a spectacle which even indifferent persons contemplate with satisfaction and delight. Still these pleasurable emotions are not unalloyed with solicitude. It is an agreeable but changeable picture of human happiness. Time in advancing carries them forward, and soon they will feel like exclaiming with the older and more serious ones round them that their youth exists only in remembrance.

There is probably not an unpolluted man or woman living who does not feel that the sweetest consolations and best rewards of life are found in the loves and delights of home. There are very few who do not feel themselves indebted to the influence that clustered around their cradles for whatever good there may be in their character and condition.

Our Baby

Anson D. F. Randolph

I. September, 1858.

 Of all the darling children
  That e'er a household blessed,
 We place our baby for compare
  With the fairest and the best;
 She came when last the violets
  Dropped from the hand of Spring
 When on the trees the blossoms hung

Those cups of odorous incense swung
When dainty robins sing.
How glowed the early morning
After a night of rain,
When she possessed our waiting hearts
To go not out again;
"Dear Lord," we said, with thankful speech,
"Grant we may love the more
For this new blessing in our cup,
That was so full before!"

II. September, 1860.
This year, before the violets
Had heralded the Spring,
And not a leaf was on the trees,
Nor robin here to sing,
An angel came one solemn night,
Heaven's glory to bestow,
And take our darling from our sight;
What could we, Lord, at morning light,
But weep, and let her go?
How dark the day that followed
That dreary night of pain;
Those eyes now closed, and nevermore
To open here again.
"Dear Lord," we said, with broken speech,
"Grant we may love thee more
For this new jewel in the crown
Where we had two before!"

The Home Circle

Golden Gems of Life

he home circle ought to be the most delightful place on earth—the center of the purest affections and most desirable associations, as well as of the most attractive and exalted beauties to be found this side of paradise. Nothing can excel in beauty and sublimity the quietude, peace, harmony, affection, and happiness of a well-ordered family, where virtue is nurtured and every good principle fostered and sustained.

The home circle is the nursery of affection. It is the Eden of young attachments, and here should be planted and tended all the germs of love, every seed that shall ever sprout in the heart—and how carefully should they be tended! How guarded against the frosts of jealousy, anger, envy, pride, vanity, and ambition! How rooted in the best soil of the heart, and nourished and cultivated by the soul's best husbandry!

Here is the heart's garden. Its sunshine and flowers are here. All its beautiful, all its lovely things are here. And here should be expended care, toil, effort, patience, and whatever may be necessary to make them still more lovely. It is around the memories of the home circle that cluster the happiest and sometimes the saddest of the recollections of Youth. There is the thought of brother and sister, perhaps now gone forever; of childish sorrow and grief; of the mother's prayer and the father's blessing.

WHEN THE CARPENTER has finished your house and hands you the key, that is not your home. It is not yet complete. I remember what happened with my own home; how, after it had been finished, came the wife, and then one child, and then another, and so by degrees ties were added and the house grew into a home.—*Henry Ward Beecher*

241

Character Formed at Home

E. H. Chapin

ome is the sphere where are most clearly displayed the real elements of character. The world furnishes occasions of trial, but it also furnishes prudential considerations. Without any absolute hypocrisy, one measures his speech and restrains his action in the street and the market. And it is easy to conceive how small men may perform great deeds, and mean men philanthropic, and cowards flourish as heroes, with the tremendous motive of publicity to urge them.

But at home all masks are thrown aside and the true proportions of the man appear. Here he can find his actual moral standard, and measure himself accordingly. If he is irritable, here breaks forth his repressed fretfulness. If he is selfish, here are the sordid tokens. If he passes in any way for more than he is worth, here you may detect the counterfeit in the ring of his natural voice, and the superscription of his undisguised life.

No, the world is not the place to prove the moral stature and quality of a man. There are too many props and stimulants. Nor, on the other hand, can he himself determine his actual character merely by looking into his own solitary heart. Therein he may discover possibilities, but it needs actuality to make up the estimate of a complete life.

He must do something as well as be something. He must do something in order that he may be something. For what he thinks is in his heart may be exaggerated by self-flattery, or darkened by morbid self-distrust. It needs some occasion to prove what is really there. And home is precisely that sphere which is sufficiently removed from the factitious motives of publicity on the one extreme, and the unexercised possibilities of the human heart on the other, to afford a genuine test.

What a man really is, therefore, will appear in the truest light under

his own roof,and by his own fireside.

I can believe that he is a Christian when I know that he faithfully takes up the daily duties and bears the crosses that cluster within his own doors. I shall think that the world rightly calls him a philanthropist, when, notwithstanding common faults and infirmities, he receives the spontaneous award of the good husband and father, and the kindness of his nature is reflected in the very air and light of his dwelling.

True Hospitality

Sir Arthur Helps

perfect host is as rare a being as a great poet, and for much the same reason, namely, that to be a perfect host requires as rare a combination of qualities as those which are needed to produce a great poet. He should be like that lord in waiting of whom Charles II said, that he was "never in the way, and never out of the way." He should never degenerate into a showman, for there is nothing of which most people are so soon weary as of being shown things, especially if they are called upon to admire them. He, the perfect host, should always recollect that he is in his own house, and that his guests are not in theirs, consequently those local arrangements which are familiar to him should be rendered familiar to them. His aim should be to make his house a home for his guests, with all the advantage of novelty. If he entertains many guests, he should know enough about them to be sure that he has invited those who will live amicably together, and will enjoy each other's company. He should show no favoritism, if possible, and if he is a man who must indulge in favoritism, it should be to those of his guests who are more obscure than the others. He should be judiciously despotic as regards all proposals for pleasure, for there will be many that are diverse, and much time will be wasted if he does not take upon himself the labor and responsibility of decision. He should have much regard to the comings and goings of his guests, so as to provide every convenience for their entrance and departure. Now I am going to insist on what I think to be a very great point. He should aim at causing that his guests should thereafter become friends, if they are not so at present, so that they might, in future days, trace back the beginning of their friendship to their having met together at his house. He, the perfect host, must have the art to lead conversation without absorbing it himself, so that he may develop the best qualities of his guests. His expense in entertainment should not be devoted to what is luxurious, but to what is ennobling and comfortable. The first of all things is that he should be an affectionate, indeed, a loving host, so that every one of his guests should feel that he is really welcome. He should press them to stay, but should be careful that this pressing does not interfere with their convenience, so that they stay merely to oblige him, and not to please themselves. In considering who should be his guests, he should always have a thought as to those to whom he would render most service by having them as his guests, such as his poorer brethren, his more sickly brethren. Those who he feels would gain most advantage by being his guests, should have the first place in his invitations, and for his considerateness he will be amply rewarded by the benefits he will have conferred.

Christianity at Home

John Angell James

Christianity begins in the home. If not there, it is nowhere. We may attend meetings, and sing hymns, and join devoutly in prayer. We may give money to the poor, and send missionaries and Bibles to the heathen. We may organize societies of every description for doing good. We may get up church fairs, and tea-parties and tableaux and picnics. We may, in short, devote all our time and all our means to doing good, and yet not be the true and earnest Christians we ought to be, after all.

If they cannot say of us in the family at home; "He, or she, is a Christian, we know it, we feel it," —if home is not a better and happier place for our living in it, if there is not an influence going out from us, day by day, silently drawing those about us in the right direction,

245

then it is time for us to stop where we are, and begin to examine our profession to the name of Christian.

Christianity. Christ-likeness. Is that ours? Are we possessed of that? Are we patient, kind, long-suffering, forbearing, seeking with all our hearts to do good, dreading with all our hearts to do evil? For if we are Christ's we shall be like Him; and the first fruits, and the best fruits, of our daily living will be in the better and happier lives of those who are about us day by day.

Tell Your Wife

Pacific Rural Press

f you are in any trouble or quandary, tell your wife—that is, if you have one—all about it at once. Her insight and invention will most likely solve your difficulty sooner than all your logic. The wit of woman has been praised, but her instincts are quicker and keener than her reason. Counsel with your wife, or mother, or sister, and be assured, light will flash upon your darkness. Women are too commonly adjudged as verdant in all but purely womanish affairs. No philosophical students of the sex thus judge them. Their intuitions, or insights, are the most subtle. In counseling a man to tell his wife, we would go farther, and advise him to keep none of his affairs a secret from her. Many a home has been happily saved, and many a fortune retrieved, by a man's full confidence in his "better-half." Woman is far more a seer and prophet than man, if she be given a fair chance. As a general rule, wives confide the minutest of their plans and thoughts to their husbands, having no involvements to screen from them. Why not reciprocate, if but for the pleasure of meeting confidence with confidence? We are certain that no man succeeds so well in the world as he who, taking a partner for life, makes her the partner of his purposes and hopes. What is wrong with his impulse or judgment, she will check and set right with her almost universally right instincts. "Helpmeet" was no insignificant title as applied to man's companion. She is a helpmeet to him in every darkness, difficulty and sorrow of life. And what she most craves and most deserves is confidence without which love is never free from a shadow.

EVE WAS MADE from a rib out of the side of Adam, not made out of his head to rule him, nor out of his feet to be trampled upon by him, but out of his side to be equal with him, under his arm, to be protected, and near his heart to be beloved.—*Matthew Henry*

The Little Children

Henry Longfellow

Little feet; that such long years
    Must wander on through hopes and fears;
Must ache and bleed beneath your load;
    I, nearer to the wayside inn,
Where toil shall cease and rest begin,
    Am weary thinking of your road.

O, little hands; that weak or strong,
    Rave still to serve or rule so long,
Have still so long to give or ask;
    I, who so much with book and pen
Have toiled among my fellow-men,
    Am weary, thinking of your task.

O, little hearts; that throb and beat
　　With much impatient, feverish heat,
Such limitless and strong desires;
　　Mine, that so long has glowed and burned,
With passions into ashes turned,
　　Now covers and conceals its fires.

O, little souls; as pure and white,
　　As crystalline, as rays of light
Direct from Heaven, their source divine;
　　Refracted through the mist of years,
How red my setting sun appears;
　　How lurid looks this sun of mine!

A Worthy Ambition

John B. Gough

oung man! If God has given you brains, heart and voice, then speak out. There are great reforms to be carried on. The whole nation needs awakening. Speak out, sir, and your speech will be welcome, wherever and on whatever particular branch of reforms you choose to make yourself heard. Lift up your voice for that which is "honest, lovely, and of good report." Not in mere wordy harangue, not in windy palaver, not in grandiloquent spouting, nor in weary, drawling verbosity—not in the jabbering garrulity which is heard only when the speaker must deliver a speech. But in words of true, sanctified earnestness, opening your mouth because you have something useful to say, saying it with the genuine, unstudied eloquence which comes right from the heart, and in all cases closing your mouth the moment you are done.

249

Influence of Character

William Taylor

he influence of character can never be over-estimated. We call it influence, indeed; but we might, perhaps—as Whately somewhere says—with more significance, style it *effluence,* for it is continually radiating from a man, and then most of all when he is least conscious of its emanation. We are moulding others wherever we are, and if we were in every respect to live according to the gospel, we should be the noblest missionaries of the cross that the world has ever seen. Books are only powerful when they are read. Sermons are only influential when they are listened to. But character keeps itself at all times before men's attention, and its might is felt by every one who comes within its sphere. Other agencies are intermittent, like the revolving light, which after a time of brightness, goes out into a period of darkness; but religious principle is continuous in its operation, and shines with the steady radiance of a star. Hence, of all the ways by which Christians may tell on the surrounding world, this is the most potent, and probably there are no means more blessed for the conversion of sinners, and the elevation of spiritual life among believers, than the habitual deportment of the disciples of Jesus. Frequently, a servant has been brought to Christ by the sight of the Christian consistency of her mistress, and not seldom all the members of a household have been benefited by the piety of a humble maiden. I have known the young men of an office seriously impressed by the sterling principle of a fellow-clerk, and sometimes the holy walk of a simple-minded artisan has won not only the admiration, but also the imitation of his neighbors. Now, this is a means of usefulness within the reach of everyone, and if we are thoroughly alive to its importance, we should be more careful than we are of our conduct. Is it not the case that, instead of commending Christ by our lives, we too frequently give occasion to the enemies of the Lord to blaspheme, and mar the force of the truth by our inconsistency? Instead of adding new energy to the gospel by our conduct, we take away from its power by our iniquities; and men say, if the life of a Christian be such as we have manifested, they will not become Christians. Who can tell how many have been thus repelled from the word of truth? And is it not a fact, that one of the strongest evidences of the divinity of our religion may be derived from the consideration that it has survived the injuries inflicted on it by the Christless conduct of its professed adherents? My brethren, is this inconsistency to continue among us? Let us today resolve that, God helping us, we shall live more thoroughly in harmony with those noble principles which Christ enforced by his teaching, and adorned by his example. In the family, let us cultivate the graces of patience, forbearance, love, and self-sacrifice. In the social circle, let us seek to manifest meekness and purity. In business pursuits, let us show that we are actuated by justice and integrity. Wherever we are, let us endeavor to have our conversation so worthy of the gospel, that men may know that we have been with Jesus.

Model Homes

Samuel Fallows

esides model schools, let us have homes crowned with the clambering vine, amid the cooling shade of trees, surrounded with the verdant lawn, with pendant berries, with golden fruits, and clusters of purple grapes. Homes graced with pictures, refined by books, and gladdened with song. Homes in which there shall be no scorching blasts of passion, no polar storms of coldness and hate. Homes in which the wife and mother shall not lose all her attractive charms by unremitting drudgery and toil, nor the husband and father starve his brain and dwarf his soul by hours of over-work. Homes in which happy children shall ever see the beauty of love, and the beauty of holiness. Homes of plenty, homes of sympathy, homes of self-sacrifice, homes of devotion, homes of culture, homes of love. Angels from the fruits, and flowers, and streams, and fellowships of the home in the upper paradise would be lured, if possible, to dwell in these earthly Edens.

H-O-M-E

T. De Witt Talmage

f you wanted to gather up all tender memories, all lights and shadows of the heart, all banquetings and reunions, all filial, fraternal, paternal, conjugal affections, and had only four letters with which to spell out that height and depth and length and breadth and magnitude and eternity of meaning, you would write it all out with these four capital letters: H-O-M-E.

The Trials of Home

W. K. Tweedie

"Sorrowing, yet always rejoicing."

hen the first death happens in a home it speaks with a voice which scarcely any other form of tribulation can equal. We read of wars, and battles, and thousands slain, but even these are far-off echoes to most, compared with our own first death. That blow falls upon the very heart, and though faith may enable even a mother to close the dying eye of her little one, and smile through her tears, exclaiming "My Savior, I do this for Thee;" yet nature may be wrung with anguish, even while grace enables the tried one to tri-

252

umph. And the pang is often rendered more acute, or the stroke more severe, by the inscrutable mystery of a little infant's death. Why the terrible convulsions? Why that low wail, that smothered cry far worse for the parent to bear than a blow! Why that little frame pining slowly away, while skill is baffled in its attempts to discover the cause? Why is every breath a sigh or a moan, till even a mother sometimes flees from the sight and the sound, and feels that it would be a relief could her little sufferer die? And when all is over—when the little one is coffined, and the marble dust is about to be borne to the tomb, why that death at all? That little hand never did sin; that little heart never thought sin; and why then, this living only to die—this infant shroud, that infant coffin and grave? "Have my sins," a parent may ask, "brought down this woe? Is this the iniquity of the fathers visited on the children?"

Of this, at least, we are sure, "death passes upon all," "In Adam all die." Thus God shows the mystery, and bids us, when we cannot understand, to be silent and adore. What we know not now, we shall know hereafter; and though our rifled homes may cause the heart to ache, yet if such bereavements urge the parents more sedulously to prepare for glory, the present tribulation will deepen and prolong the future hosannas of the tried. And nature may symbolically teach us the same lesson. When we enter a mist-cloud as it drifts or hovers along the mountain-side which we are climbing, it sometimes dissolves around us so that the sunshine becomes undimmed. In like manner, if not here, at least hereafter, all the mist-clouds will clear away from before the parent who believes. Concerning his children torn from his embrace to the tomb, he may learn to say, "For us they sicken and for us they die."

Meanwhile, could parents remember that they are encountering their cares, and weeping their tears, and bearing their cross, and seeing their hopes deferred today, or blighted tomorrow, while attempting to

train their children for God, they would be stimulated to persevere, and not "faint in their minds."

But there is one form of grief more intense than even this. The trials which crowd our homes are numerous, and no doubt, one of the reasons may be that some would make their home their heaven. Their affections center there and their family is the Alpha and Omega of their exertions, their joys, and their hopes. Now to prevent such idolatry a thorn is often placed in the nest and men find labor and sorrow where they expected only sunshine and smiles. There may be poverty, and that is bitter. Or some disaster may threaten to strip our homes bare, but it is when trials assume the character of retributions that they convulse a household the most. It was hard for David to know that Absalom was no more, and that he perished a rebel against his king and father, made the pang more poignant still. But if that father associated that death with his own home misdeeds, his sorrow would be the most acute that man is doomed to feel. His touching wail, his outcry over his lost son, thus acquires a deeper meaning than before. "Would God I had died for thee," becomes not merely pathetic but profound. And that is the climax of all anguish—to see an object of affection go down, we fear, to a darker home than the grave. It is sad for a widowed one to see the delight of her eyes, the husband of her youth, snatched away by death. It is agony to an affectionate family to see the mother who bore them, and bore with them, carried to the narrow house. But a moral death causes a deeper wound—a more remediless sorrow, and nothing but omnipotent grace can carry a sufferer through such a grief. While he drinks "the wine of astonishment" his solace may be "It is the Lord," and "the Judge of all the earth will do right." But if the mourner finds cause for self-accusation in connection with his grief, his sorrow culminates there, and amid such sadness the nightfall of life may often find us weeping over the errors of its morning. If, on the other hand, our sorrows come directly from another, our solace is more easily found. It will then be the believer's endeavor to be silent where he cannot understand, and while he prays for repentance to the wanderer, he himself will forgive, remembering that he is what he is only by the grace of God.

A babe in a house is a well-spring of pleasure,
    A messenger of peace and love, ,
A resting-place for innocence on earth;
    A link between angels and men.—*M. F. Tupper.*

Family Prayer

Matthew Henry

amilies, as such, have many errands at the throne of grace, which furnish them with matter and occasion for family prayer every day; errands which cannot be done so well in secret, or public, but are fittest to be done by the family, in consort, and apart from other families. And it is good for those who go before the rest in family devotions, ordinarily to dwell most upon the concerns of those who join in their family capacity, that it may be indeed a family prayer, not only offered up in and by the family, but suited to it. In this and other services we should endeavour not only to say something, but something to the purpose.

Five things especially you should have upon your heart in your family prayer, and should endeavour to bring something of each, more or less, into every prayer with your families.

1. You ought to make family acknowledgements of your depend-

ence upon God and His providence, as you are a family.

2. You ought to make family confessions of your sins against God; those sins you have contracted the guilt of in your family capacity.

3. You ought to offer up family thanksgivings for the blessings which you, with your families, receive from God.

4. You ought to present your family petitions for the mercy and grace which your families stand in need of.

5. You ought to make family intercessions for others also.

Home Memories

J. R. Miller

here is no need for argument to prove the influence of the home memories in the formation of character. When one's childhood home has been true and sweet its memories never can be effaced. Its teachings may long be unheeded and life may be a miserable waste. Sin may sweep over the soul like a devouring flame, leaving only blackened ruins. Sorrows may quench every joy and hope and the life may be crushed and broken, but the memory of the early home lives on like a solitary star burning in the gloom of night. Even in revels and carousals its picture floats in the mind like a vanished dream. Its voices of love and prayer and song come back like melodies from some far-away island in the sea when the lips that first breathed them out have long been silent in the grave.

There ought to be a powerful motive in this truth to lead us to watch the character of the memories we make in our homes. How will those who go out of our doors be affected in later life by what they remember of their early home? Will the memory be tender, restraining, refining and inspiring? or will it be sad, bitter and a curse?

William Cowper's mother died when he was only six years old, yet so deep was the impression made upon him by her character that he said there was not a day in all his manhood's years when he did not remember and think of her. The memory of her tenderness hung over him like a soft summer sky. Will it be so with the children who are playing now in our homes? Is the mother who reads these words so impressing the tender lives of her children with the goodness of her own character that the memory and the influence shall remain when their hairs are white with age and when she is long gone from earthly scenes?

Raising Our Children

Matthew Henry

onsider what your children are designed for in this world— they must be a seed to serve the Lord, which shall be accounted to Him for a generation. They are to bear up the name of Christ in their day, and into their hands must be transmitted that good thing which is committed to us. They are to be praising God on earth, when we are praising him in heaven. Let them then be brought up accordingly, that they may answer the end of their birth and being. They are designed for the service of their generation and to do good in their day. Consult the public welfare then and let nothing be wanting on your parts to qualify them for usefulness, according as their place and capacity is.

Consider especially what they are designed for in another world. They are made for eternity. Every child you have has a precious and immortal soul, that must be forever either in heaven or hell. Prehaps it must remove to that world of spirits very shortly, and will it not be very mournful, if through your carelessness and neglect, your children should learn the ways of sin, and perish eternally in those ways? Give them warning, that, if possible, you may deliver their souls, at least, that you may deliver your own, and may not bring their curse and God's too, their blood and your own too, upon your heads.

I know you cannot give grace to your children, nor is a religious conversation the constant consequent of a religious education; "The race is not always to the swift, nor the battle to the strong:" but if you make conscience of doing your duty, by keeping up family doctrine; if you teach them the good and the right way, and warn them of bypaths; if you reprove, exhort, and encourage them as there is occasion; if you pray with them, and for them, and set them a good example, and at last consult their souls welfare in the disposal of them, you have done your part, and may comfortably leave the issue and success with God.

Home: A Divine Institution

W. K. Tweedie

he truth is, that Home, or the family, is a divine institution expressly designed for training children in the knowledge of God. For if it be true that "the Church is a family," it is conversely as true that a family should be a church. Religion is the conscience of Rome; and the well-being of every household as completely depends upon the supremacy of the truth, as our individual well-being depends on the ascendancy of conscience.

THE CHRISTIAN FAMILY is to be devoted to God's service and glory. Since Christian families are set apart and dedicated to God's service and glory, then it is God's will that those families should solemnly worship Him. To alienate family from God, when it is supposed to be dedicated to Him, is sacrilege.—*Richard Baxter*

Patience with Children

Charles Haddon Spurgeon

n planting beans the old practice was to put three in each hill: one for the worm, one for the crow, and one to live and produce the crop. In teaching children, we must give line upon line, and precept upon precept, repeating the truth which we would inculcate, till it becomes impossible for the child to forget it. We may well give the lesson once, expecting the child's frail memory to lose it, twice. reckoning that the devil, like an ill bird will steal it, thrice, hoping that it will take root downward, and bring forth fruit upward to the glory of God.

Christ Our Home

J. C. Ryle

eaven, beyond doubt, is the final home in which a true Christian will dwell at last. Towards that he is daily travelling—nearer to that he is daily coming. "We know that if our earthly house of this tabernacle were dissolved, we have a building of God, an house not made with bands, eternal in the heavens." (2 Cor. 5:1) Body and soul united once more, renewed, beautified, and perfected, will live for ever in the Father's great house in heaven. To that home we have not yet come. We are not yet in heaven.

But is there meanwhile no home for our souls? Is there no spiritual dwelling-place to which we may continually repair in this desolate world, and repairing to it, find rest and peace? Thank God, there is no difficulty in finding an answer to that question. There is a home provided for all laboring and heavy-laden souls, and that home is Christ. To know Christ by faith, to live the life of faith in Him, to abide in Him daily by faith, to flee to Him in every storm of conscience, to use Him

260

as our refuge in every day of trouble, to employ Him as our Priest, Confessor, Absolver, and spiritual Director, every morning and evening in our lives,—this is to be at home spiritually, even before we die. To all sinners of mankind who by faith use Christ in this fashion, Christ is in the highest sense a dwelling-place. They can say with truth, "We are pilgrims and strangers on earth, and yet we have a home."

Brave Children of God

D. L. Moody

When the Lawrence mills were on fire a number of years ago, after they had fallen in there was only one room left standing, and in it were three mission Sunday school children imprisoned. The crowd got shovels, and picks, and crowbars, and were soon working to set the children free. Night came on, and they had not yet reached the children. When they were near them, by some mischance a lantern broke and the ruins caught fire. They tried to put it out but could not succeed. They could talk with the children and even pass them some food, and encourage them to keep strong. But, alas, the flames drew nearer and nearer to this prison. Superhuman were the efforts made to rescue the children. The men fought bravely to keep back the flames, but the fire gained fresh strength and returned to claim its victims. The efforts of the fireman were hopeless. When the children knew their fate, they knelt down and began to sing the little hymn they had been taught in their Sunday school days. O, how sweet: "Let others seek a home below, where flames devour and waves overflow." The flames had now reached them. The stifling smoke began to pour in their little room, and they sank, one by one, upon the floor. A few moments more and the fire circled around them and their souls were taken into the bosom of God.

The Christian's Home

Thomas Guthrie

n his best hours, home, his own sinless home—a home with his Father above that starry sky—will be the wish of every Christian man. He looks around him—the world is full of suffering. He is distressed by its sorrows, and vexed by its sins. He looks within him and he finds much in his own corruptions to grieve him. In the language of a heart repelled, grieved, vexed, he often turns his eye upward! saying, "I would not live always." No, not for all the gold of the world's mines, not for all the pearls of the seas, not for all the pleasures of her flashing, frothy cup, not for all the crowns of her kingdoms—would I live here always. Like a bird about to migrate to those sunny lands where no winter sheds her snows, or strips the grove, or binds the dancing streams, he will often in spirit be pruning his wing for the hour of his flight to glory.

Home is Like Heaven

Golden Gems of Life

he sweetest type of heaven is home. Heaven itself is the home for whose acquisition we are to strive most strongly. Home in one form or another is the great object of life. It stands at the end of every day's labor, and beckons us to its bosom. Life would be cheerless and meaningless if we did not discern across the river that divides it from the life beyond glimpses of the pleasant mansions prepared for us. Yes, heaven is the home towards which those who have lived aright direct their steps when wearied by the toils of life. There the members of the homes on earth, separated here, will meet again, to part no more.

HEAVEN

"If ye be risen with Christ, seek those things which are above, where
Christ sitteth on the right hand of God. Set your affections on things
above, not on the things of the earth. For you died, and your life is
hidden with Christ in God."—Colossians 3:1-3

"So also is the resurrection of the dead. It is sown in corruption,
it is raised in incorruption: it is sown in dishonor, it is raised in glory:
it is sown in weakness, it is raised in power: it is sown a
natural body, it is raised a spiritual body."—1 Corinthians 15:42-44.

"Lay not up for yourselves treasures upon earth, where moth
and rust doth corrupt, and where thieves break through
and steal; but lay up for yourselves treasures in heaven,
where neither moth nor rust doth corrupt, and where thieves
do not break through and steal: For where your treasure is,
there will your heart be also."—Matthew 6:19-21

"Beloved, now are we the sons of God, and it doth not yet
appear what we shall be; but we know that when He shall appear,
we shall be like Him: for we shall see Him as He is."—1 John 3:2

"Therefore we do not lose heart. Even though our outward man
is perishing, yet the inward man is renewed day by day.
For our light affliction, which is but for a moment, worketh for us
a far more exceeding and eternal weight of glory; while we look not
at the things which are seen, but at the things which are not seen:
for the things which are seen are temporal; but the things which
are not seen are eternal."—2 Corinthians 4:16-18

"And God shall wipe away all tears from their eyes; and there shall be
no more death, neither sorrow, nor crying, neither shall there be
any more pain: for the former things are passed away."—Revelation 21:4

"MOTHER IS IN HEAVEN!"

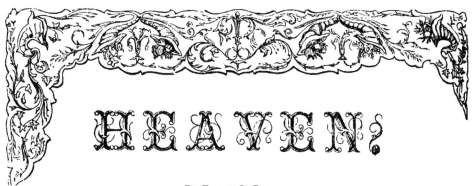

HEAVEN?

BY FANNY J. CROSBY

O! where shall human grief be stilled
    And joy for pain be given,
Where dwells the sunshine of a love
In which the soul may always rove?
    A sweet voice answered—Heaven.

O heart, I said, when death shall come
    And all thy cords be riven,
What lies beyond the swelling tide?
The same sweet voice to mine replied
    In loving accents—Heaven.

Where, where shall friendship never diet
    Nor parting hand be given?
My heart was filled with strange delight
For in that silent hush of night,
    I heard the answer—Heaven.

O, voyager on life's fitful sea;
    By stormy billows driven;
Say, what can soothe thy aching breast,
Or give thee comfort, joy and rest,
    Like Mother, Home and Heaven!

Assurance of Heaven

2 Timothy 4:6-8

Death may dissolve my body now,
    And bear my spirit home;
Why do my minutes move so slow,
    Nor my salvation come?

With heav'nly weapons I have fought
    The battles of the Lord,
Finish'd my course, and kept the faith,
    And wait the sure reward.

God has laid up in heaven for me
    A crown which cannot fade;
The righteous Judge, at that great day,
    Shall place it on my head.

Nor hath the King of Grace decreed
    This prize for me alone;
But all that love and long to see
    Th'appearance of His Son.

Jesus, the Lord, shall guard me safe
    From ev'ry ill design;
And to His heav'nly kingdom take
    This feeble soul of mine.

God is my everlasting aid,
    And hell shall rage in vain;
To Him be highest glory paid,
    And endless praise. Amen.

—*Isaac Wa*

Fountain of Consolation

John Gregory Pike

erhaps your soul may at times be cast down and distressed; b
remember, when friends are absent the Lord is present. The ch
Shepherd is forever near you and He who laid down His life for y
will doubtless make your comfort and welfare His care. Let your fai
repose aright upon the Savior's love, and nothing will seem dark on this si
of the grave, and all appears bright beyond it. If at times you sow in sorro
you will doubtless reap in joy. Hear your Lord saying, "I will never leave th

266

nor forsake thee." Above all, hear Him saying, "My grace is sufficient for thee. Lo, I am with you always, even to the end of the world." What more can you desire? Jesus always with you—can you ever indulge distress? Jesus always with you—can you then ever want a counselor? Jesus always with you—can you ever despair of final conquest? He who laid down His life for you, ever attentive to your welfare—no moment passing in which He is absent; no moment coming when He shall leave you, or His helping hand be far away. O rejoice in these promises, they are worth more than all the world.

The Gardener and the Rose

Charles Haddon Spurgeon

uppose you are a gardener employed by another. It is not your garden, but you are called upon to tend it, and you have your wages paid you. You have taken great care with a certain number of roses; you have trained them well, and they are up, and there they are, blooming in their beauty. You pride yourself upon them. You come one morning into the garden, and you find that the best rose has been taken away. You are angry. You go to your fellow-servants and charge them with having taken the rose. They will declare that they had nothing to do with it; and one says, "I saw the Master walking here this morning; I think He took it." Is the gardener angry then? No, at once he says, "I am happy my rose would attract the attention of the Master. It is His own. He has taken it. Let Him do what seems good to Him."

It is even so with your loved ones. They wither not by chance; the

267

grave is not filled by accident; men die according to God's will. Your son is gone because the Master took him. Thank Him that He let you have the pleasure of caring for him and tending him while he was here. Thank Him that He gave, and He, Himself, has taken away. Would you have cause to be angry? The Lord has done it. Can you then murmur?

Trials and Afflictions

Robert Murray M'Cheyne

Afflictions shower the power of Christ's blood, when it gives peace in an hour of trouble—when it can make happy in sickness, poverty, persecution, and death. Do not be surprised if you suffer, but glorify God.

The Christian's Future Happy Home

John Gregory Pike

Heaven is described as the Christian's future happy home. Many expressions are employed to furnish some faint ideas of its excellence and blessedness. It is represented as "a city which hath foundations, whose builder and maker is God." Heb. 11:10. A city adorned with unutterable splendor, whose walls are founded on precious jewels; whose streets are gold; whose gates are pearl; and whose light is the glory of God. These images are designed to represent the glory of the heavenly world. To it will apply the prophet Isaiah's expressive language: "Violence shall no more be heard in thy land, wasting nor destruction within thy borders; but thou shalt call thy walls Salvation, and thy gates Praise. The sun shall be no more thy light by day; neither for brightness shall the moon give light unto thee; but the Lord shall be unto thee an everlasting light, and thy God thy glory. Thy sun shall no more go down, neither shall thy moon withdraw itself, for the Lord shall be thine everlasting light and the days of thy mourning shall be ended." Heaven is represented as a "better country," purposely provided by God for His redeemed; as a kingdom which He delights to bestow upon His children—a kingdom prepared for them from the foundation of the world. It is described as the eternal Father's house in which are many mansions—dwellings of peace, of tranquil and continued stay; and in that happy home, in the presence of God, "there is fullness of joy, and pleasures for evermore."

Lord, It Belongs Not To My Care
Richard Baxter

Lord, it belongs not to my care,
    Whether I die or live;
To love and serve Thee is my share,
    And this Thy grace must give.
If life be long I will be glad,
    That I may long obey;
If short—yet why should I be sad
    To soar to endless day?
Christ leads me through no darker rooms
    Than He went through before;
He that unto God's kingdom comes,
    Must enter by this door.
Come, Lord, when grace has made me meet
    Thy blessed face to see;
For if Thy work on earth be sweet,
    What will Thy glory be!
Then I shall end my sad complaints,

And weary, sinful days;
And join with the triumphant saints,
To sing Jehovah's praise.
My knowledge of that life is small,
The eye of faith is dim;
But 'tis enough that Christ knows all,
And I shall be with Him.

A Clearer Vision

Edward Payson

have viewed God as a fixed star, bright indeed, but often intercepted by clouds. But now it is coming nearer and nearer, and spreads into a sun, so vast and glorious that the sight is too dazzling for flesh and blood to sustain." This was not a blind adoration of an imaginary Deity; for, he added, "I see clearly that all these same glorious and dazzling perfections, which now only serve to kindle my affections into a flame, and melt down my soul into the same blessed image, would burn and scorch me like a consuming fire if I were an impenitent sinner."

"My soul," he said, "instead of growing weaker and more languishing, as my body does, seems to be endued with an angel's energies, and to be ready to break from the body and join those around the throne."

Fullness of Joy in Heaven

John Gregory Pike

What varied and inconceivable good will flow from entire exemption from all evil! The cares and anxieties incident to the present state, no more distress those happy conquerors. God has wiped away their every

271

tear, and dried up every source of sorrow. They have no toilsome days, no wearisome nights. The head never aches, the heart never throbs. Pain and sickness are alike unknown. Instead of feeble, emaciated, withered forms, all are beheld happy beings, vigorous with immortal health, and clothed with celestial loveliness. Here the loveliest fade like a flower; but the flowers that fade on earth, if once transplanted to heaven, will there never fade more, but will bloom through everlasting ages in unwithering beauty. With pain and sickness, death too will cease. When this corruptible shall have put off incorruption, and this mortal immortality, death will be swallowed up in victory. The sublime language of the Redeemer will be accomplished: "I will ransom them from the power of the grave; I will redeem them from death. O death, I will be thy plagues; O grave, I will be thy destruction. Repentance shall be hid from mine eyes." (Hos. 13:14.) There shall then be no more death; no more will that last enemy daunt the children of God by his approach, nor will they ever again dread its power. The languors that precede the hour of dissolution will never be felt. The painful separations that death frequently occasions, will never be known. None will be summoned by death to leave the friends they love, or the happy country where they dwell.

The Heavenly Home

The Mother's Journal (1868)

friend once asked me this question, "What do you expect to enjoy the most when you reach the better land?" It was a question that suggested many and deep thoughts to my mind, and I stopped to reflect a moment before answering. I had been reading recently of corruption in high places, of the manifest dishonesty of men occupying positions of trust and responsibility in the

nation, who had been thought incorruptible, until some great temptation overtook them, and then for poor, weak human nature, they fell.

I was conscious of a feeling of sadness, that, in the struggle between
good and evil, the evil should often triumph. The answer came from
the fullness of my heart: "Oh! to be free from sin,—to dwell where evil
no longer reigns, and where the tendency to sin no longer exists; with
the multitude of those that have washed their robes and made them
white in the blood of the Lamb; with Christ the friend and elder brother ever near! Will not this be Heaven indeed?"

Among the thoughts suggested by this conversation concerning
Heaven as our home, I will mention a few which may be profitable to
all. I have been particularly impressed in my intercourse with Christians, that our ideas of Heaven are altogether too vague and indefinite,—that we should seek earnestly for more light upon a subject so
full of importance. As a company of believers bound for a better
Country, it is our privilege, as well as duty, to acquaint ourselves as
much as possible with all that pertains to the dwelling place which we
expect may be ours when we shall assume the spiritual body of the
saints in glory. True we can know comparatively little of the spirit
world and its inhabitants, for it is said, "It hath not entered into the
heart of man to conceive what God hath prepared for those that love
him." But all that is revealed respecting it is our privilege to know.
There are many passages of Scripture that give sweet comfort to the
soul when seeking something definite and tangible concerning the
heavenly home. Take for example those beautiful words from the
vision of John in Revelation 21:4, "And God shall wipe away all tears
from their eyes, and there shall be no more death, neither sorrow, nor
crying, neither shall there be any more pain, for the former things are
passed away."

No more tears! What a precious message to the poor and sorrowing of this earth. When friends forsake, and the deep waters of affliction threaten to overwhelm them, when eating the bitter bread of poverty and tears are their portion by day and by night. It is then their privilege to think of Heaven as their home and take this promise to their hearts, "God shall wipe away all tears from their eyes."

Then when death invades the earthly household, taking the loved ones from our fond embrace, how our hearts bleed, and how we long for their presence once more; the world seems no longer bright to us, but gloom and sadness cover everything about us. But in Heaven "there will be no more death," and "its inhabitants shall go no more out forever," for they will have put on immortality. "Neither shall there be any more pain." We have seen the children of our heart's love wasting under some painful sickness, the days and weeks of suffering wore deep furrows into our own cheeks, because we were powerless to alleviate their sufferings. How comforting the thought that in Heaven the sigh of pain is forever hushed. The pale cheek, the sunken eye, the failing breath, will no more wring our hearts with anguish for those we love, "for the former things have passed away."

Then again, "there is no night there;" "they need no candle, neither light of the sun, for the Lord God giveth them light." No fear of the midnight assassin may disturb us there. We shall no longer read the tales of horror which chill the blood, nor feel our souls sicken at the thought of the various forms of vice and crime, which the darkness covers, and over which the pitying eye of a Saviour weeps. For "there shall in no-wise enter into it anything that defiles." The golden streets, and precious stones, typical of purity and beauty,—the fountain of living waters,—the many mansions,—do not all these convey to us definite ideas of the heavenly home? May not the words of Christ be taken in their literal sense, when He speaks to His followers of the "many mansions in His Father's house, where He is going to prepare a place

for them." And was He not heard pleading in that last prayer, when about to leave His disciples, "Father I will that they also whom thou hast given me, be with me where I am, that they may behold my glory?"—John 17:24a. Here is abundant testimony from the Word of God that Heaven is a place to which we may accustom ourselves to look forward with joyful anticipations! Like the weary traveler, obliged to stop for a night at the wayside inn, who yet looks forward longingly to the pleasant home and loved ones awaiting him at his journey's end, we too may refresh ourselves by the wayside; but the true disciple will ever be looking beyond, to the green pastures and still waters of "the city of our God," to the companionship of Christ, and the dear ones gone before, and to the peace that will be so sweet after life's wearisome toils and cares are ended.

Then there will be no more temptations to overcome, for with the flesh, all these are laid aside, and all who inhabit the beautiful land will be alike pure and sinless. For, "without, are murderers, and sorcerers, and whosoever loveth and maketh a lie." How blessed to dwell continually in an atmosphere of love, and peace unbroken; where the tongue of slander will no longer seek to harm, and where no envy or malice is hidden under a smiling exterior.

This much it is given us to know of the future home of the true believer; enough, methinks, to inspire every breast with earnest desires to possess more of that spirit here which will constitute their chief joy hereafter. A little while longer to battle with principalities and powers of evil, to wrestle with the strong man of sin, and be sometimes vanquished, but to renew the conflict day by day—and then the rest of Heaven! Very brief is the time given us here to lay up golden fruit to give the Lord of the harvest at his appearing. Let us use all diligence lest at the last we bring, "In place of golden sheaves; nothing but leaves."

It will not do to sit down at ease in the enjoyment of this world. When the midnight cry was sounded, "behold the bridegroom cometh, go ye out to meet him," the foolish virgins, who were asleep, and without oil in their lamps, awoke to the terrible reality that they were shut out from the marriage, with the words full of dreadful meaning sounding in their ears, "Verily I say unto you I know ye not." Let us not grow weary in well doing, but persevere to the end, that the heavenly inheritance, and the many mansions may be ours at last.

Dying Meditations

John Willison

Oh, delightful thought! That I, who was going on in sin, should be plucked as a brand out of the burning. Oh, how will they lie on a death-bed who have nothing but their own works to fly to? With only this to depend upon, I should be the most miserable of all creatures; but the long white robe of my Redeemer's righteousness is all my desire. They are truly blessed, they alone are happy, who are enabled to exult in the garment of celestial glory which never grows old—in the illustrious robe of a Savior's consummate righteousness, which is incorruptible and immortal. This is a robe which hides every sin, of thought, word, and deed, that I have committed. Oh, how unspeakably happy are they who are justified by this all-perfect righteousness of the Lord Jesus Christ, and who therein can constantly triumph and glory!

Eternal Holiness and Happiness

John Gregory Pike

ow rapturous will be the scene of eternal holiness and happiness. An immense assemblage of happy beings, forming one glorified family, in the presence of their God and Redeemer. Angels and saints now brethren in Christ Jesus; their abode, their pleasures, their employments, and their character forever the same. Not one defect among them all, not one blemish in the character of countless millions, not one error in their conduct, not one defective disposition, not one unkind feeling ever experienced, not one unholy thought ever known. Every countenance glowing with heavenly beauty and every heart full of heavenly love, every eye the index of a soul adorned with all the lovely excellencies of its redeeming Lord. All in their measure resembling Him in glory. All like Him, and all so resembling Him in character and disposition, that His all-piercing eye shall not discern one defect in all His happy family; but even in His sight they shall be unblamable and unreprovable. Happy are they who form part of such a family.

Complete Perfection

John Gregory Pike

What is it to see God and dwell with Him? What is it to be led by the Lamb to living fountains of Immortal blessings, to be satisfied in His likeness, to possess fullness of joy and pleasures forevermore, to enjoy incorruptible and unfading inheritances, and to be honored with crowns of righteousness of glory and life that never fade away? What is it to possess a far more exceeding and eternal weight of glory—a glory too great to be described by the boldest expressions heaped on others equally bold, and continued to eternity? What is it to sit down as a happy and honored conqueror by the Savior's side? What is all this and all this additional to other blessings already contemplated—to perfect safety, to perfect holiness, to perfect freedom from every ill, from every vexing disposition, every unholy feeling, every pain and every sorrow? What is it to be all this, and possess all this, not for ages or centuries only, but for periods, compared with whose duration the whole of time, from the creation to the judgment-day, would be the twinkling of an eye? Reader, what is all this? No tongue can express—no heart can conceive, but you must have it all, or lose it all. Gain it all in Christ, or lose it all by slighting Him. Many already possess these blessings. They have reached their home. They mingle with better friends than any this world ever gave. They possess what formerly they sought. Eternity opens to them no prospects but prospects bright with gladness and joy, in infinite succession. And who are these blessed ones? Some of these were the benevolent possessors of wealth and plenty, but many of them toiled in poverty, yet in poverty they were rich. They labored in the field or the factory, in the mine or on the road. They wept, they languished, yet in affliction they were blessed. They watched, they prayed, they fled to Jesus and followed Him, and He has fixed them in their heavenly home.

Christ's Second Coming

Robert Murray M'Cheyne

hen Christ shall come in the clouds of heaven, all kindreds of earth shall wail. There will not be one unawakened person in earth or hell. Not the proudest or deadest of you will keep from trembling in that day. But ah, it is only those who believe His Word that will flee under His wings. It is not enough that you are anxious about your souls, you must be fleeing to Christ; yea, you must be in Christ, before you are safe.

Death is Gain

Samuel Rutherford

f death, which is before you and us all, were any other thing than a friendly dissolution, and a change, not a destruction of life, it would seem a hard voyage to go through such a sad and dark trance, so thorny a valley, as is the wages of sin. But I am confident the way ye know, though your foot never trod in that black shadow. The loss of life is gain to you. If Christ Jesus be the period, the end, and lodging home, at the end of your journey, there is no fear; ye go to a friend. And since ye have had communion with Him in this life, and He has a pawn or pledge of yours, even the largest share of your love and heart, ye may look death in the face with joy.

Death is but an awesome step over time and sin to sweet Jesus Christ, who knew and felt the worst of death, for death's teeth hurt Him. We know death has no teeth now, no jaws, for they are broken. It is a free prison; citizens pay nothing for the grave. The jailer who had the power of death is destroyed. Praise and glory be to the First-begotten of the dead.

Desire After Heaven

William Jay

hilip Henry often said when he had finished the delightful exercises of the Sabbath, "Well, if this be not the way to heaven, I know not what is!" Yes, these are introductory to the glory that shall be revealed; they are foretastes to endear it, and earnestness to insure it. And when you come to die—if you can say, in sincerity, "Lord, I have loved the habitation of Thy house, and the place where Thy honor dwelleth"—you may plead with confidence, "Gather not my soul with sinners, nor my life with bloody men." No, He will not gather you, in eternity, with those you never loved in time; but being let go, you shall join your own company, and "be forever with the Lord."

Realities of Eternity

John Gregory Pike

hink of the years that have elapsed from the days of Adam to the present day: eternity is longer. Think of those that may pass from this day till that when the judgment trumpet shall sound: eternity is longer. Look at the ground adorned with its green carpet, covered with innumerable millions of blades of grass: are the years of eternity as many? They are more; eternity is longer. Look at the leaves that clothe the trees with verdure: are the years of eternity countless as those leaves? They are more; eternity is longer than such a period of ages. Add to these years others as numerous as the drops of morning dew: do these describe eternity? No; eternity is longer. Count the drops of the sea; will their number represent eternal ages? No, eternity has ages far more countless. Those, compared with it, are like a drop to an ocean. Repeat these calculations, yet eternity is longer. Millions by millions multiplied give no idea of its duration; and all the years that human thought can heap together, compared with it are insignificant and nothing. Beyond them all eternity still stretches forth its immeasurable duration. This eternity awaits you.

Eternity is a duration that nothing can shorten, and that never can end. Time has an end; eternity has none. The period daily approaches nearer, when the end of time shall be announced. The last spring that shall cheer the earth with its bloom, will have passed away; the last summer will have ended; the last autumn have finished; the last harvest this earth shall ever produce be reaped; and the last winter have concluded. Time's last year will have arrived; its last day; its last hour; its last minute; its last moment; and time shall be no more. But no such end will arrive to close eternity. Let thousands of ages pass away, eternity is not shortened. Let millions more, and worlds of millions roll along, eternity remains the same. As long, as blest, as happy, or as dreadful and miserable as ever.

The joys and sorrows of time have an end, but those of eternity have none. Time brings an end to the Christian's sorrows, but eternity will bring no end to his joys. Did he sigh? There was a last sigh. Had he pangs of grief? There was a last pang, and a last grief. Did he weep? There was a last tear. Had he struggles? There was a last struggle. Did he pine in poverty? There was a last day of want. But in eternity there will be no last joy, no last rapture, no last song of praise, no last thanksgiving for redeeming love. On earth, among Christian friends, time brought a last meeting and a last parting; a last dying look, and a last farewell—but eternity will bring no last meeting, no last look, no dying eye.

As it is with the pious, so it will be, in an awfully opposite manner, with the ungodly. Time will bring to the sinner a last trifling day or festive night, a last pleasure, and a last hour of sinful gayety; but eternity will bring no last pain, no last sorrow. The sinner's pleasures will end, but not his pain; his joys, but not his griefs; his gain, but not his loss. O reader, think of this solemn eternity; and in the view of it, choose that good part which shall never be taken away from you. You may look forward and in imagination see yourself leaving this world—your funeral over, your body in a coffin, and that coffin in the grave. And after a few years, yourself so forgotten there, that no one on earth will know you ever existed, but then you will be in eternity. Before your friends have laid you in the grave, your immortal spirit will have begun to experience the joys or sorrows of eternity. Happy they who enjoy the Savior's grace; and who, when they quit this world, are welcomed by him to "everlasting habitations."

THE WAY to the crown is by the cross.—*Robert Murray M'Cheyne*

Preparing for the Happiness of Eternity

Joseph Addison

lewd young fellow seeing an aged hermit go by him barefoot, said "Father, you are in a very miserable condition if there is not another world." "True, son," said the hermit, "but what is your condition if there is?" Man is a creature designed for two different states of being, or rather for two different lives. His first life is short and transient; his second, permanent and lasting. The question we are all concerned in is this: in which of these two lives is our chief interest to make ourselves happy? Or, in other words, whether we should endeavor to secure to ourselves the pleasures and gratifications of a life, which is uncertain and precarious, and, at its utmost length, of a very inconsiderable duration—or to secure to ourselves the pleasures of a life which is fixed and settled, and will never end. Every man, upon first hearing of this question, knows very well which side of it he ought to close with. But, however right we are in theory, it is plain that in practice we adhere to the wrong side of the question. We make provisions for this life as though it were never to have an end and for the other life as though it were to never have a beginning.

Directions for Mourners

John Willison

he comfort of life does not lie so much in the abundance of things, as in the art of enjoying a little. I have lost a dear friend, but my happiness was more wrapped up in that God to whom my beloved ones have gone: and God will bring them along with him. That which beautified their character and made them so lovely was what could not be lost, but is perfected by the translation. I love them still, and take great pleasure in loving them, which helps relieve my sorrow for their absence.

Knowledge in Heaven

Isaac Watts

he blessed God himself is an infinite being. His perfections and glories are unbounded. His wisdom, His holiness, His goodness, His faithfulness, His power and justice, His all-sufficiency, His self-origination, and His unfathomable eternity, have such a number of rich ideas belonging to each of them, as no

283

creature shall ever fully understand. Yet it is but reasonable to believe, that He will communicate so much of Himself to us by degrees, as He sees necessary for our business and blessedness in that upper world. Can it be supposed that we should know everything that belongs to God all at once, which He may discover to us gradually as our capacities improve? Can we think that an infant-soul that had no time for improvement here, when it enters into heaven, shall know everything concerning God, that it can ever attain to through all the ages of its immortality? When a blessed spirit has dwelt in heaven a thousand years, and conversed with God and Christ, angels and fellow-spirits, during all that season, shall it know nothing more of the nature and wondrous properties of God than it knew the first moment of its arrival there?

Sown in Weakness

Edward Henry Bickersteth

e may surely extend the application of this sowing beyond the hour of death, to the Christian's whole life on earth, which is so often compared in Scripture to the seed-time of an eternal harvest (Gal. 6:7-8). Suffering child of Jesus, how true is it of you, "sown in weakness!" How many enjoyments are you shut out from. How many occupations must you daily resign. How many paths of intellectual activity are closed to you! Be of good cheer, your seed-time is one of weakness; your grain of wheat has been hid somewhat more deeply in the soil than others, and so has had to struggle with a heavier burden up to the pure light. But I doubt not it has struck its fibrous roots into a richer vein of mould, and when emancipated and clothed in "that body that shall be,"(1 Cor. 15:37), will be the more exquisite in hue, form, and fragrance for its long and sanctified humiliation. Cheerfully confide in the husbandry of Jesus, and you shall extract fruitful nourishment from the darkness and seclusion of your trial. He has hidden you, but He has not forgotten you. Is your soul at times refreshed? I know it is. Ah, this is the dew of His Spirit, and token of His love. Think your affliction of itself would yield you any spiritual recreation? Nay, it would be as barren as the desert sand. For it is the Lord who makes "bright clouds" and gives "showers of rain;" and that earth only "which drinketh in the rain that cometh oft upon it receiveth blessing from God."(Hebrews 6:7)

Raised in Power

Edward Henry Bickersteth

es, many and costly are the sacrifices which a Christian is called to make. The crown is a reality, and the cross is not a shadow. The joy of active service, the merriment of the family circle, the chastened cultivation of taste, the delight of Christian society, and chief of privations, the assembly in the courts of the Lord;—these and many nameless enjoyments which only they who have long been laid upon the bed of languishing can appreciate, is he daily called to resign. They seem lost and buried. But in fresh springtide of the resurrection, how shall every suspended power start into new life and effortless activity! Each one shall be raised in power. Then and there shall he enjoy the untoilsome exercise of every faculty and affection, for "His servants shall serve Him."(Rev. 22:3) We shall dwell in the mansions of our Father's house; we shall contemplate the glories of the new Jerusalem. We shall join those harpers, playing their heavenly melodies, who fill the courts above with the swell of their ceaseless hallelujahs. We shall imbibe no longer the partial, childlike knowledge on earth, but the wisdom derived immediately from Jesus, and the interchange of thought betwixt the holy intelligences of heaven. We shall have our place in the heavenly circle, when the whole family is gathered into one home, which no losses can sadden, and no fears disturb. We shall share the unutterable rapture of the worship before the throne, in the temple of God, admitted by the Son of His love, through the communion of the Spirit, into the presence-chamber of His Father and our Father, His God and our God. These things and much more are yours, suffering believer. Wait, only wait.

To Be With Christ

Richard Baxter

In this world I have had many of God's mercies and comforts, but their sweetness was their taste of Divine love and their tendency to heavenly perfection. What was the end and use of all the good that ever I saw or that God ever did for my soul and body, but to teach me to love Him, and to desire to love Him more? O my God, love is your great and special gift. All good is from you. Come into my heart! Dwell in me by your Spirit of love, and I shall dwell by love in you.

In View of Glory

Edward Payson (in a letter to a friend while on his deathbed.)

Were I to adapt a figurative language of Bunyan, I might date this letter from the Land of Beulah, of which I have been for several weeks a happy inhabitant. The Celestial City is full in my view. Its glories beam upon me, its breezes fan me, its odors are wafted to me, its sound strikes upon my ears, and its spirit is breathed into my heart. Nothing separates me from it but the river of death, which now appears but an insignificant hill that may be crossed at a single step when God shall give permission. The Sun of Righteousness has been gradually drawing nearer and nearer, appearing larger and brighter as he approaches; and now he fills the whole hemisphere, pouring forth a flood of glory, in which I seem to float, like an insect in the beams of the sun; exulting, yet almost trembling while I gaze on this excessive brightness, and wondering with unutterable wonder why God should deign thus to shine upon a sinful worm. A single heart and a single tongue seems altogether inadequate to my wants. I want a whole heart for every separate emotion, and a whole tongue to express that emotion.

But why do I speak thus of myself and my feelings? Why not speak of our God and Redeemer? It is because I know not what to say. When I would speak of them my words are all swallowed up. I can only tell you of the effects their presence produces; and even of these I can tell you but very little. O, my sister, my sister! if you could only know what awaits the Christian: if you could only know so much as I know, you could not refrain from rejoicing, and even leaping for joy! Labors, trials, troubles, would be nothing. You would rejoice in afflictions, glory in tribulations; and, like Paul and Silas, sing God's praises in the darkest night, and in the deepest dungeon. You have known little of my trials and conflicts, and I know that they have been neither few nor small; and I hope this glorious termination of them will serve to strengthen your faith and elevate your hope.

And now, my dear sister, farewell! Hold on your Christian course but a few days longer, and we will meet in heaven.

Dying Testimony of Believers

Collected From Various Authentic Sources

"Be thou faithful unto death, and I will give thee a crown of life."—Rev. 2:10.

hristianity has its living witnesses, whose testimony is "known and read of all men." In these are held forth the truth and divinity of the Christian religion, in its life, beauty, and fascinating charms of holiness. This evidence is vivid and affecting, the manifest result of divine efficacy put forth in the formation of Christian character. It is seen and known to be of God, by all who have eyes to see and hearts to understand. It is evident and quite striking and convincing. It exhibits an effect for which no human wisdom or power can ever be deemed an adequate cause. It is ever present before the eyes of men, exhibiting the same heavenly traits from generation to generation. And when a uniformly consistent and holy life is closed by a dying testimony, the evidence is then complete.

We should not, therefore, separate the consistent life of godliness from the dying testimony of the saints. The two combined constitute an invaluable living epistle to the honor of Christ Jesus and His holy religion.

Let us contemplate the dying scenes of some of the noble army of martyrs, ministers, and confessors of that true faith; and while we look upon them as they go up, may the Spirit that rested on them, descend and rest upon us!

1. We shall place at the head of them all, the Prince of Martyrs—the **Lord Jesus Christ**; for while we do, by faith, look to Him as our great High Priest, who, by His sufferings on the cross, made a perfect atonement and satisfaction to divine justice for us, —a perfect example for imitation in all ages. In His agonies in the garden, when

wrestling with the powers of darkness and anticipating the more awful agonies of the cross, he cried out, "O, my Father, if it be possible, let this cup pass from me! Nevertheless, not my will, but thine be done!" He was not afraid—not unwilling to die for us; but, O let us remember what His soul and body were then enduring under the guilt of sinners! His holy soul did shudder at the prospect; and it did set us moreover an example of willingness to suffer and die whenever God's will should require it. O what dignity! What submission! What self-possession! What meekness did the Prince of Martyrs uniformly display! "He was led as a lamb to the slaughter, and as a sheep before His shearers is dumb, so He opened not His mouth!" "The cup which my Father giveth me, shall I not drink it?" Looking in the infinitude of His benevolence upon His bloody persecutors, He set before us the great and divine model of the forgiveness of enemies—"Father, forgive them; for they know not what they do!" And then, knowing all things to be accomplished, He meekly bowed His head, as He cried with a loud voice, "It is finished!" and gave up His spirit.

Let us now turn to the noble band of martyrs and confessors, who have been imitators of God, as His dear children.

2. The martyr **Stephen** was stoned to death while calling upon God and saying, "Lord Jesus, receive my Spirit!" And he knelt down and cried, "Lord, lay not this sin to their charge!" and when he said this he fell asleep in Christ.

3. **Ignatius**, a student of and successor to the Apostle Peter in the church of Antioch, after faithfully preaching the Gospel and winning many souls to Christ, sealed the truth with his blood. By the edict of the emperor Trajan, he was dragged off to Rome, but ceased not to animate, exhort and encourage all Christians. In the Roman amphitheater he was thrown to the hungry lions, repeating, "My Love was crucified for me!"

4. **Augustine**, after a long service to God, longed to depart and be with Christ. "O Lord, shall I die at all? ... "Yes, O why not now? But Thy will be done. Come, Lord Jesus!"

5. **John Huss**, the Bohemian martyr, was burned alive in the year 1415. When he came to the place of execution, he threw himself on the ground and sang a Psalm; and looking steadfastly to heaven, he uttered his prayer, "Into Thy hands, Lord, I commit my spirit. Thou hast redeemed me, O most good and faithful God! Lord Jesus Christ, assist me, that with a firm and present mind, by Thy most powerful grace, I may undergo this most cruel death, to which I am condemned for preaching Thy most holy Gospel. Amen." When the chain was placed on his neck, he exclaimed with a smile, "Welcome this chain, for Christ's sake!" As the sticks were piled up to his neck, the Duke of Bavaria in a brutal manner called on him to abjure, and submit! "No, no," cried the Martyr; "I take God to witness I preached none but His own pure doctrines; and what I taught I am ready to seal with my blood!" The fire being kindled, Huss sung a hymn with a loud voice, which was heard above all the crackling and roaring flames. After finishing the hymn, he cried out, "Lord Jesus, thou Son of the living God, have mercy on me!" As he uttered this, he sunk down in the flames and expired!

6. The great reformer, **Martin Luther**, was well known for two chief elements of his character; fervent devotion and invincible courage. He never spent less that three hours a day in secret prayer. When any fresh trouble arose, he would say, "Come let us sing the forty-sixth Psalm." On his death-bed he grieved of two things; leaving his family to carry on without him, and not receiving the privilege of dying a martyr's death. The last words he was heard to utter were; "Into thy hands I commend my spirit. Thou hast redeemed me, O Lord God of truth!" Thus he died a happy and triumphant death.

7. **Melancthon**, his illustrious associate and close friend, also closed his career by a happy death. Raising himself up in his death-bed, he exclaimed with holy joy, "If God be for us, who can stand against us!" Being asked by his affectionate relatives if he desired anything he replied, "Nothing but heaven!" And laying himself back, he gently fell asleep in Jesus.

8. **John Knox**, the Scottish Reformer's dying words were, "Come, sweet Jesus, into Thy hands I commend my spirit; be mer-ciful, O Lord, to Thy church, which Thou hast redeemed; raise up faithful pastors." After this, calling his friends to his bedside, he broke out in these rapturous expressions: "I have been meditating on the troubled state of the Church, the spouse of Christ; I have called on God, and committed her to her head, Christ; I have fought against spiritual wickedness in high places, and have prevailed; I have tasted of the heavenly joys where presently I shall be!" "Now, for the last time, I commit soul, body, and spirit into His hands!" Uttering a deep sigh, he said, "Now, it is come!" His faithful atten-dant desired him to give his friends a sign that he died in peace. On this he waved his hand, uttering two sighs, and fell asleep in Jesus.

9. When, **Tyndale**, the Bible translator, suffered martyrdom, in 1536, the last prayer he uttered was, "O Lord, open the King of England's eyes!" He lost sight of his own afflictions in his anxiety for the welfare of the Church of Christ.

10. During the reign of King Henry VIII, the beautiful and pious **Anne Askew**, was tortured and martyred for her confession in the truth of the Gospel of Jesus Christ. Unwilling to recant her testimony, she was ordered to endure the agonies of the rack, by the wicked Lord Wriothesley. Throughout the whole of her persecution, Anne Askew had preserved the patient sweetness of her demeanor. All the cruelties of her enemies had been powerless to wring one unchristian word. She

was only 25, and life was sweet to her, but not so sweet as to sacrifice her conscience. She did not desire martyrdom, but did not shrink from it, and she bore her sufferings with a firmness and gentleness never surpassed in the annals of Christian heroism.

At length the day of her execution arrived. Anne, unable to move her arms and legs, in consequence of her torture upon the rack, was brought in a chair to the stake. Three others were condemned with her, John Lascels, Nicholas Belenean, and John Adams. They spoke words of comfort to each other while being fastened to the stakes. The renegade Bishop Shaxton mounted the pulpit and preached to the martyrs to repent, but in their eyes he was a traitor who betrayed his Lord. When he spoke truth Anne assented audibly, but when contrary to Scripture she exclaimed, "There he misseth, and speaketh without the Book."

The sermon ended, Anne was offered a pardon if she would abjure her opinions, but waved her hand and calmly exclaimed, "I am not come here to deny my Lord and Master." The other three martyrs followed the example of their heroic sister. The reeds were then kindled and the martyrs were immediately enveloped in the flames. Thus died Anne Askew, one of the noblest and purest witnesses of the truth of which the Christian church can boast.

11. Lawrence Saunders suffered martyrdom under the "bloody Queen Mary." He kissed the stake at which he was bound, and cried aloud, "Welcome the cross of Christ! Welcome life everlasting!"

12, 13. Under the same wicked Queen, Bishops **Hugh Latimer** and **Nicholas Ridley** were burned at Oxford. Latimer died in a short time in the fierce fire; but the wind kept the flames off the vitals of Ridley. His sufferings were excruciating; his lower parts were consumed before the fire reached his body! Their courage and holy resignation showed manifestly the presence of the blessed Comforter sustaining them. "Be of good heart, brother," cried Ridley, "for our God will either assuage the fury of this flame, or enable us to abide it." Latimer replied, "Be of good comfort, brother; for we shall this day light such a candle in England as, by God's grace, shall never be put out!"

14. The famous **Archbishop Cranmer**, when brought to the stake, after making a bold confession of his faith, and deploring the error into which he had fallen in the hour of temptation, thrust his right hand into the flames, (that being the hand with which he had earlier signed his denial of his Lord) exclaiming, "This hand has offended!—This unworthy hand!" and he moved it not, except once to wipe off the sweat of agony from his face, until it dropped off! He then cried aloud, "O Lord Jesus, receive my spirit!" What a triumphant death before the very eyes of Christ's enemies!

15. **John Bunyan**, having frequently exhorted all about his dying bed to faith and a godly life, he called on them repeatedly to spend much time in prayer. His last words were; "Weep not for me, but for yourselves. I go to the Father of our Lord Jesus Christ; who will receive me, though a sinner, through the mediation of our Lord; where I hope we shall ere long meet, to sing the new song, and remain happy forever, world without end. Amen."

16. **Lord William Russell**, son of the Duke of Bedford, fell victim to the tyranny of Charles II, in 1683. The evening before he was executed, he observed, "The bitterness of death is already past!" Just before he was beheaded, he said aloud, "Neither imprisonment nor fear of death have been able to discompose me in any degree. On the contrary, I have found the assurances of the love and mercy of God, in and through my blessed Redeemer. I do not question but I am going to partake of that fullness of joy which is in His presence; the hopes of which do so wonderfully delight me, that I think this is the happiest time of my life; though others may look upon it as the saddest."

17. **Samuel Rutherford**, one of the most resplendent lights that ever rose in Scotland, was the professor of divinity in the University of St. Andrew's. When parliament of Scotland summoned him for trial because he stood up for liberty and religion, he was on his dying bed. "Tell the parliament," he said to his messenger, "that I have received a summons to a higher bar; I must needs answer that first; and when the day you shall come, I shall be where few of you shall enter!" In his last moments he said to ministers around him, "There is none like Christ: O dear brethren, pray for Christ; feed the flock of God! And O beware of menpleasing!" Having recovered from a fainting fit, he said, "I feel, I believe, I joy, I rejoice, I feed on manna! My eyes shall see my Redeemer, and I shall be ever with Him! And what more would you have? I have been a sinful man: but I stand at the best pass that ever a man did. Christ is mine, and I am His! Glory shines in Immanuel's land! O for arms to embrace Him! O for a well-tuned harp!" He exulted in his Savior to the last, as one in full vision of joy and glory!

18. **James Guthrie** was a learned and godly minister. He was the leading minister of the Presbyterian Church in that afflictive period of the Scottish persecution, and was singled out as the next victim by Charles II. He met his sufferings with Christian courage and cheerfulness. His sufferings were occasioned purely by his religion and his opposition to the tyranny of the Stuart dynasty. On the scaffold, after having fully enumerated the causes of his sufferings, he said, "I take God to record on my soul, that I would not exchange this scaffold for the palace and the miter of the greatest prelate in Britain! Blessed be God who has showed mercy to me, and made me a minister of the everlasting Gospel! Jesus is my light and life, my righteousness, my strength and salvation, and all my desire! Him, O Him do I commend with all my soul unto you. Bless Him, O my soul, now and forever! Now, O Lord, lettest Thou Thy servant depart in peace, for mine eyes

have seen Thy salvation!"

19. **Hugh McKail**, who was among the first victims in the twenty-eight years' persecution in Scotland, was executed in the twenty-sixth year of his age. His great influence and popular talents as a preacher made him an object of sharp jealousy. He closed his powerful and eloquent speech on the scaffold in these sublime and touching words, "Now I leave off to speak any more to creatures, and begin my intercourse with God forever! Farewell, father and mother, friends and relations; farewell the world and all its delights; farewell food and drink; farewell sun, moon, and stars! Welcome God and Father; welcome sweet Jesus, the mediator; welcome blessed Spirit of all grace, God of consolations; welcome glory; welcome death; welcome eternal life!" And having prayed a few moments, he lifted his eyes to heaven and cried with a loud voice, "O Lord, into Thy hands I commend my spirit; for Thou hast redeemed ny soul, O Lord God of truth!" And while uttering this prayer he was launched into eternity!

20. **James Renwick** was the last that was martyred in that persecution for "liberty, religion, and the covenant." Like McKail, he was only twenty-six years of age when he suffered, and of distinguished talents and oratory. On the scaffold he was repeatedly interrupted in a brutal manner, by the tumultuous beating of the drums, in order to prevent the immense multitude from hearing his speech, a custom peculiar to those days! He smiled and said, "They will not let a dying man be heard!" His last words were, "O Lord, I die in the faith that Thou wilt not leave the Church, but that Thou wilt make the blood of Thy witnesses the seed of Thy Church, and return again, and be glorious in our land! And now, O Lord, I am ready." Then whispering to his friend on whom he leaned, he said, "Farewell, be diligent in duty; carry my love to my dear brethren in the furnace." Then turning to the multitude, and lifting his eyes to heaven, he cried, "Lord, into Thy hands I com-

mend my spirit; for Thou hast redeemed me, Lord God of Truth. Amen!"

21. **Captain John Paton.** These heroic Christian examples were not confined to ministers in that period. Capt. Paton, who served in the wars under Gustavus Adolphus, and afterwards in the army of Scotland, was a brave and judicious soldier. He died for his religion, and in the defense of Scottish liberty. His last words on the scaffold were, "I leave my testimony against the impious usurpation of Christ's prerogative and crown. I solemnly adhere to the whole work of the Reformation. I forgive all my persecutors and enemies, and pray God to forgive them. I leave my dear wife and six sweet children with the Lord, the Father of orphans and the widow's Husband! And now, farewell all worldly joys, farewell sweet Scriptures, and preaching, and reading, and praying, and singing! Welcome Father, Son, and Holy Spirit! I desire to commit my soul to Thee in well-doing! O Lord, receive my spirit!" Thus fell one of the most gallant officers of the Scottish (and God's) army.

22. The pious **James Hervey** closed his life, pouring out his soul in prayer; "How thankful am I for death! It is the passage to the Lord and Giver of eternal life! O welcome, welcome death! Thou mayest well be reckoned among the treasures of the Christian: to live is Christ, to die is gain! Lord, now lettest Thou Thy servant depart in peace, for mine eyes have seen Thy salvation!"

23. The venerable **Ralph Erskine**, a faithful and devoted minister of the Church of Scotland, was for a few hours preceding his dissolution, in great darkness and mental distress. But, shortly before he died, he raised his hands, and clapping them, he exclaimed, "Victory, victory!" Then he expired.

24. The immortal **John Locke** applied himself faithfully to the study of the Holy Scriptures for the last fourteen years of his life. To a

young gentleman he said, "If you would attain the true knowledge of the Christian religion, study the Bible, especially the New Testament. The Bible has God for its author, salvation for its end, and truth without error for its matter!" On his deathbed he exhorted all around him to study the Word of God. "Blessed be God," he said, "for what the law has shown to man; blessed be His name for justifying him through faith in Christ; and thanks be to Thy name, O God, for having called me to the knowledge of the Divine Savior!"

25. **Richard Baxter** closed his course full of the joys of the Holy Ghost. To some ministers who were comforting him he said, "I have pains; there is no arguing against sense; but I have *peace,* I have peace!" "You are now drawing near your long-desired home," said one. "I believe, I believe," was his reply. When the question was put to him, "How are you?"he promptly replied, "Almost well!" To a friend who had entered his chamber he said, "Thank you for coming." Then fixing his eye on him, he added, "Lord teach you how to die!" These were his last words.

26. **John Janeway**, a young minister of England, died a triumphant death. Not a word dropped from his lips which did not breathe of Christ and heaven. "O my friends, stand and wonder: was there ever greater kindness? Were there ever more sensible manifestations of grace? O why me, O Lord, why me? If this be dying, then dying is sweet! Let no Christian be afraid of dying. O death is sweet to me: this bed is soft: Christ's arms, His smiles, His visits, sure they would turn hell into heaven! What are all human pleasures compared to one glimpse of His glory, which shines so strongly in my soul! I shall soon be in eternity: I shall soon see Christ himself, who died for me, who loved me, and washed me in His blood! I shall soon mingle in the hallelujahs of glory! Methinks I hear the melody of heaven, and by faith I see angels waiting to carry me to the bosom of the Jesus! And I shall be forever with

the Lord! And who can choose but to rejoice in this?"

27. **Matthew Henry**, the famous gospel preacher and commentator, said to a friend a short time before his sudden death, "You have been used to take notice of the sayings of dying men. This is mine: that a life spent in the service of God and communion with Him is the most comfortable and pleasant life that anyone can live in this world!"

28. **Jonathan Edwards** died with as much calmness and composure as if going to sleep. He was in the full possession of reason to the last, and looked into eternity as into his Father's house in the heavens. "Never did anyone more fully evidence the sincerity of his profession by one continued, universal, calm, cheerful, and patient resignation to the divine will of God, than he," said his physician. "Not one murmur, not one whisper of his was heard indicating discontent. When some were deploring his departure as a frown on the college, and as a heavy stroke on the church, not being sensible that he heard them, he turned his dying eyes on them and said, "Trust in God, and you need not fear!" These were the last words this great and pious divine spoke on earth.

29. The eminent **George Whitefield** uttered this noble sentiment when a Christian friend asked him what his dying testimony would be; "My dying testimony is this: I have preached Christ a living testimony!" A sentiment perfectly in keeping with his zeal, his piety, his fervor, his incessant labors in the ministry, and his wonderful success in being used by God to win souls to Christ.

30. **Thomas Scott**, the commentator, died in 1821. As a faithful minister, a judicious writer, and a holy man, he had few equals. His dying bed may be said to have been sublimely Christian! He exhibited an awful sense of divine things, of the evil of sin, of the purity and holiness of God. And notwithstanding his progress heavenward, what self-abasement he ever manifested! "O Lord, abhor me not," he said in fervent prayer, "though I be abhorrible, and abhor myself: say not, 'Thou

filthy soul, continue to be filthy still;' but rather say, "I will be thou clean." He longed much to be gone: "I am weary of my journey, and wish to be at home, if it is God's will." "Ah! I had thought that I should close the sacred services of this day (the Sabbath) in heaven." A great part of his time he prayed and thought aloud. On one occasion he said, "Posthumous reputation! the veriest bubble with which the devil ever deluded a wretched mortal! But posthumous usefulness—aye, in that there is indeed something: that was what Moses, the prophets, and the Apostles desired; and most of all, the Lord Jesus Christ." Among the last words he uttered were these: "Lord support me—Lord Jesus, receive my spirit!" To his weeping wife and children he said with great tenderness, "Can any rational being grieve at my departure? Well, nature will have its first burst of sorrow, but you will soon learn to view it in its true light." "Christ is my all! He is my only hope!" "O to realize the fullness of joy; O to be done with temptation!" "This is heaven begun: I am done with darkness forever! Satan is vanquished! Nothing remains but salvation with eternal glory, *eternal glory!*"

31. **Augustus Toplady** closed a long and eminently holy life by a very triumphant death. He said: "O how this soul of mine longs to be gone; like an imprisoned bird, it longs to take its flight. O that I had the wings of a dove, I should flee away to the realms of bliss, and be at rest forever! I long to be absent from the body and present with the Lord." At another time he said, "O what day of sunshine has this been to me! I have no words to express it: it is unutterable! O, my friends, how good our God is! Almost without interruption His presence has been with me." Being near his end, having awakened out of sleep, he said, "O what delights! who can fathom the joys of the third heavens!" And just before he expired he said, "The sky is clear; there is no cloud: Come Lord Jesus, come quickly."

32. **Edward Payson**, the eminent, devoted and faithful minister,

had a fine mind, charming imagination and ardent love of Christ. While on his deathbed, laboring under acute pains, he exclaimed, "These are Gods arrows—but they are sharpened with love." He once exclaimed, "The victory is won forever! I am going to bathe in an ocean of purity, and benevolence, and happiness, to all eternity." Looking to his wife and children, he said, "I am going, but God will surely be with you!" His last words he was heard to whisper were, "Faith and patience, hold out!"

The Way to Heaven

Jonathan Edwards

ow poor you are if you have no heaven but only this world. You have nothing but a little part of this clod of earth, and what is it all worth! If you have a little more land than some of your neighbors, or if you are in a way to make more money than others, if your accommodations are better than others, and you have more worldly conveniences and pleasures than others, or if you are promoted a little higher among men than some others are, what a poor portion is this, and how miserable are you who have no better happiness that you can call your own! How happy do these things make you? Are such things as these the "rivers of pleasure" that you choose for your portion? O how miserable! When a few days have passed you must go to the grave and into eternity, and then your glory shall not descend after you. Then how wretched are you, if when you are done with worldly enjoyments, it may be said that you have received your consolation! (Luke 6:24)

But you have yet an opportunity to be made happy forever. The opportunity you now have to obtain the happiness of another world is worth ten thousands of this world! Do you then ask, "What must I do

in order to go to heaven?"

Your heart must be drawn to Him, and it must be pleasing and sweet to you to have heaven as a free gift, as the fruit of mercy and saving grace; you must assuredly believe that Christ is a sufficient Savior, and your must acquiesce in the way of salvation by Him, by His blood and His right-eousness, as a wise, holy, sufficient and excellent way. Your heart must incline to Jesus Christ as a Savior above your own righteous-ness and all other ways. Your delight must be in this holy way of salvation.

You must be of the same temper and disposition with the Psalmist, who says, "Whom have I in heaven but Thee? And there is none on earth that I desire besides Thee." You must esteem and relish the enjoyment of Him far above all other things. You must be brought to see that there is in the enjoyment of God, and communion with Him, what is far better than all kinds of happiness you could devise.

In heaven they are not idle, but they are continually employed, and their employments are holy employments; they spend their time wholly in holy exercises: in contemplating God, in praising and serving Him. "And there shall be no more curse: but the throne of God and of the Lamb shall be in it; and His servants shall serve Him." (Rev. 22:3). If ever you are to go to heaven your heart must be brought beforehand to such a temper as freely to choose such employments, you must have a relish of them, and must count them excellent and delightful.

You must hate and abhor all sin, and allow none in your life. Sin must become to you a great burden. You must loathe yourself for it, and fight and strive against it, to purge yourself more and more from it; striving more and more to mortify sin, earnestly desiring and seeking to be more holy, more conformed to the will of God, and to walk more becoming a Christian.

Heaven must be to you like the treasure hid in a field, or like the pearl of great price. If you would have heaven, you must take it as your whole portion; you must, in your heart, part with all other things for it; and it must be your manner actually to part with them whenever they stand in the way of your getting forward towards heaven. If you would have heaven, you must sell worldly profit, and your credit, and the goodwill of your neighbors, your worldly pleasures and conveniences, and whatever else stands in your way.

Some expect to get to heaven who are not walking in a narrow way. The way they are walking in is a way indulging in ease and of shifting off the hard and difficult parts of religion. It is not the way of self-denial, and toil, and laboriousness; but they walk in a broad way, a way wherein they are not perplexed, but can go on without labor and watchfulness, or bearing the cross. But such as these, let their hopes be what they may, and their pretenses to experience what they may, are not likely to get to heaven.

To some the way the Scripture has laid out is too narrow and straight, therefore they are endeavoring to get to heaven by a broad way; but it is vain for you to contrive this. If you can find out any way of getting to heaven that is not the straight and narrow way, it will be a way that is your own invention and not of God. If you go thither, you must go in the way of the footsteps of the flock. If you would go to heaven, you must be content to go there in the way of self-denial and sufferings. You must be willing to take up the cross daily and follow Christ, and through much tribulation enter the kingdom of heaven.

Perfection of the Soul

Joseph Addison

There is not, in my opinion, a more pleasing and triumphant consideration in religion than that of the perpetual progress which the soul makes toward the perfection of its nature, without ever arriving at a period in it. To look upon the soul as going on from strength to strength, to consider that it is to shine forever with new accessions of glory and brighten to all eternity; that it will be still adding virtue to virtue and knowledge to knowledge, carries in it something wonderfully agreeable to that ambition which is natural to the mind of man. Nay, it must be a respect pleasing to God himself to see a creation forever beautifying in his eyes, and drawing nearer to him by greater degrees of resemblance.

No Cross, No Crown

John Bunyan

You must understand that there is no man that goes to heaven without first going to the cross. The cross is the standing waymark, by which all they that go to glory must pass. "If any man will come after me," says Christ, "let him deny himself and take up his cross daily, and follow me." The cross! It stands, and has stood, from the beginning, as the way to the kingdom of heaven.

Are you enquiring the way to heaven? Why, I tell you, Christ is the way; and you must go to Him to be justified. And if you are in Him, you will see the cross. You must go close by it; you must touch it; you must take it up, or else you will find yourself out of the way that leads to heaven, and turn up some of those crooked lanes that lead into the chambers of death.

It is the cross that keeps back those that are kept from heaven. Some men, when they come to the cross, can go no farther; but back again to their sins they must go. Others stumble at it and break their necks. Others again when they see the cross approaching, turn to the left or right, and so think to get to heaven another way. But they are deceived. "For all that will live godly in Christ shall," mark it, "shall suffer persecution!" There are but few when they come to the cross, cry, "Welcome cross!" as some of the martyrs did to the stake at which they were burned.

Therefore, if thou meet with the cross in thy journey, be not daunted and say, "Alas! What shall I do now?" But rather take courage, knowing that by the cross is the way to the kingdom.

He Cares for You

John Gregory Pike

oes affliction cloud your sky? Do sorrows overwhelm your sinking spirits? Yet forget not that God is kind: "He cares for you." Gracious declaration! What words can be more expressive of His tender interest in your happiness? "He cares for you." Not only gives you blessings, but cares for your welfare, makes your little interests His concern. Surely all must be right that so gracious a Friend appoints; all must tend to good that so kind a Father ordains: "He that spared not his own Son, but delivered him up for us

304

all, how shall he not with him also freely give us all things?" Did He thus give His best Beloved for you, and can you think that He will refuse you any real good? Are you oppressed with sickness and pain? God could give you health: to give you health would be a little thing, compared with giving you Christ. Surely, if He does not give you health, the reason must be, He sees it best to appoint you sickness. Are you poor? God could give you wealth. He gave you Christ; and if He keeps you poor, the cause must be, that poverty is best for you. Were riches best, He who gave Christ would give you riches. Whatever fancied good you may desire, you may argue, if this were real good, God would give it me. He who gave Christ, that great and precious son, would not refuse this trifling gift, if this would prove a blessing to me. A suffering Christian, after a night of pain, observed, "It has been a night of great pain, but it was a night appointed me by Jesus Christ, and sure it must be a good one that He appoints." Thus reason respecting your heavenly Father's conduct. Doubt not His love who gave a Saviour. Depend on His interest in your happiness, through the few moments of time, who sent His only begotten Son into the world, to make you happy to eternity.

John Sudlow

Anecdotes for the Young

ohn Sudlow, died of the plague in London in the year 1655, at about the age of twelve. From the time he was four, he had a great reverence for God, and a strong sense of the important realities of the other world. The death of a little brother first led him to such serious thought, and induced him to inquire how he might go to heaven; and he learned the way of salvation through Christ.

When he was seized with the awful malady which laid him in the grave, he discovered great patience and resignation to the will of God. Upon his deathbed he exclaimed, "The Lord shall be my physician; for He will cure both body and soul. Heaven is the best hospital. It is the Lord, let Him do what seems good in His eyes. It is the Lord that taketh away my health; but I will say with Job, 'Blessed be the name of the Lord!' If I should live longer, I would only sin against God." When a minister came to him, he said, "This is a wicked world; yet, it is good to live with my parents, but better to live in heaven."

An hour before his death he was asked if he was not afraid to die. He answered, "No, the Lord will comfort me in that hour." When the minister asked him how he could expect comfort, he replied, "If I had my way, I would have been in hell long ago;" and added that he expected comfort and salvation in Christ alone. In this manner he died, to be forever with Jesus.

GOD HIMSELF hath infinite goodness in Him, which the creature cannot take in at once, but which they are taking in eternally. The saints see in God still things fresh, which they saw not in the beginning of their blessedness.—*Thomas Goodwin.*

My Little Playmate and Her Grandfather

Theodore Thinker

inny Willson was very nearly my own age. We used to play together, when we were little children; and many a pleasant hour have we spent in company, listening to the music of the birds, and gathering honey-suckles and anemones. Her father died before her recollection; and she could not have been more than six or seven years old, when God sent kind angels to conduct her mother to heaven. Little Virginia was then an orphan, and well do I remember how she wept as she told me that they had laid her dear mother to sleep in the cold ground. But Virginia had a very kind and good grandfather, who adopted her as his own child, when her mother died. He was an excellent old gentleman. How he loved the Bible! Many a time I have seen him teaching his young charge out of this precious book.

"Theodore," said she to me, one day, as we were going to gather some water-cresses in my father's meadow, "Theodore, you don't know how happy I have been for a week past. Grandpa has been showing me such sweet verses in the Bible. I didn't know how good that book was before. It says, "When my father and my mother forsake me, then the Lord will take me up." Oh, how kind it was for God to make such a book, and to write such things in it. And grandpa says, that verse was put in the book for little girls like me. You know I have lost my dear father and mother"—here the tears started from Virginia's eyes, and, for a little while, she cried so much that she could not speak; but by and by she commenced again, and her countenance was even more bright and cheerful than it was before—"My father and mother are gone away; but the Lord has taken care of me. And grandpa has been telling me, too, how the Saviour came down from heaven into this world, and how he died for little children, and grown up people. Theodore, I have been praying that God would make me good, like my mother, so that I may go and live with her again by and by. I dreamed last night that she came back to see me, and I seemed to hear her say, 'Virginia, my child,' just as she used to, before she died, 'Virginia, be a good girl, and learn to love Jesus Christ.' I thought I saw the angels, too, all dressed in white; and some of them flew to me, and seemed to beckon me away from the world. I don't know why it is, but it seems to me that I am not going to live here long. And how strange it is! I used to be afraid to die; but it is not so now. Death seems to me like going on a pleasant journey."

For a long time we talked together about dying, until we quite forgot our water-cresses. We indulged a multitude of childish fancies. We wondered whether we should know each other in heaven, and whether the Saviour would speak to little children. I could not see how Virginia should be willing to die, and leave so many beautiful things. She tried to tell me how it was, but I could not understand her. Virginia was a feeble child; but to me it did not seem possible that she could die. I thought of what she said often, after this ramble in the meadow, and wished I could feel as she did about dying.

Little Virginia did not stay long in the world. She died before the leaves began to fall. She died, as a bud withers, ere it has unfolded. And as the angels came to convey her to heaven, she said to her young playmates, "When my father and mother forsake me, then the Lord will take me up."

———

DO LIVE AS MEN that must shortly be buried in the grave, and their souls appear before the Lord, and as men that have but little time to do all for their everlasting life. O live as men that are sure to die, and not sure to live till tomorrow.—*Richard Baxter*

The House of God

Jonathan Edwards

eaven is the house where God dwells with His family. God is represented in Scripture as having a family; and though some of this family are now on earth, yet in so being they are abroad and not at home, but all going home: Ephesians 3:15, "Of whom the whole family in heaven and earth is named." Heaven is the place that God has built for himself and his children. God has many children, and the place designed for them is heaven; therefore the saints, being the children of God, are said to be of the household of God, Ephesians 2:19: "Now therefore ye are no more strangers and foreigners, but fellow-citizens with the saints, and of the household of God." God is represented as a householder or head of a family, and heaven is His house.

Heaven is the house not only where God hath His throne, but also where He doth as it were keep His table, where His children sit down with Him at His table and where they are feasted in a royal manner becoming the children of so great a King; "That ye may eat and drink at my table in my kingdom" (Luke 22:30); "But I say unto you, I will not drink henceforth of this fruit of the vine until that day when I drink it new with you in my Father's kingdom." (Matthew 26:29)

God is the King of kings, and heaven is the place where He keeps His court. There are His angels and archangels that as the nobles of His court do attend upon Him.

The Departed Child

Samuel Rutherford

Your child is not sent away, but only sent before; like unto a star, which going out of our sight, doth not die and vanish, but shines in another hemisphere; you see her not, yet she doth shine in another country. If her glass were but a short hour, what she wants of time, that she has gotten of eternity; and you have to rejoice that you have now some furniture up in heaven. Build your nest upon no tree here; for you see God has sold the forest to death; and every tree, whereupon you would rest, is ready to be cut down, to the end that we might fly and mount up and build upon the Rock, and dwell in the holes of the Rock.

Soul and Body Glorified in Heaven

John Bunyan

would speak a little of the state of our body and soul in heaven, when we shall enjoy the blessed eternal state of salvation.

The soul will then be filled in all the faculties of it with as much bliss and glory as ever it can hold.

Our understanding will then be perfect in knowledge. "Now we know in part,"—we know God, Christ, heaven, and glory, but in part; "but when that which is perfect is come, then that which is in part shall be done away." Then we shall have perfect and everlasting visions of God, and that blessed One his Son Jesus Christ; a good thought of whom doth sometimes so fill us, while in this world, that it causes joy unspeakable.

Then will our conscience have that peace and joy, that neither tongue or pen of men or angels can express.

Then will our memory be so enlarged as to perfectly retain all things that happened to us in this world; so that with unspeakable aptness we shall call to mind all God's providences, all Satan's malice, all our weaknesses, all the rage of men, and how God made all work together for His glory and our good, to the everlasting ravishings of our hearts.

For our body, it shall be raised in power, in incorruption, a spiritual body and glorious.

It is compared to the brightness of the firmament, and to the shining of the stars forever! It is said that then our vile body shall be made like the glorious body of Jesus Christ. Their state is then to be equally glorious with angels.

And when body and soul are thus united, who can imagine what glory they both will possess? They will both be in capacity without jarring to serve the Lord; with shouting, thanksgivings, and with a crown of everlasting joy upon their head.

In this world there cannot be the harmony and oneness of body and soul that there will be in heaven. Here the body sometimes sins against the soul; and the soul vexes the body. While we are yet in this world, the body oft hangs this way, and the soul quite the contrary; but there in heaven they shall have such perfect union as never to jar more. The glory of the body shall so suit the glory of the soul, and both so perfectly suit with the heavenly state, that it passes words and thoughts.

Oh sinner, what sayest thou? How dost thou like being saved? Doth not thy mouth water? Doth not thy heart twitter at being saved? Why, come then! The Spirit and the Bride say "Come; and let him that heareth say, Come; and let him that is athirst, Come; and whosoever will, let him freely take the water of life."

The Pearly Gates Ajar

Emily Judson

I gazed down life's dim labyrinth,
　　A wildering maze to see,
Crossed o'er by many a tangled clue,
　　And wild as wild could be:
And as I gazed in doubt and dread,
　　An angel came to me.

I knew her for a heavenly guide,
　　I knew her even then,
Though meekly as a child she stood
　　Among the sons of men
By her deep spirit-loveliness,
　　I knew her even then.

And as I leaned my weary head
　　Upon her proffered breast,
And scanned the peril-haunted wild
　　From out my place of rest,
I wondered if the shining ones
　　Of Eden were more blest.

For there was light within my soul,
　　Light on my peaceful way,
And all around the blue above
　　The clustering starlight lay;
And easterly I saw upreared
　　The pearly gates of day.

So, hand in band, we trod the wild,
    My angel love and I—
Her lifted wing all quivering
    With tokens from the sky.
Strange my dull thought could not divine
    'Twas lifted but to fly!

Again down life's dim labyrinth
    I grope my way alone,
While wildly through the midnight sky
    Black, hurrying clouds are blown,
And thickly, in my tangled path,
    The sharp, bare thorns are sown.

Yet firm my foot, for well I know
    The goal cannot be far;
And ever, through the rifted clouds,
    Shines out one steady star—
For when my guide went up, she left
    The pearly gates ajar.

Employment in Glory

Jonathan Edwards

Though the employment and happiness of all the heavenly assembly shall in the general be the same, yet 'tis not improbable that there may be circumstantial differences. We know what their employment is in general, but not in particular. We know not how one may be employed to subserve and promote the happiness of another, and all to help one another. Some may there be set in one place for one office or employment, and others in another, as 'tis in the Church on earth. God hath set every one in the body as it hath pleased Him; one is the eye, another the ear, another the head.

Future Usefulness

Horatius Bonar

N o man's usefulness ever ends. The true becomes truer; the powerful becomes more powerful; the noble becomes nobler; the fruitful becomes more fruitful; the successful multiplies successes; and without fear of reverse, or failure, or weariness, the liberated saint rejoices in the anticipation of an eternal future of usefulness—in all respects illimitable, far beyond that of his most productive days on earth. The corn of wheat, before it fell into the ground,was comparatively barren, but having fallen into the ground and died it brings forth much fruit.

Meditating on Future Life

John Calvin

W hatever be the kind of tribulation with which we are afflicted, we should always consider the end of it to be, that we may be trained to despise the present, and thereby stimulated to aspire to the future life. For since God well knows how strongly we are inclined by nature to a slavish love of this world, in order to prevent us from clinging too strongly to it, he employs the fittest reason for calling us back, and shaking off our lethargy. Every one of us, indeed, should aspire and aim at heavenly immortality during the whole course of life.

314

This life, though abounding in all kinds of wretchedness, is justly classed among divine blessings which are not to be despised. Wherefore, if we do not recognize the kindness of God in it, we are chargeable with no little ingratitude towards him. To believers, especially, it ought to be a proof of divine benevolence, since it is wholly destined to promote their salvation. Before openly exhibiting the inheritance of eternal glory, God is pleased to manifest himself to us as a Father by minor proofs, viz., the blessings which he daily bestows upon us. Therefore, while this life serves to acquaint us with the goodness of God, shall we disdain it as if it did not contain one particle of good? We ought, therefore, to feel and be affected towards it in such a manner as to place it among those gifts of the divine benignity which are by no means to be despised.

Were there no proofs in Scripture (they are most numerous and clear), yet nature herself exhorts us to return thanks to God for having brought us forth into light, granted us the use of it, and bestowed upon us all the means necessary for its preservation. And there is a much higher reason when we reflect that here we are in a manner prepared for the glory of the heavenly kingdom. For the Lord hath ordained, that those who are ultimately to be crowned in heaven must maintain a previous warfare on the earth, that they may not triumph before they have overcome the difficulties of war, and obtained the victory. Another reason is, that we here begin to experience in various ways a foretaste of the divine benignity, in order that our hope and desire may be whetted for its full manifestation. When once we have concluded that our earthly life is a gift of the divine mercy, of which, agreeably to our obligation, it behooves us to have a grateful remembrance, we shall then properly descend to consider its most wretched condition, and thus escape from that excessive fondness for it, to which, as I have said, we are naturally prone.

Glimpses Through Life's Windows

J. R. Miller

N o one can ponder the great theme of immortality for an hour and not feel the stir and glow of a better, nobler life in him. In our more prosaic moods we are like men shut up in a narrow cell. We see for the time nothing but the little patch of dusty floor at our feet and the cold, cheerless walls that encircle us. We are occupied with our little round of duties. Burdens press, sorrows pour bitter tears into our cup, our hopes are shattered; or we have our short-lived joys, we see our plans succeed, and play at living like children in their mimic fancies. Now and then we have intimations of a wider and more glorious world outside our walls, stretching away beyond the small circle in which we dwell. Faint voices appear to come to us from without. Or there are glimmerings as if of memory, like the visionary gleams of a past and forgotten life, which flash before us in our higher moods. But to most of us pent up in this earthly life these are only merest intimations, faintest whispers, dreamlike suggestions. We go on living in our narrow sphere, oppressed by its limitations, our faculties and powers stunted by its gloom.

Did you ever climb the winding staircase in the interior of some great monument or tower? At intervals, as you ascended, you came to a window which let in a little light, and through which, as you looked out, you had a glimpse of a great expanse of fair and lovely world outside the dark tower. You saw green fields, rich gardens, picturesque landscapes, streams flashing like flowing silver in the sunshine, the blue sea yonder, and far away, on the other hand, the shadowy forms of great mountains. How little, how dark, how poor and cheerless, seemed the close, narrow limits of your staircase as you looked out upon the illimitable view that stretched from your window!

Life in this world is like the ascent of such a column. But while we

316

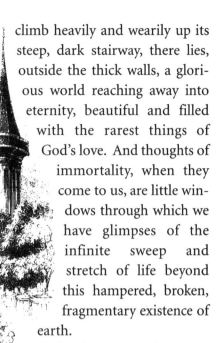

climb heavily and wearily up its steep, dark stairway, there lies, outside the thick walls, a glorious world reaching away into eternity, beautiful and filled with the rarest things of God's love. And thoughts of immortality, when they come to us, are little windows through which we have glimpses of the infinite sweep and stretch of life beyond this hampered, broken, fragmentary existence of earth.

The doctrine of the resurrection is one of these windows. It opens to us a vista running away beyond the grave. Death is a mere episode, a mere experience, an incident on the way. Even the grave, which seems to quench all the light of life, is but a chamber in which we shall disrobe ourselves of the infirmities, blemishes and imperfections of mortality and be reclothed in the holy, spotless vesture of immortality. Thus we sleep at night, and sleep seems like death; but we awake in the morning, our life unharmed, unwasted, made fairer, fuller, fresher, stronger. Winter comes, and the leaves fall, the flowers fade, the plants die, and snow wraps the earth in a blanket of death. But spring comes again, and the buds burst out anew, the flowers lift their heads and the grasses shoot up once more. From beneath the great drift, the gentlest and most delicate forms of life come as fresh and fragrant as if they had been nourished in a conservatory. Nature rises from the grave of winter in dew beauty and luxuriance. In place of the faded loveliness and exhausted vigor of autumn, there is now all the splendor of new creation. Every leaf is green, every pore is flowing full of vital sap, and every flower pours sweet fragrance in the air.

The grave is life's winter, from whose darkness and chill we shall come with unwasted beauty. Then, far beyond this strange experience, as we look out the window, we see life going on, expanding, deepening, enriching.

When the truth of immortal existence comes into our personal consciousness, it opens a wonderful vista before us. It gives life a new glory. It furnishes one of the most powerful motives for noble living.

The weakness of most lives, even of most Christian lives, is the absence of this motive. For, however firmly we may cling to the truth of immortality as a belief, there are but few lives in which it is so realized as to be a ruling inspiration, a strong, masterful conviction. How it would widen out all our thoughts, conceptions, hopes and plans if the walls that divide life here and hereafter were broken down and our eyes could see our own existence in perspective, stretching away into eternity, as real, as personal, as fraught with interest beyond the grave as on this side of it! How it would lift up, dignify, ennoble, inspire, awaken and deepen all our life if we could but hold the truth of personal immortality in our consciousness all the while as vividly and as really as we hold tomorrow!

The grave would not then be the end of anything save of mortality and of the sins, weights and infirmities which belong to, this earthly state. It would break up no plans. It would cut off nothing. If we see life only as a narrow stage bounded by the curtain that falls at death, ending there for ever, how poor and little and limited does existence appear! We can have no plans that require more than earth's brief day for their completion. We can start no work that cannot be finished before the end comes. We may cherish no joys that will reach over into the life hereafter.

We may sow no seeds that will not come to harvest this side of the grave. Our souls may be thrilled by no aspirations and hopes that have their goal beyond the shadows. But how different if we see life with the veil torn away! The future is as much in our vision and as real as the little present. We may begin works here which shall require ten thousand years to complete. There is no hurry, for we shall have all eternity in which to work. We may scatter seeds which we know shall not come to harvest for long ages. We may cherish hopes and aspirations whose goals lie far away in the life to come. We may endure sacrifices, hardships and toils which cannot bring any recompense or reward in this world, knowing that in the long yearless future we shall find a glorious return.

Life may seem a failure here, crushed like a lily under the heel of wrong or sin, broken, trampled, torn. But it may yet become a glorious success. Many of the truest and best of God's children know only defeat in this world. They are evermore beaten back and thrust down. The burdens are too heavy for them. They are overmastered by sorrows. The world's enmity treads them in the dust. They are not worldly-wise, and while others march by to great earthly success they live obscurely, oppressed, cheated, wronged, and lie buried away in the darkness of failure. If the vista did not reach beyond the bare and cold room in which these unsuccessful ones breathe their last, we might drop a tear of pity over their sad story of defeat. But when the curtain is lifted and we see millions of years of existence for them on the other side, we dry our tears. There will be time enough for them to retrieve the failure of earth. Through the love and grace of Christ, the defeated Christian life that goes out in the darkness here may be restored to beauty and power, and in the long ages beyond death may realize all the hopes that seemed utterly wrecked in this world.

Indeed, it may be that those who have failed here, as men phrase it, are the very ones who shall win the highest success in the after-life if they have kept their garments clean amid the struggles and toils. It has been said that heaven is probably a place for those who have failed on earth. Certainly, for the Christian, the realization of the truth of immortality takes away the bitterness of earthly defeat. There will be time enough for victory and for the most glorious success in the unending eternity.

There are lives that are cut off here before any of their powers are developed. A thousand hopes cluster about them. Dreams of greatness or of beauty fill the visions of loving friends. Then suddenly they are stricken down in the dim dawn or the early morning. The bud had not time to open out its beauties in the short summer of earthly existence. It is borne away still folding up in its closeshut calyxes all its germs and possibilities of power, loveliness and life. Sorrow weeps bitterly over the hopes that seem blighted and cuts its symbols of incompleteness upon the marble; and yet, with the warmth of immortality pressing up against the gates, what matters it that the bud did not open here and unfold its beauties this side the grave? There will be time enough in heaven's long summer for every life to put out all its loveliness and glory. No hopes are blighted that are only carried forward into the immortal years. No life is incomplete because it is cut off too soon to ripen, in an earthly home, into majesty of form and glory of fruitage; for death does not come to the Christian as a destroyer. It dims no splendor. It blots out no beauty. It paralyzes no power. It only takes out of life whatever is dull, earthly and opaque, whatever is corrupt and mortal, and leaves it pure, brilliant, glorious.

Death only sweeps away the limitations, breaks down the walls,

shatters the crust of mortality, washes out the stains, and then life expands into perfect freedom, fullness, joy and power. The translation of a Christian life from earth to heaven is like the removal of a tender plant from a cold northern garden, where it is stunted and dying, into a tropical field, where it puts out most luxuriant growths and covers itself with splendor.

There ought to be wondrous comforting power in the truth of immortality for those who carry here the burdens of sickness, infirmity or deformity; and there are many such. Many lovely bodies are full of disease and they stagger under life's lightest burdens. Then there are many who carry imperfect bodies, and old age comes to the strongest and the fairest, stealing away the strength and touching the loveliness, and it fades. But the resurrection body will be forever free from disease and pain. There will be no decrepitude, no bowed forms, no pale cheeks, no wasting or decay. How pleasant it is to the old to know that they will get back their bodies with all the marks of age removed, and will begin life again with all the glow of immortal youth! Not only does age leave no traces of wasting, but the immortal life is a growth ever toward youth and freshness of existence rather than toward senescence and decay.

There is another bearing which the truth of immortality must have upon the life that truly realizes it. It is in the intensifying of all its best activities and powers. If there were to be no life after this brief existence, why should we deny ourselves and spend our strength in serving others? Why should we sacrifice our own ease and comfort for the sake of those who are degraded and unworthy? How cold and hard all duty seems without this motive! But when this truth of immortality comes and touches these austere duties, how they begin to glow! The certainty of a hereafter bright with all manner of rewards and joys is a wondrous inspiration. No matter that there is no apparent result when we toil and sacrifice; that the word we speak seems to float away into oblivion; that the impression we seek to make on a life fades out while we gaze. Somewhere in the long years to come we shall find that not the smallest deed done for Christ, or the feeblest word spoken, or the faintest touch given, has been in vain. In the highest sense do we work towards eternity. The brightest clouds lose their splendor while you gaze, but work done in human souls will appear in unfading hues, brightening forever.

Thus the glimpses we get through the little dim windows in the walls of our earthly life should give a new meaning to our existence here and to all our multiplied relationships. With immortality glowing before us, our brief years on earth should be marked by earnestness, reverence, love and faithfulness. Soon we shall break out of our narrow circle and traverse the boundless fields that we see now only in the far-away and momentary glimpse. But it will be a blessed thing if we can get into our hearts even here something of the personal consciousness of our immortality, with its limitless possessions and possibilities, and feel something in our souls of the power of an endless life.

Use of Afflictions

Robert Murray M'Cheyne

Sickness brings out graces that cannot be seen in times of health. It is the treading of the grapes that brings out the sweet juices of the vine; so it is affliction that draws forth submission, weanedness from the world, and complete rest in God. Use afflictions while you have them.

Heaven is the treasury of everlasting joy.—*Shakespeare*

323

In Mother's Place

"In mother's place"—so father said,
His kind hand resting on my head,
While all the burden of the day,
The care and trouble, fell away!
New purpose seemed to grow in me
To struggle for the victory,
And by the fireside's happy light
I breathed a silent prayer tonight!
The children, crowding at my side,
Need me, and will not be denied!

The home her presence made so
    bright
Needs me, and I must be its light!
The girls and boys too soon will go
From sheltering arms of love,
    I know
May the sweet influence of home
Be theirs wherever they may
    roam!
Yes! It is little I can do;

Yet faith in God will bear me
    through,
And give me wisdom to fulfill
My duty, since it is His will
That these, who need a mother's
    care,
Should find in me—bereft of her,
And longing for her loving face—
A guide and friend in mother's
    place.

324

WHEN I GET TO HEAVEN, I shall see three wonders there. The first wonder will be to see people there I did not expect to see; the second wonder will be to miss many persons whom I did expect to see; and the third and greatest wonder of all will be to find myself there.

—John Newton

Precious Comfort from Sickness

Charles Haddon Spurgeon

ickness in the believer is intended for the glory of God, and in part this design is answered during the trial. It is to be feared that the Lord gets but a small revenue of glory from some of us. Sickness takes out a warrant against ingratitude, and surcharges us for our defalcations, by bringing our negligences to remembrance. God gets many a song from his caged birds which might never be heard if they had strength to wanton on the wing. Psalms and hymns, like music on the water, sound sweetly from the depths of suffering. Moreover, God is glorified in the results of sanctified pain, by the gentleness, meekness, quietness, and unction which adorn the spirit of the experienced believer. Until the oyster is sick it yields no pearls. Heavy damps of adversity make souls verdant. Saints, unlike the plants of earth, grow fastest in the sharpest weather. We make most progress in our voyage heavenward when the wind is rough. Calms are more pleasant than profitable; better for comfort than for commerce; fairer in the present than in the retrospect. Affliction cuts the facets of the Lord's diamonds, and so they shine with a greater luster to his honor. What the church owes to the file and the hammer no tongue can tell.

Would the church triumphant have been so glorious as it now is, if its members had been spared the great tribulation out of which they passed to their crowns? Would half the grace which now beautifies the

325

church militant have been discernible at all, if severe trials had not developed it? Would the Lord have had honor among us if the chastening rod had been laid aside? For the world to see how a Christian can endure hardness, is a great glory to God. The great hospital of saintly suffering is a grand exposition in which the choice works of the Holy Spirit are exhibited to all who have eyes to see. Our covenant God is magnified by the virtues peculiar to tried believers, quite as much as by those which adorn his active servants.

How Sin Appears in Heaven

Edward Payson

f we could see our sins as they appear to God, that is, as they really are; we must place ourselves as nearly as possible in His situation and look at sin through His eyes. In order to do this, we must leave our dark and sinful world, where God is unseen and almost forgotten, and where the evil of sinning against Him cannot be fully perceived,—and mount up to heaven, the peculiar habitation of His holiness and glory.

Let us then attempt this adventurous flight. Let us follow the path by which our Savior ascended to heaven and soar upwards to the palace and throne of the great King. As we rise, the earth fades from our view; now we leave worlds, and suns, and systems behind us. Now a new light begins to dawn and brighten upon us. It is the light of heaven, which pours a flood of glory from its wide open gates, spreading continual meridian day far and wide through the regions of ethereal space. Passing swiftly onward through this flood of day, the songs of heaven begin to burst upon your ears and voices of celestial sweetness, yet loud as the sound of many waters and of mighty thunderings, are heard exclaiming, Alleluia! for the Lord God omnipotent reigns! A

326

moment more, and you have passed the gates—you are in the middle of the city, you are before the eternal throne, you are in the immediate presence of God, and all His glories are blazing around you like a consuming fire. Flesh and blood cannot endure it; your bodies dissolve into their original dust, but your immortal souls remain, and stand naked before the great Father of spirits. With a voice which reverberates through the wide expanse of His dominions, you hear Him saying, "Be ye holy; for I, the Lord your God, am holy." And you see His throne surrounded, you see heaven filled with by those only who perfectly obey this command. You see ten thousands of thousands of pure, exalted, glorious intelligences, who reflect His perfect image, and seem to be so many concentrations of wisdom, knowledge, holiness and love; a fit retinue for the thrice holy Lord of hosts, whose glory they unceasingly proclaim.

And now, if you are willing to see your sins in their true colors; if you would rightly estimate their number, magnitude, and criminality, bring them into this hallowed place. Here, in the midst of this circle of seraphic intelligences, with the infinite God pouring all the light of His countenance round you, review your life, contemplate your offenses, and see how they appear. Recollect that the God in whose presence you are, is the Being who forbids sin—the Being, of whose eternal law sin is the transgression, and against whom every sin is committed.

Patience Under Trials

William Jay

More than once you have been appalled in the prospect of a trial, but when the evil day came there came with it mercy and grace to help. Perhaps you even gloried in tribulation. Perhaps you would not refuse to pass through some of those distressing exercises again to enjoy the same peace and comfort.

Is there not much ignorance and inconsideration in this impatience! How do you know that it is better to escape from these troubles than to bear them! Not one of them has befallen you by chance. May you not infer the righteousness of them all from their very Author? Is not His work perfect? Are not His ways just? He doth all things well. Does He detain you in distress because He does not love you! Yea, He loved you with an everlasting love; and withheld not His own Son from you. You may, therefore, entirely confide in Him, assured that if He does not release you, it is because He waits to be gracious; and also equally assured, that blessed are all they that wait for Him; for it is good for a man not only to hope, but quietly wait for the salvation of the Lord.

We are detained here to be useful; and we are often most useful in our trials. Nothing strikes like facts. The passive graces are the most impressive. They are better than a thousand sermons; better to arrest the careless, to instruct the ignorant, to encourage the timid, to comfort the desponding. It was well Bunyan did not escape from the prison at Bedford, or we should not have had his *Pilgrim's Progress*, and his *Holy War*. Paul was a prisoner, and knew that to depart and be with Christ was far better; nevertheless, because it was more needful for the Philippians, he was willing to abide in the flesh, and acquiesced in the delay of his deliverance and bliss. And here you also may be wanted. Perhaps you have a venerable mother, and are required to rock the cradle of her age who rocked the cradle of your infancy. Perhaps you are a parent, and a rising family is dependent on your care, instructed by your wisdom, edified by your example. We are all placed in circumstances where we may prove a blessing; and this is our only opportunity. We may glorify God in heaven; but not in the same way as now, by submission, patience, and self-denial. This is an advantage we have above the glorified. They cannot exercise candor, and forgive injuries, and relieve distress, and lead souls. Life is ours as well as death. For all the days of our appointed time let us wait, till our change comes.

Eternal Choice

John Gregory Pike

ake your choice. Decide as in God's sight; but know, you must decide, and the decision is for eternity! Behold that eternal good which God, in His Word, has graciously unveiled to your contemplation. See those mansions of peace, those crowns of life, that blessedness which flows in an eternal stream. Behold those happy immortals—many of them once poor, despised, and suffering, now so changed. Hearken to the praises which they render; to the anthems of delight they sing. Witness their raptures in perfect safety. Belonging to Jesus leads to all this. Will you be His? Or will you madly and wickedly refuse? Will you embrace religion and secure that heaven, or trifle with religion and find ruin? *One you must do.* Which will you do? Is it difficult for you to become decidedly pious? Will not eternal life compensate every struggle? Are your enemies many? Must your sacrifices be great? Still, what are they when compared with the blessings of eternity? How small is the loss of what you soon must leave forever, and how rich the gain of blessings you will never lose! How momentary the loss and how eternal the gain! Even now, the hope of heaven would give you blessings far greater than any the world can ever give, while you would be looking forward to still greater good hereafter. How sweet now is the anticipation! What will be the possession? O ye blessed scenes of perfection and peace, shall ye be mine, and mine soon; and then mine forever? O happy heaven! Glorious abode! Where for me eternal love has prepared a mansion of peace, and where for me elder brethren wait. Shall I soon see thy walls of Salvation, and thy gates of Praise? Ye happy angels, shall I, a poor traveller on earth, soon be equal with you—as blest, as rich, and as safe as you? Thou Lamb of God, once slain for my transgressions, and now my life, shall I soon see thee as thou art, and wear thy lovely image? Shall I be done with toil and care, with worldly labors and earthly sorrows; and all to me be rest, and peace, and praise—the enduring calm and the victory of heaven? Shall all this be mine, when "a few more suns have rolled their cares away?" Then what need I fear the trials of this wilderness? To thee, my Lord, and to the heaven thy love has prepared, will I look with many a longing desire. There shall I see thee as thou art, and there praise thee better through eternal days.

The Happy Blind Girl

J. C. Ryle

Dear Children, Would you like to know who was the happiest child I ever saw? Listen and I will tell you.

I met this young girl while travelling on the train. We were both on our way to London, and we travelled many miles together. She was only eight years old and she was quite blind. She had never been able to see at all. She had never seen the sun, and the stars, and the sky, and the trees, and the flowers, and all those pleasant things which you see every day of your lives,—but still she was quite happy.

She was by herself, poor little thing. She had no friends or relations to take care of her on her journey and be good to her, but she was quite happy and content. She said when she got into the carriage, "please tell me how many people there are in the carriage, I am quite blind and can see nothing?" A gentleman asked her if she was afraid. "No," she said, "I am not frightened; I have travelled before, and I trust in God, and people are always very good to me." But I soon found out the reason why she was so happy—and what do you think it was? She loved Jesus Christ and Jesus Christ loved her. She had sought Jesus Christ, and she had found Him.

I began to talk to her about the Bible, and I soon saw that she knew a great deal about it. She went to a school where the teachers used to read the Bible to her; and she was a good girl, and had remembered what her teachers had read.

Dear children, you cannot think how many things in the Bible this poor little blind girl knew. I only wish that every grown-up person knew as much as she did. But I must tell you some of them.

She talked to me about sin. She knew how it first came into the world when Adam and Eve ate the forbidden fruit, and it is seen everywhere now. "Oh!" she said, "the very best people in all the world have many sins every day, and I am sure we all waste a great deal of time, if we do nothing else wrong. Oh! We are all such sinners! There is nobody who has not sinned."

And then she talked about Jesus Christ. She told me about the agony of Gethsemane, about His sweating great drops of blood, about the soldiers nailing Him to the cross, about the spear piercing His side, and blood and water coming out. "Oh!" she said, "how very good it was of Him to die for us, and such a cruel death! How good He was to suffer so for our sins."

And then she talked about wicked people. She told me she was afraid there were a great many in the world, and it made her very unhappy to see how many of her schoolmates and acquaintances went on in their sin. "But," she said, "I know the reason why they are so wicked, it is because they do not try to be good—they do not wish to be good—they do not ask Jesus to make them good."

I asked her what part of the Bible she liked best. She told me she liked the history of Jesus Christ, but the chapters she was most fond of were the last three chapters of Revelation. I took out my Bible, and read these chapters to her as we went along.

When I had finished, she began to talk about heaven. "Think," she said, "how nice it will be to be there. There will be no more sorrow, nor crying, nor tears. And then Jesus Christ will be there, for it says, 'The Lamb is the light thereof,' and we shall always be with Him; and besides this, there shall be no night there. They will need no candle nor light of the sun."

Dear children, just think of this poor little blind girl. Think of her taking pleasure in talking of Jesus Christ. Think of her rejoicing in the account of heaven!

The World to Come

American Tract Society

Is there a world to come? Who believes it? See that rich man reposing in ease, surrounded with splendor, filled with abundance, and living only to himself—does he believe it?

See that poor man, pining in want, murmuring at his lot, and envious of the rich—does he believe it?

That man of pleasure, busy only in contriving new means of ministering to his passions and appetites—does he believe it?

The thoughtless multitudes that gaily pass along our streets, heedless of death and judgement—do they believe it?

Yet there is a world to come. Conscience gives warning of it; the eager craving, the fond anticipations of a mind that can never be satisfied with earthly good, foretell it. Above all, the Bible, the sure word of inspiration, clearly reveals it. Yes, there is a world to come. It is coming rapidly. It will soon be here; and you, my reader, and I shall very soon have ex-changed our dwelling here for a habitation in that world to come.

What kind of world is it? Very unlike this world. This world is transient: "the fashion of it passes away." The dearest objects on which our hearts fasten, perish. Riches, honors, pleasures, friends, are all mortal. The very "heavens shall pass away with a great noise, and the elements shall melt with fervent heat; the earth also, and the things that are therein, shall be burned up." But the world to come is eternal. Its inhabitants, its scenes, its destinies, all will last forever. Days, months, and years are lost in the boundless duration of eternity.

This world is changing. Scarcely anything remains the same today that it was yesterday. Circumstances change—reducing the prosperous to adversity; raising the poor and wretched to competence and joy; characters are changed—the virtuous and moral become profligate, and there is hope that the vicious may be reclaimed. But in the world to come all is unchanging. Its pleasures and its pains, its sorrows and its joys, and the conditions of its inhabitants, will be the same forever. Character also will be fixed. "He that is holy," will be "holy still; and he that is filthy," will be "filthy still."

But O, how different will it be in the world to come. There He will bestow the rewards or inflict the woes for which men have been prepared in this world. Some will be raised to seats of honor and glory and blessedness "at His right hand," where is "fullness of joy," and where are "pleasures for evermore." Others will "depart accursed into everlasting fire, prepared for the devil and his angels;" "where their worm dieth not, and the fire is not quenched," and where is "weeping and gnashing of teeth."

The world to come is perfect. Everything here is imperfect. The best are imperfect, and the worst have some good traits of character, at least as it respects their fellow-men and their condition here. The purest happiness here has some alloy, and the deepest woe some mitigating circumstances. But there, everything will be fixed, settled, perfect. The heavenly city will be furnished and fitted in the most perfect manner to make its inhabitants happy. The world of woe will be perfectly fitted to express the awful wrath of God against sin. The spirits of the just will be made perfect, in character and in bliss. Not a pain, not a sorrow, not a want, not a sin will be found among all the hosts of heaven. And in the pit of darkness not a joy will thrill the bosom, not a hope cheer the heart. It will be "the blackness of darkness forever."

My friend, are you prepared for the world to come? Not if your heart is placed supremely on this world. The two worlds are so unlike, that he who loves this world will find no corresponding object of affection in that which is to come. Place him in the midst of heaven, and he would be completely miserable, for he would not find in all its glories an object that he could love, or that could minister delight. All his sources of happiness are gone forever and there is nothing to supply their place.

You are not prepared unless you have experienced a great change—a change which is called in the Scriptures being "born again;" "created anew in Christ Jesus;" having "passed from death unto life." If you have experienced this change, you have repented of your sins, humbly mourning over them, confessing them to God, and forsaking them. You have believed in the Lord Jesus Christ, renouncing all dependence upon your own righteousness, and trusting in Him alone for salvation.

What then is your condition? What does your conscience say? Let me urge you immediately to set about preparation—yes, immediately, for you have no time to lose. "This night thy soul may be required of thee."

Do you ask what is to be done? Give up this world as the object of your love. It is impossible for you to be saved, so long as you cleave to this world as your portion. "Ye cannot serve God and mammon." If you cannot give up the world; if its honors, or riches, or pleasures have such a hold upon you that you can not renounce them for Christ, then settle it in your mind that, continuing as you are, your damnation is sure. Go then, humbly and penitently confess your sins to God, and in the name of Christ, ask his forgiveness. Trust no longer in yourself; but by a living faith commit your guilty soul to the Savior, to be washed and purified through his all-cleansing blood. Resolve at once, in dependence upon the Holy Spirit, that henceforth you will live to God; that you will make His glory the end, and His will the rule of all your future life.

Are these "hard sayings!" You will not think so when you shall have entered the world to come. You will then see that these were the most reasonable and easy terms that God could give, and the only ones consistent either with his own honor or your happiness. They must be complied with or you are lost forever. They never can be given up, or relaxed. God will not change. You must change, or die.

My dear reader, why should you hesitate a moment? You have everything to gain by complying—everything to lose by refusing. Why will you die? Your soul is precious. Remember, it is a choice between eternal happiness and eternal woe. Can you hesitate? O decide for God and heaven; decide now, and forever. The God of infinite mercy help you to fix the purpose, accept the consecration, and make you eternally blessed.

Consider What Heaven Is!

Edward Reynolds

ho can tell the joys and pleasures that are in Heaven! O that you were willing to go and see, and taste them. You will find at last that it was well worth all your pains and care. There are all the springs of life, and peace, and bliss. There dwells the eternal God, in whose presence is fullness of joy forevermore. There dwells the Lord Jesus, who will fill you with happiness by the light of his countenance. There dwell the happy angels, and there the holy souls that are gone from the world, who are now made perfect, and will make you joyful. If all this does not affect you, if heaven and its inhabitants are despised, if your own soul is slighted, then what will you do? Yet, once more, be entreated to think on these things! Will not the meditation of them do you good? Will it not tend to make you better and wiser, more fit for death and a better world? The Lord help you to understand and seek the things that make for your eternal peace, before it is too late.

Glimpses at Immortality

J. R. Miller

onsciousness of immortality is a mighty motive in life. If we think only of what lies in the little dusty circle about our feet we miss the glory for which we were made. But if we realize even dimly the fact that we are immortal, a new meaning is given to every joy of our life, to every hope of our heart, to every work of our hands.

The realization of this truth of immortality in our personal consciousness is partly at least a matter of education. We may train ourself to think of our life in its larger aspect. We may allow our mind to dwell

New York Photo Electrotype Co.

337

only on material things, and keep our eyes on the narrow patch of earth on which we walk in our daily rounds. Or we may persist in lifting our thoughts to things that are unseen and eternal. This really is most important in the truest religious training and discipline, and we should lose no opportunity to get glimpses of things that are imperishable.

We live in our narrow sphere in this world, treading round and round in the same little circle. Life's toils and tasks so fill our hands, that we scarcely have time for a thought of anything else. Its secularities and its struggles for bread keep us ever bent down to the earth. The tears of sorrow dim our vision of God and of heaven. The dust and smoke of earth's battles hide the blue of heaven. We need continually to get far looks to rest us, and to keep us in mind of the great world that stretches away beyond our close horizons. The glimpses of eternity which flash upon us as we read our Bible or look into Christ's face, tell us anew what we so easily forget, that we are immortal, that our life really has no horizon.

There is comfort in this for those whose life seems a failure here,—crushed like a trampled flower under the heel of wrong or sin, broken, torn. There will be time enough in the immortal days for such broken lives to grow into strength and loveliness. Think of living a thousand years, a million years, in a world where there shall be no sin, no struggle, no injustice, no failure, but where every influence shall be inspiring and enriching, for in the immortal life all growth is toward youth, not toward the decrepitude of age. The truth of immortality gives us a vision also of continued existence in love and blessedness for those who have passed from us and beyond our sight. We miss them and we ask a thousand questions about them, yet get no answer from this world's wisdom. But looking through the broken grave of Christ, as through a window, we see green fields on the other side, and amid the gladness and the joy we catch glimpses of the dear faces we miss from the earthly circle.

What a countless multitude of mothers there are, for example, whose little children have been lifted out of their arms and borne away! The bud did not have time to open in the short summer of earth. It is carried from us, still folding in its closed-up calyxes all its possibilities of loveliness, power and life. Sorrow weeps bitterly, almost inconsolably, over the hopes which seem blighted, and cuts on the marble shaft an unopened bud, a torn branch, or some other symbol of incompleteness. Yet when we believe in immortality, what matters is that the bud did not open here and unfold its beauty this side the grave? There will be time enough in heaven's long summer for every life to put forth all its loveliness. Faith in immortality lifts the veil and eyes of love find these sweet infant faces again in the beautiful land.

I wonder! Oh! Wonder, where the little faces go, that come and smile and stay awhile, and pass like flakes of snow.

Comfort for the Bereaved

John Chrysostom

o you say, a dead man experiences corruption and becomes dust and ashes. And what then beloved hearers? For this very reason we ought to rejoice. For when a man is about to rebuild an old and tottering house, he first sends out its occupants, then tears it down and rebuilds a new a more splendid one. This occasions no grief to the occupants, but rather joy; for they do not think of the demolition which they see, but of the house which is to come, though not yet seen. When God is about to do a similar work, he destroys our body and removes the soul which was dwelling in it, that he may build it anew and more splendidly, and again bring the soul into it with

greater glory. Let us not, therefore, regard the tearing down, but the splendor which is to succeed.

If a man has a statue decayed by rust and age, he breaks it up and casts it into a furnace, and after the melting he receives it again in a more beautiful form. As then the dissolving in the furnace was not a destruction but a renewing of the statue, so the death of our bodies is not a destruction but a renovation. When, therefore, you see as in a furnace our flesh flowing away to corruption, dwell not on that sight, but wait for the recasting. Be not satisfied with the extent of this illustration, but advance in your thoughts to a still higher point; for the statuary, casting into the furnace a brazen image, does not furnish you in its place a golden and undecaying statue, but again makes a brazen one. God does not thus; but casting in a mortal body formed of clay, he returns to you a golden and immortal statue—for the earth, receiving a corruptible and decaying body, gives back the same, incorruptible and undecaying. Look not, therefore, on the corpse lying with closed eyes and speechless lips, but on the man that is risen, that has received glory unspeakable and amazing, and direct your thoughts from the present sight to the future hope.

We differ from unbelievers in our estimate of things. The unbeliever surveys the heavens and worships it, because he thinks it a divinity. He looks to the earth and makes himself a servant to it, and longs for the things of sense. But not so with us. We survey the heaven, and admire Him that made it; for we believe it not to be a god, but a work of God. I look on the whole creation, and am led by it to the Creator. He looks on wealth and longs for it with earnest desire. I look on wealth and condemn it. He sees poverty and laments. I see poverty and rejoice. I see things in one light, he in another. Just so in regard to death. He sees a corpse, and thinks of it as a corpse. I see a corpse, and behold sleep rather than death. We all see what takes place with the same eyes, but not with the same understanding and judgment. Since, therefore, in all other things we differ from them, shall we agree with them in our sentiments respecting death?

Consider to whom the departed has gone and take comfort. He has gone where Paul is, and Peter, and the whole company of the saints. Consider how he shall arise, with what glory and splendor. Consider, that by mourning and lamenting thou canst not alter the event which has occurred. Consider whom you imitate by so doing, and shun this companionship in sin. For whom do you imitate and emulate? The unbelieving, those who have no hope; as Paul has said—"That ye sorrow not, even as others who have no hope."

We ought, therefore, to thank God not only for the resurrection, but also for the hope of it; which can comfort the afflicted soul, and bid us be of good cheer concerning the departed, for they will again rise and be with us. If we must have anguish, we should mourn and lament over those who are living in sin, not over those who have died righteously. Thus did Paul; for he says to the Corinthians—"Lest when I come to you God shall humble me among you and I shall bewail many." He was not speaking of those who had died, but of those who had sinned and had not repented of the lasciviousness and uncleanness which they had committed; over these it was proper to mourn. For often while lamenting these, we amend our own faults; but to bewail the departed is senseless and hurtful. Let us not, then, reverse the order, but bewail only sin. All other things, whether poverty, or sickness, or untimely death, or false accusation, or whatever human evil befalls us, let us resolutely bear them all. For these calamities, if we are watchful, will be the occasions of adding to our crowns.

Beating Me Home

Annie Johnson Flint

"I shall go to him." (2 Samuel 12:23)

Through the shady lane, ere the sun has set,
    We strolled together, my boy and I;
Far above our heads, where the treetops met
    And the blue sky shone through a lacy net,

The birds were singing a lullaby.
    The small boy chattered, as small boys can,
    Of all that he meant to do and be;
How he'd grow and grow to a great big man
    And the short arms stretched to their
             utmost span;

And work his hardest, and all for me.
    At the end of the lane he stayed his feet,
With wistful eyes on the way that led,
    From the sleepy calm of the village street
To the city's noise and the city's heat:

'Oh, why do we never go there?' he said.
    So I answered again the old demand,
The road was dusty and hard and long;
    And I gathered closer the little hand,
For I fain would keep him in childhood's land,

Untouched by sorrow and pain and wrong.
    Then, his quest forgotten in eager play,

343

He turned to the home land, cool and green,
    He loosed my hand as he sped away
And I heard him calling me, clear and gay,

When swaying branches had dropped between.
    Now his words are echoing o'er and o'er,
Through my empty heart and the empty air:
        'Mother, dear, I'm beating you home once more,
        I'll go ahead and open the door,

Just follow me slow and you'll find me there!
    Oh, the Home he 's reached is safe and sweet,
And slow my walk through a long, long lane
    As I follow the prints of his flying feet,
And list for his laughter mine ears to greet,
    Follow and listen, and not in vain.

I have done forever with all my fears;
    No care shall sadden his joyous song,
And his eyes shall never be dimmed by tears,
For the child heart beats through the
            endless years
Untouched by sorrow and pain and wrong.

And I know, though the silence hurts me sore
    And still to my longing his voice is dumb,
He has only "beaten me home" once more,
He has 'Gone ahead to open the door,'
    And there he's waiting for me to come.

Look Upwards

Jonathan Berridge

fflictions, desertions, and temptations, are as needful as consolations. Jonah's whale will teach a good lesson as well as Pisgah's peak; and a man may sometimes learn as much from being a night or a day in the deep, as from being forty days in the mount. I see Jonah come out of a Whale and cured of rebellion; I see Moses go up into the mount with meekness, and come down in a huff and break the tables. Further, I see three picked disciples attending their Master into the mount, and falling asleep there. It is well for you to be clothed in sackcloth while you tarry in the wilderness. Look upwards and press forwards. Heaven's eternal hills are before you, and Jesus stands with arms wide open to receive you. One hour's sight and enjoyment of the Bridegroom in his place above will make you forget all your troubles on the way.

Death of the Little Scholar

Charles Dickens

e followed the old woman who had summoned him into another room, where his infant friend, half dressed, lay stretched upon a bed.

He was a very young boy, quite a little child. His hair still hung in curls about his face and his eyes were very bright, but their light was of heaven, not earth. The schoolmaster took a seat beside him and, stooping over the pillow, whispered his name. The boy sprang up, stroked his face with his hand, and threw his wasted arms around his neck, crying out that he was his dear, kind friend.

"I hope I always was. I meant to be, God knows," said the poor schoolmaster.

"Who is that?" said the boy, seeing Nell. "I am afraid to kiss her, lest I should make her ill. Ask her to shake hands with me. The sobbing child came closer up and took the languid hand in hers. Releasing his again, after a time, the sick boy laid his gently down.

"You remember the garden, Harry," whispered the schoolmaster, anxious to rouse him, for a dullness seemed gathering upon the child, "and how pleasant it used to be in the evening time? You must make haste to visit it again, for I think the very flowers have missed you, and are not as happy as they used to be. You will come soon, my dear, very soon now—won't you?"

The boy smiled faintly—so very, very faintly—and put his hand upon his friend's gray head. He moved his lips too, but no voice came from them—no, not a sound.

In the silence that ensued, the hum of distant voices borne upon the evening air came floating through the open window. "What's that?" said the sick child, opening his eyes.

"The boys at play upon the green."

He took a handkerchief from his pillow, and tried to wave it above his head. But the feeble arm dropped powerless down.

"Shall I do it?" said the schoolmaster.

"Please wave it at the window," was the faint reply. "Tie it to the lattice. Some of them may see it there. Perhaps they'll think of me and look this way."

He raised his head and glanced from the fluttering signal to his idle bat that lay with slate and book and other boyish property upon a table in the room. And then he laid him softly down once more and asked if the little girl were there, for he could not see her.

She stepped forward and pressed the passive hand that lay upon the coverlet. The two old friends and companions—for such they were, though they were man and child held each other in a long embrace, and then the little scholar turned his face to the wall and fell asleep.

The poor schoolmaster sat in the same place, holding the small hand in his, and stroking it. It was but the hand of a dead child. He felt that, and yet he stroked it still and could not lay it down.

How many of the mounds in that old church-yard where Nell had lately strayed grew green above the graves of little children! And though she thought as a child herself, and did not perhaps sufficiently consider to what a bright and happy existence those who die young are borne, and how in death they lose the pain of seeing others die around them bearing to the tomb some strong affection of their hearts (which makes the old die many times in one long life), still she thought wisely enough to draw a plain and easy moral from what she had seen that night, and to store it deep in her mind. Her dreams were of the little scholar; not coffined and covered up, but mingling with the angels and smiling happily.

HEAVEN! It is called the paradise of God—a paradise, to show how quiet, harmless, sweet, and beautiful heaven shall be to them that possess it.—*John Bunyan*

The Last Enemy

Edward Henry Bickersteth

he last enemy is death: it may be a hard struggle—it may be a dark valley; yet look where Stephen looked; and lo, Jesus is standing at the right hand of God, waiting to receive you unto Himself. Oh sweet death, when Christ is waiting to receive you. Behold, He stretches out His hands to receive your departing spirit. Breathe it into His hand saying, "Lord Jesus, receive my spirit."

Having an Eternal View

John Gregory Pike

ternity is a duration that is long beyond calculation and beyond comprehension. Think of the years that have elapsed from the days of Adam to the present day: eternity is longer. Think of those that may pass from this day till that when the judgment trumpet shall sound: eternity is longer. Look at the ground adorned with its green carpet, covered with innumerable millions of blades of grass, are the years of eternity as many? They are more, eternity is longer! Look at the leaves that clothe the trees with verdure, are the years of eternity countless as those leaves? They are more, eternity is longer than such a period of ages. Add to these years others as numerous as the drops of morning dew, do these describe eternity? No, eternity is longer. Count the drops of the sea, will their number represent eternal ages? No, eternity has ages far more countless. Those, compared with it, are like a drop to an ocean. Repeat these calculations, yet eternity is longer. Millions by millions multiplied give no idea of its duration; and all the years that human thought can heap together, compared with it, are insignificant and nothing. Beyond them all eternity still stretches forth its immeasurable duration. This eternity awaits you!

Eternity is a duration that nothing can shorten, and that can never end. Time has an end; eternity has none. The period approaches nearer, when the end of time shall be announced. The last spring that shall cheer the earth with its bloom, will have passed away; the last summer will have ended; the last autumn have finished; the last harvest this earth shall ever produce be reaped; and the last winter have concluded. Time's last year will have arrived; its last day; its last hour; its last minute, its last moment; and time shall be no more. But no such end will arrive to close eternity. Let thousands of ages pass away, eternity is not shortened. Let millions more, and worlds of millions roll along, eternity remains the same. As long, as blest, as happy, or as dreadful and miserable as ever.

As it is with the duration of eternity, so it is with its blessings and its sorrows. The joys and sorrows of time have an end, but those of eternity have none. Time brings an end to the Christian's sorrows, but eternity will bring no end to his joys. In eternity there will be no last joy, no last rapture, no last song of praise, no last thanksgiving for redeeming love. On earth, among Christian friends, time brought a last meeting, and a last parting; a last dying look, and a last farewell. But eternity will bring no last meeting, no last look, no dying eye.

Earthly Affections and Hope of Heaven

William Gurnall

et your hope of heaven moderate your affections on earth. Nothing more unbecomes a heavenly hope than an earthly heart. You would think it an unseeming thing to see some rich man who has a vast estate among the poor gleaners in harvest time as busy to pick up the ears of corn that are left in field as the most miserable beggar in the company. Oh, how all the world would cry shame of such a poor man! Well, Christian, be not angry if I tell you that you do a more shameful thing by far, if you, who pretends to hope for heaven, be as in the pursuit of this world's trash as the poor carnal wretch is who expects no portion except what God has left him to pick up in the field of this world. Certainly your hope is either false, or at best very little. The higher the summer sun mounts above the horizon, the more force it bears to clear and heat the air with his beams. If your hope of salvation advanced to any ordinary height in your soul, it would scatter these inordinate desires after this world, with which you are now choked up, and put you into a greater heat of affection after heaven. Augustine, relating what sweet discourse once passed between his mother and himself concerning the joys of heaven says, "Lord, thou knowest how vile and contemptible this sorry world was in our eye in that day when our hearts were warmed with some sweet discourse of that blessed place." And I doubt not but every gracious person finds the same,—the nearer to heaven he gets in his hopes, the farther he goes from earth in his desires. When he stands upon these battlements of heaven, he can look down upon this dunghill world as a little dust-heap, next to nothing.

WITHDRAW YOURSELVES oft into secrecy, and there think of the end for which you were made, of the life you have lived, the time you have lost, the sin you have committed, of the necessity of conversion and living a holy life, of the nearness of death and judgement, and of the certainty and excellency of the joys of heaven.—*Richard Baxter*

Heaven, a Place

D. A. Harsha

Heaven is a place as well as a state. Among the last words of our Redeemer before he left this vale of tears, we find this cheering declaration and promise, I go to prepare a place for you. And if I go and prepare a place for you, I will come again, and receive you unto myself; that where I am, there ye may be also. Precious words from a loving Friend! But follow Him to the land of promise. Christ has now gone to prepare that place for us! O what a place will Jesus prepare for his dear children! What a place will infinite love make! How attractive will it be!

Language fails to describe the beauties of Immanuel's land, and the human mind to conceive its blessedness. "All the glories of kingdoms, all the beauties of gardens, all the splendor of palaces, yea all the riches of creation, form but a faint sketch of the sublime original." We cannot know what heaven really is until we enter into "the holy place" and sit down under the shadow of the tree of life in the midst of the Paradise of God. Then shall we see in the light of glory that it is a happy region—a happy home indeed.

Heaven is a holy place where the King eternal, immortal, invisible, the only wise God, unveils his glorious perfections in full effulgence. In that blessed place, the Lamb of God, the Saviour of sinners, dwells in his glorified humanity. There triumphant saints are gathered home to Christ. There they are made pillars in the temple of God and go no more out. There the host of heaven dwell in the blissful presence of the King of glory.

This blessed place should attract us. We should look beyond this fleeting world. We should endeavor to raise our eyes to Canaan's happy shores, and obtain a glimpse of those everlasting hills whence cometh our help.

Let the Christian ascend the mount of meditation, and by the help of God's word, survey those fair regions which lie beyond the Jordan of death.

How consoling to think that every child of God shall finally be brought to that celestial world, to gaze with wondering eyes on its untold glories! What gratitude do we owe to God for providing such an inheritance for us. To Him we should continually raise our hearts in grateful songs of praise. We should call upon our souls and all that is within us to bless his holy name.

Heaven is that "pleasant land" to which all Christian pilgrims are travelling. We are now in a wilderness world, where the winds of adversity blow upon us, and the tempests of sorrow sweep along our pathway. But this is not our home. Our march is heavenward—to the glorious land. Guided by the Captain of our salvation we are coming up from the wilderness, and our feet shall soon stand on the glorious mount of God. Our conversation is in heaven, our future inheritance lies there, and we are looking on it as our eternal home. No wonder then that it should appear so attractive in our eyes. No wonder that we should long to behold the good land which is afar off. All true believers desire that "better country." They feel that they are strangers and pilgrims here. They look beyond this world to those regions of perpetual delight where they expect to spend countless ages.

Heaven is a promised land. We are journeying unto the place of which the Lord said, 'I will give you.' God's Word is true. Every saint that has lived on earth shall be brought to this heavenly world, where Jesus reigns in all his glory. Cheer up then, ye drooping saints. View that happy world where your Saviour reigns, and where you are shortly to reign with him.

In that celestial city, there shall be no night. Eternal day beams with unclouded splendor in the city of Immanuel. No natural or moral darkness shall ever overspread the landscape of glory. Thy sun shall no more go down, neither shall thy moon withdraw itself; for the Lord shall be thine everlasting light, and the days of thy mourning shall be ended.

But look again at that celestial city. Emanating from God's eternal throne, the river of life flows through its midst. And he showed me a pure river of the water of life, clear as crystal, proceeding out of the throne of God and the Lamb. The heavenly Jerusalem is enriched with "the river of God, which is full of water." This is the stream that makes

Immanuel's land to bloom with immortal joys. This is the river of pleasure—the river whose streams shall make glad the city of God, the holy place of the tabernacle of the most High. There, the inhabitants of Zion may bathe in the pure fountains of immortality "fast by the throne of God," and drink freely of those swelling streams of purest joy which flow through the realms of glory.

In the city of our God is the tree of life, of whose delicious fruit the saints eat, and under whose ambrosial bowers, they dwell in eternal repose, and celestial bliss. In the midst of the street of it, and on either side of the river, was there the tree of life, which bare twelve manner of fruits, and yielded her fruit every month; and the leaves of the tree were for the healing of the nations.

There is much in the heavenly Jerusalem to attract you—many crowns of glory—many mansions of bliss—many songs of praise—much that the eye has never seen, the ear never heard, nor the human mind never conceived. Strive then to obtain an interest in Jesus, that you may "have right to the tree of life, and may enter in through the gates into the city." How cheering is the promise of the Saviour, To him that overcometh will I give to eat of the tree of life, which is in the midst of the Paradise of God! Then fight the good fight of faith, lay hold on eternal life, and you will come off more than a conqueror through Him that loved you and gave himself for you.

There is something peculiarly attractive in this description of heaven. How sweet is even an earthly home, but how endeared will be that home above, where we shall meet with our Heavenly Father, with our elder Brother, with our dear Christian friends, who went to glory before us—with the whole household of faith! In that house not made with hands, there are "many mansions" for our enjoyment. There is ample room and provision for all God's children in the sanctuary, everything to render them happy, unspeakably happy to all eternity.

Entering the Celestial City

John Bunyan (from Pilgrim's Progress)

ow just as the gates were opened to let in the men, I looked in after them, and behold the city shone like the sun; the streets, also, were paved with gold, and in them walked many men with crowns on their heads, palms in their hands, and golden harps to sing praises withal. There were of them that had wings; and they answered one another without intermission, saying, 'Holy, holy, holy is the Lord.' And after that, they shut up the gates; which when I had seen, I wished myself among them.

Life Through Death

Horatius Bonar

t is strange that in a world made by God the only wise and infinitely good, there should be such a thing as death. It is more wonderful that this death should come out of a thing so glorious as life. But beyond these, there is a wonder greater still, that life should grow from death, and corruption be the seed and parent of incorruption.

Yet this last is the process which God has been carrying on in our earth since the threatening took effect, against Adam; "In the day that thou eatest thereof thou shalt surely die."

It needs no great power to bring death out of life. Man can effect that without an effort. But to bring life out of death needs other power than man's. Man can kill, but God only can make alive. It is the Creator alone that can quicken; and hence the apostle sets these two things together when he says, "God who quickeneth all things, and calleth those things which be not as though they were" (Rom. 4:17). The power to destroy life has been given to the creature; but the power to impart it is a prerogative of Godhead and a function of Omnipotence. Thus all of death that is in us we owe to ourselves; and all of life that is in us we trace solely to God; to Him whose name is "Jehovah," who not merely is King "eternal and immortal," but who only hath immortality (I Tim. 6:16).

It is by falling that we rise; by going down into the depths of the valley that we find our way up to the mountains of immortality beyond. It is through winter that we pass into spring. It is by dying that we are made to live,—live forever. For the life that is not reached by death seems but half secure. The life that lasts,—the life that is truly immortal and eternal, is only obtained by dying. It is resurrection-life that is the truest as well as the highest form of life—the surest as well as the most glorious immortality.

The Joys of Earth are Fleeting

Harriet E. Francis

"Mine, mine !" cried the Earth, as with a glancing view,
    She gazed at her robe of rich emerald hue;
"I'm decked out in splendor, more beautiful far
    Than sun, moon, or comet, or bright twinkling star."
But ere months passed away the earth, with a wail,
    Was mourning her beauty 'mid frost, snow, and hail.

"Mine, mine," cried a boy, with blue, laughing eye,
    "O, mine is this insect of beautiful dye!
I've followed it far this warm, sunny day,
    And now with it long I gently will play."
He opened his hand to gaze at the prize

The butterfly flew aloft in the skies.

"Mine, mine," said a maiden, with dark, wavy hair,
    O, mine is the love of one noble and fair!
The dream that I've cherished so long in my heart
    The bridal hath bound it, no more to depart."
But a year scarce had passed ere the deep-scalding tear
    She bitterly wept o'er her husband's low bier.

"Mine, mine," spoke a mother, in tenderest tone,
    As she gazed at her child, her cherished, her own,
"O, mine is this loved One, and, e'er by his side,
    I'll shield him from evil, to virtue will guide."
But time fled away, and deep furrows of care
    Were written, alas! on his forehead so fair.

"Ours, ours," was the shout of a happy throng,
    As they entered heaven's gates with a joyous song,
"O, ours is this home where no sorrow can dwell,
    Where joys are sweeter than words could e'er tell!"
And ages rolled on, yet their home was as bright
    As when first, in beauty, it broke on their sight.

MY TIME IS SHORT; I must be up and doing; I must go briskly on with my work, leaving it to my Lord to find me strength for it, and success in it. His blessing I expect here and forever—not for anything I have done; and yet I would labor as hard as if heaven was to be the reward of my labors.—*William Romaine*

Time and Eternity

John Flavel

ow little do many of you think, in the hurry of business, in the pursuits of literature, of gain, and of pleasure, in the strength of manhood, in the heedlessness of youth—how little do you think of the hour of death, of the darkness and the worm—the dust and oblivion to which yon are hastening! O, my dying fellow sinners, pause, I beseech you, pause and think, What is your life? Strive to live every day and hour under the impression that it is even a vapor. Let all your worldly schemes be based upon this great truth—that you know not what shall be on the morrow.

Contrast Between Earth and Heaven

James Hamilton

here are some things which those in Heaven never do. They do not want,—do not weary,—and they do not weep. "They shall hunger no more, neither thirst any more neither shall the sunlight on them, nor any heat ... And God shall wipe away all tears from their eyes."

And now, if any of your friends have slept in Jesus, is it not blissful to know how they are engaged? You and they once journeyed together; but a sudden door opened, and your father, or brother, or child was snatched from your side; and ere you could follow, or glance in, the door closed again. But the Lord has opened a crevice in the enclosing wall, and bids you look and see. See where they are,—see what they are doing now. You are in great tribulation,— it is even your tribulation to be deprived of them; but they come out of all tribulation. You often find it hard to reach the throne of grace—hard to prevail with yourself to pray. They never quit the throne of God, but serve him day and night in his temple. It is only by faith that you can walk with Jesus. They see God and follow the Lamb withersoever he goeth. You suffer much from sickness, and langor, and bodily discomfort, our summers are too sultry, and our frosts too keen,—and you lose much time through infirmities of the flesh. They hunger no more, neither thirst any more; neither does the sunlight on them, nor any heat. Your heart is often like to break. Betwixt the unkindness of some and the sufferings of others you have fears to drink in great measure. God himself has wiped away all tears from their eyes. And your best frames and most blessed services are very brief. There is only one sabbath in your week, and that is soon gone. There are few white days in your history—few days when you see the luster of that robe with which God has already clothed you, and find your soul drawn forth in full-toned gratitude and praise. Their palm never withers. Their hallelujahs never cease. Their congregation never breaks up. Their sabbath knows no end. Wherefore, comfort one another with these words.

The Blood of the Lamb

Octavius Winslow

s if to illustrate the nature and test the efficacy of His great and gracious expedient of saving sinners, it pleased the redeeming God that the first subject of death should be a believer in the Lord Jesus. Scarcely had the righteous Abel laid his bleeding lamb upon the altar—that altar and that lamb all expressive of the truth, and radiant with the glory of the person and work of the coming Savior—ere he was called to seal with his blood the faith in Christ he had professed. But if the first victim, he was also the first victor. He fell by death, but he fell a conqueror of death. He lost the victory, but he won the battle. Thus was the "last enemy" foiled in his very first assault upon our race. The point of his lance was then turned, the venom of his sting was then impaired, and robbed of his prey, he saw in the pale and gory form his shaft had laid low the first one of that glorious race of confessors, that "noble army of martyrs," who in all succeeding ages should overcome sin, hell, and death, by the blood of the Lamb.

SORROWS are often like clouds, which, though black when they are passing over us, when they are past become as if they were the garments of God, thrown off in purple and gold along the sky.

—*Henry Ward Beecher*

The Word Made Flesh

Horatius Bonar

f the fullness treasured up for us in the, "Word made flesh" is to come forth, then Christ must die. There must be the pouring out of the soul unto death. Even He is not at liberty to communicate His love and joy to us, save through His own death—His death as the payment of the righteous penalty and the ful-fillment of the unchangeable sentence, "the soul that sinneth it shall die." He, though the true wheat, must "abide alone," except He die.

He has died, the Just for the unjust, dying the sinner's death, and bearing the sinner's curse. Thus He "brings forth much fruit." All that made this fruitful One barren has been taken away. Death has done what life, in all its divine vigour, could not do. In the sinner's grave, to which the Surety went down, the dissolution of legal bonds has been effected, whereby the fullness hitherto pent up and imprisoned comes forth and flows over earth, like the fresh verdure bursting up and spreading itself over earth at the new breath of spring.

We Shall See in Heaven

Ladies' Repository

Mother," said a sweet, blind girl, "shall I see in heaven?" "Yes, dear," as her eyes filled with tears, and her voice choked with emotion; "we shall all see in heaven, there will be no darkness there."

As the words of the young girl fell upon my ear my heart responded, "Yes, we shall see in heaven." My mind reverted to the past, with its lights and shadows, and even penetrated into the future, even to the time when darkness shall be made light, and hidden things be revealed. And my soul reveled in glorious anticipations, till the trials of earth dwindled into insignificance, and the words, "we shall see in heaven," seemed as a sort of talisman to cheer me amid earth's cares and sorrows. Christian pilgrim, does the hand of the Lord seem heavy? "Do friends forsake and foes prevail?" Has the worldly substance for which you have spent many an anxious thought, melted away like dew before the sun? Can you not now see? Walk carefully. Hereafter you shall see in heaven, and earth's burden being dropped, rest will be all the sweeter. The green grass waves over the grave of the fair blind girl, but when assailed by trials from without, or temptations from within, I seem to hear a voice saying, "Shall we see in heaven?" and to my troubled heart comes the sweet response, "We shall see in heaven, and there will be no darkness there."

The Blessing of Affliction

Golden Gems of Life

rief or misfortune seems to be indispensable to the development of intelligence, energy, and virtue. The trials to which humanity are subject are necessary to draw them from their lethargy, to disclose their character. Afflictions even have the effect of eliciting talents which, in prosperous circumstances, would have lain dormant. Suffering, indeed, seems to have been as divinely appointed as joy, while it is much more influential as a discipline of character. Suffering may be the appointed means by which the highest nature of man is to be disciplined and developed. Sometimes a heartbreak rouses an impassive nature to life.

How uncertain is human life! There is but a breath of air and a beat of a heart betwixt this world and the next. In the brief interval of painful and awful suspense, while we feel that death is present with us, we are powerless and he all powerful. The last faint pulsation here is but the prelude of endless joys hereafter. In the midst of the stunning calamity about to befall us, when death is in the family circle, and some loved one is about to be taken from us, we feel as if earth had no compensating good to mitigate the severity of our loss. But we forget that there is no grief without some beneficent provisions to soften its intensities. Thus in the presence of death there is also a consolation. Has the life been stormy? There is now rest—rest for, the troubled heart and the weary head. And it can be known only by experience with what a longing, many hearts thus look forward to the rest of death. Many whom the world regards as peculiarly blessed by Providence carry with them such corroding, anxious cares that it is with a feeling of relief that they contemplate the approach of death. To them death comes in its most beautiful form. He borrows the garb of gentle sleep, lays down his iron scepter, and his cold hand falls as warm as the hand of friendship over the weary heart now ceasing to beat.

Think it not unkind when afflictions come to you; it is all for the best that they are sent. God calls those whom he loves, and why should he not claim his own jewels to shine in his house, though our own be made dreary? It may seem hard under such circumstances to say that it is all for the best. The human heart is prone to give over to grief and lamentations; but wait—soon, when like the tired pilgrim you shall fall sick and weary, He will take you home to rejoice in finding friends from whom you have been separated. Then how true will be the saying that "it was all for the best!"

To A Better Land

Robert Murray M'Cheyne

It is true they are gone from you, but remember that they have gone into far tenderer hands. You stood up to bend over their dying body, but the Lord Jesus stood up to receive their undying soul. Your feeble, but affectionate hands stretched out to smooth their dying pillow, but the almightly hands of the Savior formed a sweeter, softer bed for their departing soul.

Jesus Knew it All!

Octavius Winslow

When you stand in the presence chamber of Jesus you prefer no request, breathe into His ear no sorrow, unveil to His eye no infirmity, with which, in all its most minute detail, He was not already infinitely better acquainted than yourself. Long ere the sadness had shaded your brow, or a tear had dimmed your eye, or the burden had pressed your spirit, or the perplexity had woven its web

around your path, or the archer had bent his bow and winged his shaft—Jesus knew it all, had appointed it all, had anticipated it all. It was no surprise to Him! Precious truth! Christ had entwined my perplexity with His thoughts, had wrapped my grief around His heart, had provided a haven for my safety ere a pebble had paved, or a cloud had shaded, or a whisper of the storm had breathed over my path.

Dealing With Sorrows

J. R. Miller

Few things of life could be sadder than dwelling ever in the glooms and shadows of past griefs. It is the will of God that we should turn our eyes away from our sorrows and let the dead past bury its dead, while we go on with reverent earnestness to the new duties and the new joys that await us. By standing and weeping over the grave we cannot get back what we have lost. When David's child was dead, he dried his tears and went at once to God's house and worshiped, saying, "Now he is dead, wherefore should I fast? Can I bring him back again? I shall go to him, but he shall not return to me." Instead of weeping over the grave where his dead was not, he turned his eyes forward toward the glory in which his child was waiting for him, and began with new ardor to press toward that home. He turned all the pressure of his grief into the channels of holy living.

That is the way every believer in Christ should deal with his sorrows. Weeping inconsolably beside a grave can never give back love's vanished treasure. Nor can any blessing come out of such sadness. It does not make the heart any softer. It develops no feature of Christlikeness in the life. It only embitters our present joys and stunts the growth of all beautiful things. The graces of the heart are like flower-plants—they grow well only in the sunshine.

365

It is Well With Your Child

Charles Haddon Spurgeon

Now, let every mother and father here present know assuredly that it is well with the child, if God hath taken it away from you in its infant days. You never heard its declaration of faith ; it was not capable of such a thing, it was not baptized into the Lord Jesus Christ, not buried with him in baptism; it was not capable of giving that answer of a good conscience toward God; nevertheless, you may rest assured that it is well with the child, well in a higher and better sense than it is well with yourselves; well without limitation, well without exception, well infinitely, "well" eternally.

Bereaved parents, could you for a moment see your own offspring above, I think you would very speedily wipe away your tears. There among the sweet voices which sing the perpetual carol may be heard the voice of your own child, an angel now, and you the mother of a songster before the throne of God. You might not have murmured had you received the promise that your child should have been elevated to the peerage; it has been elevated higher than that,—to the peerage of heaven. It has received the dignity of the immortals; it is robed in better than royal garments; it is more rich and more blessed than it could have been if all the crowns of earth could have been put upon its head.

IT HAS BEEN SAID that some of the greatest treasures in heaven will be the blunders God's children have made when trying to show their love. A mother said that the most sacred treasure in her home was a puckered handkerchief which her little girl, now in heaven, had tried to hem for her.—*J. R. Miller*

Nothing is Forgotten

Charles Dickens

here is nothing—no, nothing—beautiful and good, that dies and is forgotten. An infant, a prattling child, dying in its cradle, will live again in the better thoughts of those who loved it, and play its part, though its body be burned to ashes or drowned in the deepest sea. There is not an angel added to the hosts of heaven, but does its blessed work on earth in those who loved it here. Dead! Oh, if the good deeds of human creatures could be traced to their source, how beautiful would even death appear! For how much charity, mercy, and purified affection would be seen to have their growth in dusty graves!

Go Tell Jesus!

Octavius Winslow

ontemplate Him in the bereaved home of Bethany! Martha and Mary are mourners. Lazarus their brother is dead. Jesus, their brother's Friend and theirs, is come—but He has come too late! "Lord, if thou hadst been here, my brother had not died." No! not too late! It was just the moment that Jesus should come. He timed His visit of sympathy and help with their grief and need. Beloved, Jesus never approaches you a moment sooner, or a moment later than your case demands. He will come—but it will be at the very instant that you most need Him. There shall be more than an angel's chime of His sympathy with your sorrow—the most perfect and exquisite blending. If He come a moment too soon, your grief would not be matured enough for His sympathy; if a moment too late, that grief might have crushed you. Now, mark the thoughtfulness and skill, the delicacy and sympathy of Jesus. All is inscribed in one brief but expressive sentence: "Jesus wept!"

To this weeping Jesus go! You return to the house of mourning from the grave where repose the ashes of one once animated and glowing with a spirit that blended with your own—you seem to have entombed a second self—all that gave existence an object, or life its charm. But rise, and go to Jesus. Tell Him what a wreck your heart is, what a blank life seems, and what wintry gloom enshrouds all the landscape of human existence. Tell Him how mysterious to your view seems the event—how heavy falls the blow—what hard, dark, rebellious thoughts of God now haunt your perturbed mind. Lay your grief upon Jesus' breast. Think not that you are alone in your sorrow—that there is not one in this wide, wide world, one who can appreciate your loss, or enter into all the peculiar features of your afflictions, the delicate shadings of your sadness—Jesus can, and Jesus only. The vacancy, too, death has made in your love and friendship,—whatever be the relation, Jesus can fill.

No Pain in Heaven

Isaac Watts

n heaven, where there is no pain, there shall be no sighing or groaning, nor any more crying, as my text expresses. There shall be nothing to make the flesh or the spirit uneasy and to break the eternal thread of peace and pleasure that runs through the whole duration of the saints: not one painful moment to interrupt the everlasting felicity of that state. When we have done with earth and mortality, we have done also with sickness and anguish of nature, and with all sorrow and vexation forever. There are no groans in the heavenly world to break in upon the harmony of the harps and the songs of the blessed; no sighs, no outcries, no anguish there to dis-

turb the music and the joy of the inhabitants. And though the soul shall be united to the body new-raised from the dead, to dwell forever in union, yet that new-raised body shall have neither any springs of pain in it, nor be capable of giving anguish or uneasiness to the indwelling spirit forever.

Nor will the body at the final resurrection of the saints be made for a medium of any painful sensations. All the pains of nature are ended, when the first union between flesh and spirit is dissolved. When this body lies down to sleep in the dust, it shall never awake again with any of the principles of sin or pain in it; though it be sown in weakness, it is raised in power; though it be sown in dishonor, it is raised in glory; and we shall be made like the Son of God without sorrow and without sin forever.

Blessings Beyond Our Losses

J. R. Miller

e should remember that the blessings which have gone away are not all that God has for us. This summer's flowers will all fade soon enough when winter's cold breath smites them, and we shall not be able to find one of them in the fields or gardens during the long, cold, dreary months to come. Yet we shall know all the while that God has other flowers preparing, just as fragrant and as lovely as those which have perished. Spring will come again, and under its warm breath the earth will be covered once more with floral beauty as rich as that which faded in the autumn. So the joys that have gone from our home and our heart are not our only joys. God has others in store just as rich as those we have lost, and in due time he will give us these to fill our emptied hearts.

Oh, Come Thou Down To Me,
Or Take Me Up To Thee

Elizabeth Prentiss

I would be with Thee, dearest Lord, I long Thy face to see,
I long that each succeeding day should bring me nearer Thee;
Wilt Thou come down to dwell with me, wilt Thou with me abide;
Wilt Thou go with me where I go, be ever at my side?

Thy home is with the humble; Lord, that blessed truth I know;
But cannot change my heart myself; do Thou, then, make it so;
Oh come, my Saviour, come to me, it is not life to live,
Unless Thy presence fills my soul, except Thyself Thou give.

Or if Thou canst not come to me, a weak, a sinful child,
If Thou, alas, dost find in me no temple undefiled,
Oh then, my gracious Lord, send down a messenger for me,
And strip my sinfulness away and take me up to Thee.

I care not where I find Thee, Lord, whether here or there,
I only know I want to find and love Thee, everywhere;
This world with all its tears and groans, would be my chosen
        place,
If Thou shouldst plan it for the scene in which to show Thy face.

And heaven with all its peace and rest, would be no heaven to me,
If I might dwell forever there, without a glimpse of Thee;
It is not life, or life's best joys, it is not heaven I want,
But oh, Thou risen Christ, for Thee, for Thee alone, I pant!

God's Relationship to Children

John Guthrie

ur Father in Heaven, the infinite Parent of us all, and the Savior, who did what no parent has done,—shed His blood to redeem them,—have a closer relation to our children, and a better right to them, than we. Be it the endeavor, then, of mourning parents to exclaim with the bereft patriarch, and as much as possible in Job's spirit and power, "The Lord gave, and the Lord hath taken away; blessed be the name of the Lord." Yea, let them overflow with hallelujahs, that in the Atonement of Jesus, they have such an impregnable ground of hope in respect to their deceased children. The fact that these children are in heaven, among the shining throng, white-robed, and vocal with the praises of redeeming love, should endear Jesus to them the more, through the ransom of whose precious blood their darlings are now in an infinitely happier than the parental home. This will help you, desolate parent, better to appreciate and real-ize the claims of that bright world to which they have been summoned. You know not what use God may have for them there. Who knows to what glorious account Jesus, even now while you weep, may there be turning their little radiant spirits? He has the ripened spirits there of "just men made perfect;" and with these He gems and jewels His crown of many stars. But He has also use there for the infant spirit in its love-liness. If the ripened saints are the stars that grace His crown, He whose delight is to take the lambs into His arms may well cull also the buds and flowerets of childhood to cluster as a garland round His bosom of love. Your children's precious dust is at present in the hands of the enemy; but that enemy,— "the last enemy," —shall be destroyed, and you and the tender objects of your regret, if you are only faithful to that Savior whose blood has saved them, and persevere in the faith and love of Him to the end, will meet again ere long, triumphant over death, the grim foe that has despoiled you, and spend a long and happy forever in the presence of your Lord.

We would say, in conclusion, to the bereft parent, through whose heart grief has driven its rude ploughshare, and whose wounds, it may be, are yet green, "Mourn not as those who have no hope," for as respects your children, "there is hope in their end." In their material part only, they are like Rachel's of old, "in the land of the enemy:" their nobler part is in the land, and in the embrace, of the Infinite Friend. Nor is that Friend forgetful of their sleeping dust. It is precious in His sight. "The redemption of the body" is as sure as "the redemption of the soul." That enemy, "the last enemy," shall one day be destroyed; and on that eventful day, "your children shall come again." Only see to it, now, like David, that you will, by faith, "go to them," and Jesus will see to it then that they shall "come to you." "Thus saith the Lord; refrain thy voice from weeping and thine eyes from tears; for thy work shall be rewarded, saith the Lord; and they shall come again from the land of the enemy." What a rapturous prospect for the Christian parent!

Heavenly Homesickness

Charles Haddon Spurgeon

ave you ever felt heavenly homesickness? Surely, when your heart has been full of the Bridegroom's beauty, and your soul has been ravished with his dear and ever precious love, you have said, "When shall the day break, and the shadows flee away? Why are His chariots so long in coming?" You have swooned, as it were, with love sickness for your precious Savior, thirsting to see Him as He is, and to be like Him. The world is black when Christ is seen in His beauty. The world is a poor heap of ashes when Jesus is altogether lovely to us.

Living for Immortality

J. R. Miller

esus appeared to Mary after He had come again from death, yet death had not extinguished one beam of His brightness. The resurrection was a type and prophecy of the future resurrection of all who believe in Him and sleep in Him. It shows us therefore that death does not mean destruction, is not the end of life. It is but an incident, an experience, and life goes on afterward without loss or marring. We ought to try to learn this blessed truth. Life is not worth living which is bounded by earth's little horizon and does not reach out into immortality. Indeed we do not really begin to live until we are living for immortality.

Children Before the Throne

Thomas Boston

read your letter of May, 1726, with the affecting account of your loss of a dear child. I travelled that gloomy road six times, and learned that God has other use for children than our comfort—a use far more honorable and happy for them. The parents come to see afterwards that it is a peculiar kindness to the poor babes they were so early carried off. It likewise serves to let into that Word in particular, in its sweetness, "I will be your God, and the God of your seed," while parents are taken up for the salvation of their dying little ones, and look about to see what the Word says with relation to the case. Oh, do not grudge the freedom the Lord has used with you, in pitching upon a precious thing for Himself, and taking it away. Both of you have offered your all to the Lord; and though, when it comes to the pinch, the heart is ready to misgive; yet in calm blood I am sure you will stand to the bargain, and check yourselves for any

semblance of repenting. The next time you see your child, you will see him shining white in glory, having been washed in the blood of the Lamb, who was an infant, a child, a boy, a youth, as well as a grown man. He became a Savior of infants and little children, as well as of persons come of age.

Little Ones in Heaven

Robert Ferguson

Christian parent, dry up your tears. If you must weep, make a rainbow of your tears. Let joy rise above grief as heaven rises above earth. If the birth of your child filled your breast with emotions which no human words can express, and if on his being born again you became the subjects of feelings yet more tender and peculiar, then think of him now amid the beatitudes and the blessedness of the heavenly world, sinless in character, deathless in life, exhaustless in energy, ceaseless in activity, and through the ages, ever moving in the light of the throne, expatiating amid its unquenchable glories, and upholding communion with the Eternal Life.

What Really Matters

J. R. Miller

Eternal life is the only thing worth living for. No matter how much pleasure, or how great success, or how high honor, one may gain in this world, if at the end of threescore years a man passes into eternity unsaved, of what comfort to him will it be to remember his pleasant life on this earth?

A rich man failed in business. When he had gathered together the fragments of his wrecked fortune he had in all a few thousand dollars.

He determined to go to another part of the country to start again. He took all his money, and had built for himself a splendid car, furnishing it in the most luxurious style, and stocking it with provisions for his journey. In this sumptuous car he travelled to his destination. At length he stepped from the door of his rolling palace, and only then thought for the first time of his great folly. He had used the last cent of his money in getting in this magnificent way to his new home, and had nothing on which to begin life anew.

We see in this illustration the folly of those who think only of this life, and make no provision for eternity. They use up all their time, their opportunities, their life's strength, in getting to the gate of the grave, and find themselves forced to begin eternity with nothing—no treasure laid up. The only true success is that which makes a man rich for eternity.

The Triumphant Death-bed Scene

Mother's Magazine

he following death-bed conversation of a beloved daughter, detailed to us by her mother, exhibits such sweet resignation and trust in God. It should be that we all might be prepared to resign this life with cheerfulness, and with like hopes enter upon that world which is to come!

"Mother," she said, "I once thought I could be a Christian without making a profession of religion, but when God took my little Burnet from me, I knew He did it to subdue the pride of my heart and bring me to the foot of the Cross. Satan has been permitted to tempt me, but the Savior has always delivered me from his snares."

I was absent from her one day for a short time; when I returned she looked at me with such a heavenly expression, and said:

"Mother, I thought just now I was dying. I went to the foot of the Cross with my burden of sins and sorrows, and left them there. Now all is peace. I am not afraid to die."

Her father coming, she took his hand in hers and said:

"My dear father, if I have prayed for one thing more than another, it has been for your salvation, but God, doubtless, saw that my death (which will, I know, be one of the greatest trials you have ever met with) is necessary to save you. Although I love my parents, husband and children dearly as any one ever did, and have every thing in this world that I could wish for, yet I am willing to die—Here, Lord, take me."

Her sister coming in, she said to her, "My dear Caroline, you see what a solemn thing it is to die. What an awful thing it must be for those who have no God. Dear sister, learn to love the Savior, learn to pray, do not be too much taken up with the world, it will disappoint you."

After saying something to each one present, turning to me, she said, "My dear mother, I thank you for your kind care of me, for keeping me from places of dissipation. I thought once you were too strict, but now I bless you for it. I shall not be permitted to smooth your dying pillow, but I shall be ready to meet you when you land on the shores of Canaan. Dear mother, come soon."

To Mr. H. she said, "Dear husband, you were the loadstone that held me longest to the earth, but I have been enabled to give you up at last. I trust you are a Christian, and we shall meet in heaven. Take care of our children, train them up for Christ, keep them from the world." She then prayed for them. After lying still for some time, she said, "Mother, I thought I was going just now, and I tried to put up one more prayer for my husband, children, and friends, but (looking up with a smile), would you believe I could not remember their names, and I just said, 'Here they are, Lord, take them, and make them what you would have them, and bring them to your kingdom at last."

When she was almost cold, and her tongue stiffened, she motioned me to put my head near her. "My dear child," I said, "it seems to distress you to talk, don't try."

"Oh, mother, let me leave you all the comfort I can, it is you who must still suffer—my sufferings are now over—I am passing over Jordan, but the waves do not touch me. My Savior is with me and keeps them off. Never be afraid to go to him. Farewell! And now, Lord Jesus, come, O come quickly. My eyes are fixed on the Savior, and all is peace. Let me rejoice! Let me rejoice!"

Saints Among Us

Elizabeth Prentiss

t is not true that as soon as human beings reach a certain point in the divine life, they are snatched out of this; saints move about us and among us every day. They live to be our examples; to be our dearly beloved and cherished ones; to remind us of Heaven, whose spirit they have won; to pray for us, and with us; to inspire and to cheer us. They are saints, but they see not the mark in their foreheads; they wrestle with the powers of the air, and with their own spiritual infirmities; they err sometimes, though sorely against their will, but they are bearing right onward, and are more than conquerors through Him who hath loved them.

IF WE COULD SEE the end as God does, we should see that every event is for the good of the believer. When we get to heaven, we shall see that every wind was wafting us to glory.—*E. H. Bickersteth*

A Mother's Comfort

Sure to the mansions of the blest,
*　　Where infant innocence ascends,*
Some angel brighter than the rest,
*　　The spotless spirit's flight attends.*
There at th'Almighty Father's hand,
*　　Nearest the throne of living light,*
The choirs of infant seraphs stand,
*　　And dazzling shine where all are bright.*
When thus the Lord of mortal breath
*　　Decrees his bounty to resume,*
And points the silent shaft of death,
*　　Which speeds our infants to the tomb.*
Oh! Think the darlings of thy love,
*　　Divested of this earthly clod,*
Amid innumber'd saints above,
*　　Bask in the bosom of their God.*

With Great Delight

Elizabeth Prentiss

> *I sat down under His shadow with great delight.*
> *I will abide under the shadow of the Almighty.*

With great delight! Yes, so I sat and rested in His shade
    When of the burden of the day, and of its glare afraid;
I felt myself protected, saved, looked up and saw His face,
    How beautiful in tenderness, how wonderful in grace!

With great delight! Life pressed me sore, I knew not where to flee,
    In all the world I saw no room, no sphere, no work for me;
He called me to this sheltered spot, rebuking my despair,
    I went, and oh the joy I found, the peace I tasted there!

With great delight! A loving friend had fallen at my side,
    My eyes were blinded by my tears, my heart within me died;
I staggered from the empty world, into this dear retreat,
    And found my bitter grief assuaged, yea, found my
        sorrow sweet.

With great delight! My heart is fixed, its endless wants I know,
    Forth from this shelter I henceforth will never, never go;
Here in the shadow of God's love forever I'll abide,
    So glad, so blest, so sure, so safe; so more than satisfied!

LET US LOOK BEYOND this valley of tears and keep our eyes fixed on that better country where the Savior ever reigns in glorious majesty; where the fountains of bliss ever flow; where the tree of life ever spreads its delightful shade, and yields its immortal fruits; where all is unending joy, and love, and peace, and felicity!—*D. A. Harsha*

A Sweet Sorrow

Philip Schaff

ow, farewell, my precious boy! Till I see you again, farewell! With a saddened heart have I performed the last act of earthly love, and now I resign you into the hands of higher and better parental care. Short was your visit in this rough and tempestuous world! The heavenly gardener has early transplanted the fragrant lily of your life into a milder and purer clime. Your life was not yet darkened and imbittered by the fearful curse of sin and death. As a tender lamb of Christ, you did bear your cross in friendly innocence, like the infants of Bethlehem, who were slain by the tyrant-sword of Herod, as the first martyr fruits offered to the new-born Savior, to whom the ancient church has devoted the third day after Christmas as an anniversary-day of special remembrance. You are now happy with them, and with the pleasant angels, far away from the sultry and sickly atmosphere of earth and sin, in serene celestial heights, in the green peaceful bowers of Paradise, led and fed, and refreshed by the Great Shepherd of the sheep and of the lambs, who was Himself once a child, that He might sanctify the tender age of infancy, and who, in the days of His flesh, pressed infants to His bosom, speaking those words of comfort: "Suffer little children to come unto me, and forbid them not: for of such is the kingdom of God." You were His by birth, and as He formed your beautiful body, so did He also, by His Holy Spirit, silently, and unconsciously to you, early prepare your spirit for that holy world where now you are at home. It was He that taught you to lisp, as you did in the midst of your suffering, with infant joy: "Heaven is a beautiful place: God is there, Christ is there, the angels are there, all good people are there!" Yes, my hopeful, pious boy! They are all there, old and young, great and small,—all who have overcome in the blood of the Lamb! There also you bloom forever in the unfading beauty of the loveliest age! Thither also do your parents, by God's grace, hope to arrive, when their hour shall strike, to embrace you, the beloved of their hearts, in glorified youth, and to lose you no more forever! Oh, the joy of such a meeting!

Perfection

Edgar Guest

> The Master was painting a picture and we children were ranged
> all about,
> Entranced by the charm of his colors and the way he was
> working it out;
> And we'd run every morn to discover some beautiful touch
> which was new,
> And we'd talk and we'd dream and we'd wonder just what he
> intended to do.
> The Master spake little while working, but oft as he heard us
> he'd smile,
> Though we begged him to tell all about it, held answer:
> 'You'll know in a while.'
> But one morning he put down his brushes, and then with
> a turn of his head

To our grief and our great consternation:
    'The picture is finished,' he said.
'Oh, Master,' we begged and implored him, 'don't put all your
    brushes away:
Please paint something more on the canvas, paint on to the
    end of the day.
Paint more, for we're eager to watch you, paint on for we love
    it so much.'
'It is perfect, my dears,' said the Master. 'I should spoil it by
    adding one touch.'
So with us God is painting a picture, and little we know of
    His plan,
We took at the lad whom we cherish and are eager to see him
    a man;
But God knows the soul He is shaping, and though for more time
    He's beseeched,
He hurts us beyond understanding, but He stops when perfection
    is reached.

Gateway to Glory

J. R. Miller

hen we look at the sepulcher of Jesus, we see how hopeless everything seemed for the time. He on whom the disciples had leaned as the Messiah is now silent in death, His work apparently finished. All the expectations based on Him depended on His living to ascend a throne. It certainly seemed now to His friends that all was over. Yet the grave was simply the low gateway to glory. As we see it now, in the light that streams from the gospel, it interrupted no plan, quenched no light, destroyed no hope. When shall

we learn to bring the truth of immortality into our own faiths and hopes? We stand by the graves of our Christian friends almost as disconsolate as were these friends of Jesus about His grave. Why shall we not learn faith? Death ends nothing for those who die in the Lord—nothing but struggle, sorrow, and sin. No hopes persist when a Christian is buried. Just beyond is glory.

NEXT TO FAITH in God comes patience. I see that more and more, and few possess enough of either to enable them to meet the day of bereavement without dismay.—*Elizabeth Prentiss*

The Bloom Falling Into Christ's Lap

Samuel Rutherford

f our Lord has taken away your child, your lease of him is expired; and seeing Christ would want him no longer, it is your part to hold your peace, and worship and adore the sovereignty and liberty that the Potter has over the clay that He gave life unto. And what is man, to call and summon the Almighty to his lower court down here? For He giveth account of none of His doings. And if you will take a loan of a child, and give him back again to our Lord, smiling as His borrowed goods be returned to Him, believe he is not gone away, but sent before; and that the change of the country should make you think, he is not lost to you who is found in Christ. He is now before you and the dead in Christ shall be raised again. A going-down star is not annihilated, but shall appear again. If he has cast his bloom and flower, the bloom is fallen in heaven in Christ's lap. As he was lent awhile to time, so is he given now to eternity, which will also take you. The difference of your shipping and his to heaven and Christ's shore, the land of life, is only in a few short years, which wears every day shorter. Some short and soon reckoned summers will give you a meeting with him, and with the Chief and Leader of the heavenly troops, that are riding on white horses, that are triumphing in glory.

Hard Couch of Sorrow

Henry Law

When the Lord told Moses, "You can be sure I have seen the misery of My people in Egypt. I have heard their cries for deliverance from their harsh slave drivers. Yes, I am concerned about their suffering." —Exodus 3:7

Exquisite tenderness melts in these words.
Assurance of compassion is most sweetly stated.
Let no believer faint in the hour of trial.
His feet may travel in affliction's road.
He may be called to lie on the hard couch of sorrow.
Troubles may roll over him as wave upon wave.
But the eye of love ever watches him,
    the heart of love ever throbs sympathetically for him,
    the ear of love ever listens to his cry,
    the hand of love will in due season be outstretched to help him.

The patient sufferer will sing with David, "He led me to a place of safety; He rescued me because He delights in me."—Psalm 18:19

Behold Your King

Elizabeth Prentiss

o not let the thought of what those who love you must suffer in your loss, diminish the peace and joy with which God now calls you to think only of Himself, and the home He has prepared for you. Try to leave them to His kind, tender care. He loves them better than you do; He can be to them more than you have been; He will hear your prayers and all the prayers offered for them, and as one whom his mother comforts, so will He comfort them. We who shall be left here without you, cannot conceive the joys on which you are to enter, but we know enough to go with you to the very gates of the City, longing to enter in with you to go no more out.

All your tears will soon be wiped away. You will see the King in His beauty. You will see Christ your Redeemer, and realize all He is, and all He has done for you. How many saints whom you have loved on earth will be standing ready to seize you by the hand and welcome you among them. As I think of these things my soul is in haste to be gone. I long to be set free from sin and self, and to go to the fellowship of those who have gone with them forever, and are perfect and entire, wanting nothing.

A Dying World

J. C. Ryle

eath is continually about us and near us, and meets us at every turn. Few are the family gatherings, when Christmas comes round in which there are not some empty chairs and vacant places. Few are the men and women, past thirty, who could not number a long list of names, deeply cut for ever in their hearts, but names of beloved ones now dead and gone. Where are our fathers and mothers? Where are our ministers and teachers? Where are our brothers and sisters? Where are our husbands and wives? Where are our neighbours and friends? Where are the old grey-headed worshippers, whose reverent faces we remember so well, when we first went to God's house? Where are the boys and girls we played with when we went to school? How many must reply, "Dead, dead, dead! The daisies are growing over their graves, and we are left alone." Surely a world so full of death can never be called a home.

Awake From Your Sleep!

John Wesley

wake, thou everlasting spirit, out of your dream of worldly happiness! Did not God create you for himself? Then you cannot rest until you rest in Him. Return, O wanderer! Fly back to your ark, for this is not your home. Think not of building tabernacles here. You are but a stranger, a sojourner upon earth; a creature of a day, but just launching out into an unchangeable state. Make haste! Eternity is at hand! Eternity depends on this moment. An eternity of happiness or an eternity of misery!

THIS IS THE TESTIMONY of all the good books, sermons, hymns, and memoirs I read,—that God's ways are infinitely perfect; that we are to love Him for what He is, and therefore equally as much when He afflicts us as when He prospers us; that there is no real happiness but in doing and suffering His will, and that life is but a scene of probation through which we pass to the real life above.—*Elizabeth Prentiss*

Flee From the Wrath to Come!

John Wesley

h, who shall warn this generation of vipers to flee wrath to come! Not those who lie at their gate, or cringe at their feet, desiring to be fed with the crumbs that fall from their tables. Not those who court their favor or fear their frown; none of those who mind earthly things. But if there be a Christian upon earth, if there be a man who has overcome the world, who desires nothing but God, and fears none but him that is able to destroy both body and soul in hell. You, oh man of God, speak, and spare not. Lift up your voice like a trumpet! Cry aloud, and show these honorable sinners the desperate condition wherein they stand! It may be one in a thousand may have ears to hear; may arise and shake himself from the dust; may break loose from these chains that bind him to the earth, and at length lay up treasures in heaven.

Your Inheritance

Octavius Winslow

"He who overcomes will inherit all things, and I will be his God and he will be my son."—Rev. 21:7

ow vast, how illimitable, then, the inheritance of the saints—inheriting "all things!" This is a beautiful idea of heaven; it is a lovely picture, on which the eye of faith delights to dwell. The earthly heir looks at his inheritance, surveys it, walks through it, luxuriates amidst its beauties, and anticipates its full possession. The heir of glory has his inheritance too, it is heaven! He looks to it, he longs for it, and soon the Savior will come in personal glory, and institute him into its full and eternal possession!

Life in Jesus

Mary Winslow

e must not expect much in this base world. All our richest blessings are to come. This world is but a preparatory state. We are disciplining and preparing for the glorious inheritance above. But how often, through wretched unbelief, we seem to wish to have our all here. And although, from bitter experience, we feel and acknowledge that this poor world is polluted, and it is not our rest, yet more or less we go on, often repining, because we cannot have things just as we wish. Oh, to leave ourselves in a loving, tender Father's hands! He knows what we need and what we ought to have, and will deny us no good thing. But He must judge for us, who are but as babes, who cannot judge for ourselves.

Heavenly Prayer

D. A. Harsha

Blessed Jesus, we beseech You to show us Your glory and to raise our hearts, our hopes, and our desires, to that blessed world to which You have ascended. O may our souls be daily rising, in holy thought, towards our home where the ransomed of the Lord shall forever obtain joy and gladness. May our thoughts become heavenly and our hearts be attuned to those songs with which the arches of heaven shall resound to all eternity! O my Savior, wean my heart from earth and enable me to place my affection on things above.

The Mother's Jewels

M. C. Bowman

> I have a little darling
>   That sleepeth near my heart,
> Whose beauty and whose sweetness
>   Ten thousand joys impart.
> Love smileth on her features,
>   And warbleth on her tongue,
> And guideth all her actions,

So innocent and young.
A joyous little creature,
    All full of mirth and glee;
Now nestling on my bosom,
    Now dancing on my knee;
More precious far than rubies,
    Or diadems of gold,
Is she, my little darling,
    Who's scarcely one year old.
I have a little daughter,
    Whose face is very fair,
With eyes of heaven's azure,
    And soft and silky hair.
Her tiny, dimpled fingers
    Are ever at their play,
While her unceasing prattle
    Doth mimic all I say.
She saith her little prayers
    Low bowing on my breast;
And giveth all a sweet good-night
    Ere she repairs to rest.
O grant, my blessed Savior,
    That her young heart and mind,
In childhood's tender hours,
    Be heavenward inclined!
I have another jewel,
    The brightest of the three
A precious hidden treasure,
    Which now I cannot see.
Far, far away in heaven

This lovely gem doth shine;
And though I cannot see him,
    I know he yet is mine.
And when life's woes are ended,
    And all my toil is done,
Again I shall embrace him,
    My own, my cherub son.
How oft our sore bereftments
    Are blessings in disguise!
God has prepared a mansion
    For us above the skies."
And thus to bring us to him,
    In his unbounded love,
Untwines the spirit's tendrils here,
    And fastens them above.

God's Lasting Goodness

Elizabeth Prentiss

he peaceful fruits of sorrow do not ripen at once; there is a long time of weariness and heaviness while this process is going on; but I do not, will not doubt that you will taste these fruits and find them very sweet. One of the hard things about bereavement is the physical prostration and listlessness, which make it next to impossible to pray and quite impossible to feel the least interest in anything. We must bear this as a part of the pain, believing that it will not last forever, for nothing but God's goodness does.

"God's angels coming down on errands sweet,
Our angels going home."

395

Home at Last!

Mother's Journal

ome at last! With what joy does the seaworn traveler utter these words. How does his heart bound, when he sees once more his own native hills, and feels that he is indeed at home. He has seen other countries, very beautiful it is true., but he felt that he was among, strangers, far away from all that were near and dear to him. But especially did he long for his home, when he felt himself in danger, when the waves threatened to engulph his little bark, and he felt there was but a plank between him and eternity.

Oh, then he would have given all that he had to find himself safe at home.

We are like the traveler, for we are all pilgrims and sojourners here, and this is not our home. it is sweet to think, when storms of sorrow rise, that they will soon be over, and the more trouble we have before we reach that home, the sweeter will it be when we have gained it. But though we are all strangers on the earth, does every one love his home?

It is far different, for there is a large class who are like another kind of traveler. One who becomes enchanted with foreign scenes, and cares not to return. Yes, sad to say, there are some who look upon this world as their chief good, and care not for that other one to which they are all rapidly hastening. They see this world all fair and beautiful,and as yet no storms have arisen, and they seem to forget that they are not to live here always, for that home which is so precious to others is not so to them. Then when sorrow comes, how sad is their condition. Looking back, they see their brightened hopes frustrated; looking forward all is dreary and dark, for they are without God in the world.

We are all too prone to forget our heavenly home and to set our affection on things of earth. How earnestly should we pray against this and endeavor to keep our eyes constantly fixed on those "distant hills."

The Glory of Heaven

D. A. Harsha

eaven is a glorious place. Its glory should attract us. How delightful to think of heavenly glory! How it raises the soul above earth! Let us soar on high and view the glory of the New Jerusalem, and of the saints in light. We have seen that the glory of God and the Lamb irradiates the celestial world. There, the Sun of Righteousness always shines, and his beams gladden the hearts of a ransomed host. There God smiles and the nations of the saved walk in the light of his countenance. There is one perpetual noontide of glory in the mansions above. There is glory—"an exceeding and eternal weight"—reserved in heaven for them that love God.

Glory shines in Immanuel's land. The city, the mansions, the inhabitants, are all glorious. Every believer in Jesus will be crowned with everlasting glory. Though we could not bear the effulgence of heaven's glory, should it now beam upon us, yet we know that when we awaken to immortality, that glory shall be revealed in us. We know that when Christ, our glorious Head, shall appear, we shall be like him; for we shall see him as he is. O, to be like the blessed Jesus! What heart can desire more? If we are His people we shall soon be like him. Our bodies shall shine like his—that wondrous Personage whose original glory once beamed on Mount Tabor, when his face shone as the sun, and when his raiment was white as the light. In heaven, the wonders of Mount Tabor will ever be exhibited; and there the pure radiance of the Savior's glory, will always beam upon redeemed millions. Who can conceive this blessedness? How desirable, how attractive does it appear to an immortal mind! From those heights of bliss every soul will be ready to exclaim with Peter, "Lord, it is good for us to be here." But more than this. The saints will be made partakers of the Redeemer's glory. "The glory which thou gavest me, I have given them." "The Lord will give glory." Amazing love! That Christ should exalt his followers to such bliss, and crown them with such glory!

There, a gracious God will bestow upon us the "riches of his glory," and we shall shine to all eternity, in the garments of glory and of beauty. We shall inherit a glorious kingdom, and wear a glorious crown. Our bodies shall be fashioned like unto Christ's "glorious body;" and we shall obtain an exceeding and eternal weight of glory in the smile and presence of God.

In view of our future glory, how insignificant do these present afflictions appear? "For I reckon, that the sufferings of this present time are not worthy to be compared with the glory which shall be revealed in us." Let the afflicted Christian remember, that his momentary trials and sufferings here, are preparing for him a weighty crown of glory hereafter.

"Our light affliction, which is but for a moment, worketh for us a far more exceeding and eternal weight of glory." How animating is this hope of a glorious immortality? O joyful hope! It cheers us amidst the surrounding gloom of life; it illuminates our pathway to the tomb; it sheds its radiance beyond the grave; it enables the believer to exclaim, when he is just finishing his earthly course and about to embark upon the boundless ocean of eternity, "Hence-forth there is laid up for me a crown of righteousness, which the Lord, the righteous Judge, shall give me at that day; and not to me only, but unto all them also that love his appearing."

Let us run with patience, the race that is set before us, and soon we shall reach the goal of immortal blessedness. Then shall the glory of heaven gladden our blissful sight, and the streams of Paradise refresh our weary souls. Let every reader be attracted by the glory of heaven. Let him look to a bleeding Savior for salvation, and press onward with eagerness to receive the crown of glory that fades not away.

SHE IS AT HOME; she is well, she is happy, she will never know a bereavement or a day's illness, or the infirmities and trials of old age; she has got the secret of perpetual youth. The only real comfort is, that God never makes mistakes; that He would not have snatched her from us if He had not had a reason that would satisfy us if we knew it.

—*Elizabeth Prentiss*

Infants in Glory

John Newton

I am willing to believe, till the Scripture forbids me, that infants of all nations and kindreds, without exception, who die before they are capable of sinning "after the similitude of Adam's transgression," who have done nothing in the body of which they can give account, are included in the election of grace; and that the words of our Lord with respect to another class of persons, are applicable to them; "It is not the will of your Father in heaven that one of these little ones should perish."

John Calvin

"Suffer the little children to come unto me, and forbid them not, for of such is the kingdom of God."—Matt. 19:14. All infants are liable to the misery in which the guilt of Adam's sin has involved our race. Yet, when taken away [in death] in infancy, are capable of regeneration, being redeemed from these evils by the blood of the Lamb. If infants are left among the children of Adam, they are left in death, for in Adam we can only die. On the contrary, Christ commands them to be brought to him. Why? Because He is life. To give them life before He makes them partakers of Himself, while these men, by driving these young children away from Him, adjudged them to death.... God adopts infants and washes them in the blood of His Son, and they are regarded by Christ as His flock.

In this passage, Christ is not speaking of the general guilt in which all the descendants of Adam are involved, but only threatening the despisers of the gospel who proudly and obstinately reject the grace that is offered them, and this has nothing to do with infants. I likewise oppose any contrary argument. All those whom Christ blesses are exempted from the curse of Adam and wrath of God; and as it is well known that infants were blessed by Him, it follows that they are exempted from [eternal] death.

Thomas Smyth

Think of your child not as dead but as living, not as a flower that is withered. but as one that is transplanted as touched by divine hand—blooming in richer colors and sweeter shades than those of earth, though to your eyes these last may have been beautiful, more beautiful than you will hope to see again.

William Perkins

Infants have no works whereby they may be judged, seeing they do neither good nor evil. Therefore, all shall not be "judged according to works." These passages of Scripture that refer to such are not to be extended to all, but must be restrained to such as have actual works, and knowledge to discern between good and evil, which infants have not. For besides that they are destitute of works, they are also want the use of reason, and therefore they shall not be judged by the book of conscience, but by the book of life.

As for the places of Scripture that mention justification and salvation by faith, they are to be restrained to men of years. Whereas infants dying in their infancy, and therefore wanting actual faith, which none can have without actual knowledge of God's will and word, are no doubt saved by a special working of God's Holy Spirit.

Augustus Toplady

I testify my firm belief, that the souls of all departed infants are with God in glory—that in the decree of predestination to life, God hath included all whom He intended to take away in infancy; and that the decree of reprobation hath nothing to do with them.

No Night There

Margaret Sangster

No night in the better land,
    No bitter night of woe!
No weary march o'er the desert sand,
    While the shadows come and go.
No sighs in the better land,
    No sighs o'er hidden grief,
No joys to drop from the trembling hand,
    As beautiful as brief.
No tears in the better land,
    Falling in burning rain;
For the Father's gentle and loving hand
    Shall banish weeping and pain.
But light in the better land;
    Light on the crystal sea;
Light flashing back from the golden sand,
    Light in the spirits free!
And songs in the better land,

Swelling out loud and clear,
To the Savior, whose strong, protecting hand
Hath brought his ransomed here.
Bliss in the better land,
Undimmed by the shivering dread
Of an hour of parting close at hand,
Of the farewell tears to shed.
Rapture and fullest peace,
In the land of light and love;
Glory forever to increase,—
Night enters not above!

Just Like the Plan!

James McConkey

oes it seem to you, dear sad heart, that your life, because of the loss of your loved one, has come to an abrupt ending? Is there nothing left for which to live? Have you ever thought that your bereavement may be part of His plan?

Do you know the story of the engineer of the Brooklyn bridge? During its building he was injured. For many long months he was shut up in his room. His gifted wife shared his toils, and carried his plans to the workmen. At last the great bridge was completed. Then the invalid architect asked to see it. They put him upon a cot, and carried him to the bridge. They placed him where he could see the magnificent structure in all its beauty. There he lay, in his helplessness, intently scanning the work of his genius. He marked the great cables, the massive piers, the mighty anchorages which fettered it to the earth. His critical eye ran over every beam, every girder, every chord, every rod. He noted every detail carried out precisely as he had dreamed it in his dreams, and wrought it out in his plans and specifications.

And then as the joy of achievement filled his soul, as he saw and realized that it was finished exactly as he had designed it. In an ecstasy of delight he cried out, "It's just like the plan; it's just like the plan."

Some day we shall stand in the glory and looking up into His face, cry out: "O God, I thank you that you did let me gather up one by one, the golden threads of your great purpose for my life. I thank you, as like a tiny trail creeping its way up some great mountain side, that pathway of life has gone on in darkness and light, storm and shadow, weakness and tears, failures and falterings, you have at last brought me to its destined end. And now that I see my finished life, no longer 'through a glass darkly' but in the face to face splendor of your own glory, I thank you, O God. I thank you that, it's just like the plan; it's just like the plan."

Blessed Are the Dead Which Die in the Lord

E. H. Bickersteth

"I heard a voice from heaven saying unto me, Write, Blessed are the dead which die in the Lord from henceforth: Yea, saith the Spirit, that they may rest from their labors; and their works do follow them."—Rev. 14:13.

Hush! Blessed are the dead
    In Jesus' arms who rest,
And lean their weary head
    For ever on His breast.
O beatific sight!
    No darkling veil between,
They see the Light of Light,

Whom here they loved unseen.
For them the wild is past
    With all its toil and care;
Its dry sirocco blast,
    Its fiery noonday glare.
Them the Good Shepherd leads,
    Where storms are never rife,
In tranquil dewy meads
    Beside the Fount of Life.
Ours only are the tears,
    Who weep around their tomb
The light of bygone years
    And shadowing years to come.
Their voice, their touch, their smile—
    Those love-springs flowing o'er
Earth for its little while
    Shall never know them more.
O tender hearts and true,
    Our long last vigil kept,
We weep and mourn for you;
    Nor blame us—Jesus wept.
But soon at break of day
    His calm Almighty voice,
Stronger than death, shall say,
    Awake—weep not—rejoice.

I HAVE LIVED to see that God never was so good to me as when He seemed most severe.—*Elizabeth Prentiss*

Daily Trials

John Newton

he evil of yesterday is gone, that which is appointed for tomorrow is not yet arrived. Would it not be well if we could live with the Lord by the day? This reminds me of a fable. A father asked his young child to carry a large wood pile. The child tried, but it was beyond his strength; he could not lift it. Then the father took off the bands and said, "Carry one stick at a time." This the child did easily, till he had removed the whole pile. Thus the troubles of a month or year, which would be too heavy for us if they came all together, are parceled out by our wise and gracious Lord into daily portions. We have, as it were, to carry one stick every day. But often, when we have carried the stick all day, we cannot or will not lay it down at night. And we take up the sticks allotted for future days or weeks long before the appointed time. It is no wonder that we say "Oh, what a heavy burden! Oh, how weary am I." Well, the day is coming when we hope to drop every load, and to bid farewell to sin, sorrow, and care forever.

A Well Founded Hope

George Herbert

y hope is that I shall shortly leave this valley of tears and be free from all fevers and pain, which will be a more happy condition. I shall be free from sin and all the temptations and anxieties that attend it. This being past, I shall dwell in the New Jerusalem; dwell there with men made perfect; dwell where these eyes shall see my Master and Savior Jesus; and with him see my dear mother and all my relations and friends. But I must die, or not come to that happy place.

Victory Over Death

Horatius Bonar

he issue of the conflict between the saints and death was decided when the Lord arose. He met the enemy on his own territory, his own battlefield, and overcame. He entered the palace of the king of terrors, and there laid hold of the strong man, shaking his dwelling to its foundations as he came forth, carrying away its gates along with him, and giving warning of being about to return, in order to complete his conquest by "spoiling his goods," and robbing him of the treasures which he had kept so long,—the dust of sleeping saints.

The Christian in Glory

Charles H. Spurgeon

ow different will be the state of the believer in heaven from what it is here! Here he is born to toil and suffer weariness, but in the land of the immortal, fatigue is never known. Anxious to serve his Master, he finds his strength unequal to his zeal. His constant cry is, "Help me to serve Thee, O my God." If he be thoroughly active, he will have much labor; not too much for his will, but more than enough for his power, so that he will cry out, "I am not wearied of the labor, but I am wearied in it." Ah! Christian, the hot day of weariness lasts not forever. The sun is nearing the horizon, and it shall rise again with a brighter day than you have ever seen, upon a land where they serve God day and night, and yet rest from their labors. Here, rest is but partial, there, it is perfect. Here, the Christian is always unsettled. He feels that he has not yet attained. There, all are at rest. They have attained the summit of the mountain and they have ascended to the bosom of their God. Higher they cannot go. Ah, toil-

worn laborer, only think when you shall rest forever! Can you conceive it? It is a rest eternal—a rest that "remains." Here, my best joys bear "mortal" on their brow; my fair flowers fade; my dainty cups are drained to dregs; my sweetest birds fall before Death's arrows; my most pleasant days are shadowed into nights; and the flood-tides of my bliss subside into ebbs of sorrow. But there, everything is immortal. The harp abides unrusted, the crown unwithered, the eye undimmed, the voice unfaltering, the heart unwavering, and the immortal being is wholly absorbed in infinite delight. Happy day! Happy day, when mortality shall be swallowed up of life, and the Eternal Sabbath shall begin.

Night of Weeping, Joy in the Morning

Horatius Bonar

ur night of weeping has taken much of its gloom and sadness from these rending asunder. The pain of parting, in the case of the saints, has much to alleviate it, but still the bitterness is there. We feel that we must separate, and though it be only for a while, still our hearts bleed with the wound.

But there is reunion. And one of the joys of the morning is this reunion among the saints. During the night they had been scattered, in the morning they are gathered together. In the wilderness they have been separated, but in the kingdom they shall meet. During this age they have been like the drops of the fitful shower. In the age to come they shall be like the dew of Hermon, the dew that descended upon the mountains of Zion, one radiant company, alighting upon the holy hills, and bringing with them refreshment to a weary earth.

Satisfied!

Elizabeth Prentiss

What shall I find in heaven? The faces dear
    Upon whose love and smiles I feasted here?
Shall I rejoice that naught can there divide
    United hearts, and so be satisfied?

What shall I do in heaven? Shall I be blest
    With a long luxury and endless rest?
Conflict and labor over, shall I ride
    Through seas untroubled, and be satisfied?

What shall I be in heaven? A messenger
    Passing from sainted ones to those who err
And suffer still on earth? Mid fields so wide,
    Shall I, who love to work, be satisfied?

I know not, care not; when life's fetters break,
    When from death's blessed restful sleep I wake,
Whate'er Thy love withhold, or may provide,
    Being like Thee, I shall be satisfied!

HERE GOD GIVES his people some taste, that they may not faint. And he gives them but a taste, that they may long to be at home, that they may keep humble, that they may sit loose from things below, that they may not break and despise bruised reeds, and that heaven may be more sweet to them at last.—*Thomas Brooks*

Sanctified Affliction

Watchman and Reflector

fflictions if sanctified, are good. They ungrasp our hold upon the world, and lift the eye to God. Temptations are good. They make us flee to Christ and cling closer to his hands. Like spies from the enemy of souls they serve to keep us on the alert. Good are our inward conflicts with sin, they make us yearn for heaven. God plucks from us our earthly friends that we may look upon Him as he is—our very best friend. He foils our earthly hopes that we may not fail of the hope of heaven. He plunges us into

410

sorrow here that we may escape the sorrow that is to come. He plants around the tree of pleasure angry briers, that we may be induced to pluck the fruit of the tree of life. He, at times, gives this life a bitter taste only to give us a keener relish for the life to come. If sanctified, every trial is a treasure; each wound a scar of glory; each drop of grief will glitter a diamond in the Christian's crown of bliss.

Are our trials sometimes great? Great is our reward. Sometimes the victims of disappointment here are tantalized by the hope often offered but seldom tasted good. The branches of the tree of life do not withdraw themselves from the hand, and the water of the river of life never retires from the lip.

The mariner in the midst of a storm longs for the break of day. The storm-tossed Christian, too, sometimes feels that his night is long and dark and wearisome. Let him be of good cheer, behind it all is coming up a brighter day. By the eye of faith and the aid of revelation we can already see its streaks. At times we can almost feel the winds of that fresh morning breaking in upon us! Christians, never despond in temptation, nor weary under losses, nor murmur in afflictions. Bear them with a smile, for the eternal joys of heaven far exceed the brief sufferings of earth.

He who was in afflictions, distresses, tumults, labors,—who was beaten, stoned, shipwrecked, imprisoned; was in journeyings often, in perils of robbers, in perils in the city, in the wilderness, in the sea; who was in stripes, in prisons, and in deaths often,—could say, I take pleasure in infirmities, necessities, reproaches, distresses, and persecutions. Why? For I reckon that the sufferings of this present time are of no account in comparison with the glory hereafter to be revealed in us.

If that white-robed company would be permitted to speak to us, we should hear them from the heights of bliss exclaim, in triumph, "Weeping may endure for the night, but joy cometh in the morning.

The night is already past, the day is at hand. Then lift up your heads, for the time of your redemption draweth nigh."

And from the Captain of our salvation—made perfect through sufferings—there comes the exhortation, "Forasmuch as Christ hath suffered in the flesh, arm yourselves likewise with the same mind; for if you suffer with him, you shall also reign with him. These light afflictions which are but for a moment, work out a far more exceeding and eternal weight of glory!" "The cup which my Father giveth me, shall I not drink?"

"Why should I murmur?" said Henry Martyn, in his last sickness; "weakness, peril, and pain are but the ministering angels whose office it is to conduct me to glory." "Oh, what owe I," says Samuel Rutherford, "to the file, to the hammer, to the furnace of my Lord Jesus!"

THROUGHOUT the whole web of national existence we trace the golden thread of human progress toward the higher and better estate.

—*James A. Garfield*

Sunshine for the Sorrowing

Theodore L. Cuyler

Among the readers of this paper there must be many who "wear mourning." Every minister, as he runs his eye over his congregation, sees the black badge of sorrow in every part of the house. Yet many of the deepest and sorest griefs of the heart do not reveal any outward signal of distress. Know that God sees ten-fold more sorrow than the human eye ever detects.

What a clear streak of sunshine our Lord let into this region of sorrowing hearts when he pronounced that wonderful benediction

"Blessed are they that mourn!" Perhaps some poor Galilean mother who came up that day to hear Jesus of Nazareth, with her eyes red from weeping over a lost child, whispered to herself, "That is for me; I am a mourner." "Ah!" thought some penitent sinner who felt the plague of his guilty heart, "that means me; I am in trouble today." It did mean them. Christ's religion is the first and only religion ever known in this world which recognizes human sorrow, and has any sunshine of consolation for broken hearts. Do cold-blooded infidels realize that fact when they attempt to destroy men's faith in the Gospel of Calvary? We are apt to limit this benediction of Jesus to one class of sufferers. We take this sweet little text into sick-rooms, or to funerals, or into the lonely group which gather around a mother's deserted chair or a little empty crib. It was meant for them. It has fallen upon such stricken hearts like the gentle rain upon the new-mown grass. Many of us know full well how good the balm felt when it touched our bruised and bleeding hearts. I remember how, when one of my own "bairns" was lying in his fresh-made grave, and another one was so low that his crib seemed to touch against a tomb. I used to keep murmuring over to myself Wesley's matchless lines, "Leave, oh leave me not alone, still support and comfort me!"

In those days I was learning (what we pastors have to learn) just how the arrow feels when it enters, and just how to sympathize with our people in their bereavements. Somehow a minister is never fully ready to emit the fragrance of sympathy for others until he has been bruised, himself. There is a great lack about all Christians who have never suffered. Paul abounded in consolation because he had known sharp tribulations in his own experience. What a precious spilling of his great sympathetic heart that was when he overflowed into that sublime passage which ends the fourth and begins the fifth chapter of his Epistle to the Corinthians. The outward man perishing—the inward man renewed day by day. The affliction growing "light" in proportion to the transcendent weight of the eternal glory! The old tent dropping to pieces and the heavenly mansion looming up so gloriously that his homesick soul longed to quit the fluttering tent, and to "be present with the Lord." These are indeed mighty consolations to bear with us into our houses of mourning. They are the foretastes which make us long for the full feast and the seraphic joys of the marriage-supper of the Lamb.

GOD DEMANDS an account of the past that we must render hereafter. He also demands an improvement of the present and this we must render now.—*William Jay*

A New Creation

Horatius Bonar

his corruptible shall put on incorruption!" There will be an entire casting aside of mortality with all its wrappings of corruption, with all its relics of dishonor. Every particle of evil shall be shaken out of us, and "this vile body" transfigured into the likeness of the Lord's own glorious body. We entered this world mortal and corruptible, all our life long we are imbibing mortality and corruption, becoming more and more thoroughly mortal and corruptible. The grave sets its seal to all this, and crumbles us down into common earth. But the trumpet sounds, and all this is gone. Mortality falls off and all pertaining to it is left behind. No more of dross or disease in our frame. We can then defy sickness, pain, and death. We can say to our bodies, be pained no more; to our limbs, be weary no more; to our lips, be parched no more; to our eye, be dim no more.

Thoughts of Heaven

William Pearce

I love to think of heaven, it seems not far away,
    Its crystal streams refresh me as I near the closing day;
Its balmy winds are wafted from the heavenly hills above
    And they fold me in an atmosphere of purity and love.
I love to think of heaven, I long to join the choir,
    To sing the song of. Jesus my soul would never tire;
The loved ones gone before me, are joining in the song,
    They cast their crowns before the Lamb who sits upon the
        throne.
I love to think of heaven, where the weary are at rest,
    No sorrow there can enter the mansions of the blest;
All tears are wiped away by the Savior's loving hand,
    And sin and death are banished from that glorious happy land.
I love to think of heaven, and the greetings I shall meet,
    From the loving band of loved ones, who walk the golden
        street;
And the patriarchs and prophets I shall know them every one
    It is written in the Word, "We shall know as we are known."

WE HAVE, AMID ALL CHANGES, three unchangeables—an unchangeable covenant, an unchangeable God, and an unchangeable heaven. While these three remain "the same yesterday, today, and forever," welcome the will of our Heavenly. Father in all events that may happen to us. Come what will, nothing can come amiss.—*Rev. Matthew Henry*

The Way to Heaven

J. R. Miller

way always leads somewhere. Jesus is the way from earth to heaven, and also from heaven to earth. Through Him we get to God, and through Him God comes to us. He is the true and only ladder whose foot rests on the earth, and whose top reaches up to the very glory of God. In His humanity Jesus comes down to the lowest depths of human need and sorrow. Had He been God only, and not man, He could not have done this. The incarnation was the letting of the ladder down until it rested in the deepest valleys. There is now no spot of shame or guilt in this world from which there is not a ladder of light, with its celestial steps leading upward to God and heaven.

For while Christ's humanity brings the ladder down to earth's places of sorest need, His divinity carries the ladder up past the shining stars, into the very midst of the glory of God. On one page of the New Testament we find Jesus on a cross, dying in darkness and shame, between criminals. We open another page, and we see that same Jesus in the midst of the heavenly brightness, wearing still the wound marks, but crowned in glory. Behold the ladder from earth to heaven!

A ladder is a way for feet to climb. Christ is the way, therefore, by which sinners can go up out of their sins to the purity and blessedness of heaven. One thing to mark specially is that there is but one way. Christ is the only Mediator. We can enter the Father's family only through Him. Grace can come to us only through Him. There is, then, no choice of ways. If we do not go by this one way we can never reach home. Nor must we forget that a way is meant to be walked in. We must put our feet on this ladder and go up rung by rung until we reach the topmost step, which will be heaven.

Ties Not Broken in Heaven

Henry Harbaugh

We delight greatly in the hope that the ties which bind us to our sainted friends are not broken in death—that while we are loving them still, they love us too. While we long to find them again they are watching with holy interest over us, and are alluring us, by sweet mysterious influences, into their holy society, and into a participation with them of celestial joys. Seeing we are compassed about with so great a cloud of witnesses, we are animated to lay aside every weight—even that of the body itself in death—that we may fly to their embraces and be near them as they are near the Lord.

Jesus, Come to Me

Bernard of Clairvaux

Forgive, blest shade, the tributary tear,
    That mourns thine exit from a world like this:
Forgive the wish that would have kept thee here,
    And stayed thy progress to the realms of bliss.
When my dying hour must be,
    Be not absent then from me:
    In that dreadful hour I pray,
    Jesus, come without delay,
        See and set me free.
    When Thou biddest me depart,
    Whom I cleave to with my heart,
    Lover of my soul be near,
    With Thy saving cross appear,
    Show Thyself to me.

The Christian in Heaven

John S. C. Abbott

he question is often asked, "If Christians in heaven know all that is transpiring upon earth, suppose a sainted mother sees a son or a daughter here going in the ways of ruin, how can she be happy?"

This is a mystery which God has not yet explained to us. It seems to us now, impossible that a mother can be happy in heaven with her child forever banished from her. But let us remember that God is more truly the parent of every being on earth than its earthly father or mother can possibly be.

We are God's sons and daughters in a far higher sense than we are the sons or daughters of our earthly parents. God made our bodies and our spirits. God became man, and by his own humiliation and sufferings upon the cross, made atonement for our sins. Year after year, with yearning utterance, God has cried out to us, "My son, my daughter, give me your heart." Yes, God is our father in a far more exalted sense than any earthly parent can be. Earthly love is frail and variable. God's love is unchanging.

Sympathy of the Two Worlds

Charles Haddon Spurgeon

here is joy in the presence of the angels of God over one sinner that repenteth." It seems as if these words show me a bridge by which I might crossover into eternity. It does, as it were, exhibit to me certain magnetic wires which convey the intelligence of what is done here to spirits in another world. It teaches me that there is a wonderful connection between this lower world and that which is beyond the skies, where God dwelleth, in the land of joy.

Our Departed Friends in Glory

Dwight. L. Moody

I f there is anything that ought to make heaven near to Christians, it is knowing that God and all their loved ones will be there. What is it that makes home so attractive? Is it because we have a beautiful home? Is it because we have beautiful trees around that home? Is it because we have beautiful paintings upon the walls inside? Is it because we have beautiful furniture? Is that all that makes home so attractive and so beautiful? Nay, it is the loved ones in it. It is the loved ones there.

I remember after being away from home some time, I went back to see my honored mother, and I thought in going back I would take her by surprise, and steal in unexpectedly upon her, but when I found she had gone away, the old place didn't seem like home at all. I went into one room and then into another, and I went all through the house, but I could not find that loved mother, and I said to some member of the family, "Where is mother?" and they said she had gone away. Well, home had lost its charm. It was that mother that made home so sweet to me, and it is the loved ones that are going to make heaven so sweet to us all.

> The path of sorrow, and that path alone,
> Leads to the land where sorrow is unknown;
> No traveler ever reached that blest abode,
> Who found not thorns and briars on his road.
> —*William Cowper*

Two Funerals

Charles Haddon Spurgeon

here are two funerals for every Christian. One the funeral of the body and the other the soul—rather it is the marriage of the soul, for angels stand ready to carry it to the Savior. The angels, imitating husbandmen, as they near the gates of heaven may shout "Harvest Home." There is a holiday whenever a saint enters and there is praise to God, while life, or thought, or being lasts or immortality endures.

Delights of Heaven

Isaac Watts

There is a land of pure delight,
    Where saints immortal reign;
Infinite day excludes the night,
    And pleasures banish pain.
There everlasting spring abides,
    And never-with'ring flowers;
Death, like a narrow sea, divides
    This heavenly land from ours.
Sweet fields beyond the swelling flood,
    Stand dress'd in living green
So to the Jews old Canaan stood,
    While Jordan roll'd between.
Could we but climb where Moses stood,
    And view the landscape o'er,
Not Jordan's stream, nor death's cold flood,
    Should fright us from the shore.

Our Friends in Heaven

Jonathan Edwards

ow beautiful is the belief of man's immortality! The dead alive again, and forever. "Earth to earth, ashes to ashes, dust to dust," is only spoken over the body, when consigned to "the house appointed for all the living." Not such the requiem of the soul. A refrain of immortality concludes earth's history and announces eternity's beginnings. "Not lost, but gone before." Such is the cherished and beautiful faith of man in all ages and lands; a mere glimmering indeed in minds unirradiated with divine truth; and only a power and a joy when God's voice audibly falls upon the ear in words of counsel and prophecy.

The sainted dead dwell in life; beholding the king in his beauty; "shining" as the brightness of the firmament, and as the stars forever and ever." They fade no more, nor realize pain. A wealth of love is theirs, a heritage of goodness, a celestial habitation and in them thoughts, hopes, feelings expand and move forward in ceaseless progressions. We may feel sad because they are lost to us, but while we weep and wonder, they are wrapped in garments of light and warble songs of celestial joy. They will return to us no more, but we shall go to them and share their pleasures, emulate their sympathies, and compete with them in the path of endless development. We would not call them back. In the homes above they are great, and well-employed, and blest. Shadows fall upon them no more, nor is life ruled with anxious cares. Love rules their life and thoughts, and eternal hopes beckon them forever to the pursuit of infinite good.

To whom are these thoughts strange and dull? Who has no treasure in Heaven—well-remembered forms hallowed by separation and distance—stars of hope illumining with ever-increasing beauty life's utmost horizon? What family circle has remained unbroken—no

empty chair—no cherished mementoes—voices and footsteps return-
ing no more—no members transferred to the illimitable beyond?
Where is he who has stood unhurt amid the chill blasts that have
blighted mortal hopes, and withered mortal loves? Alas! The steps of
death are everywhere. His voice murmuring in every sweep of the
wind; his ruins visible on towering hill and in sequestered vale. We all
have felt or seen his power. Beneath the cypress we rest and weep. Our
hearts riven with memories of the loved and lost, and yet hope springing eternal from earth's mausoleums to penetrate and possess the
future.

Heaven is ours. For is it not occupied by our dead? Heaven and
earth lay near together in the myths of the ancients, and shall it be otherwise in the institutions of Christianity? We need faith. Our paths are
surrounded by the departed. Our assemblies multiplied by their presence. Our lives bettered by their ministries. From beneath night shadows we look forward into the approaching day, and while we gaze the
beams of the morning spread light and loveliness over the earth. It is
not otherwise, as from beneath the night of time we peer anxiously
after the pure day of Heaven.

And communion with the dead, whom we have known and loved
on earth will make Heaven more real and attractive to us, dissipating
the vagueness of the notion with which it is too often regarded; beget-
ting within us abiding attachments for celestial seats. God, who created the world, and whose providence is everywhere visible in promot-
ing our welfare, is there. And Jesus, who, died for us, and with whom
we have grown familiar in his earthly history; and the Holy Spirit, the
sanctifier of the church, and whose gentle influences we have felt within us, is there. And our friends are there,—changeless, loving spirits
now, yet with lineaments familiar and forms well remembered. The
homes of the blest are no longer vague, indistinct, poorly defined. We

see them—the beautiful city, the outlined hills of immortality—the on-flowing river making glad the palaces of God. And we can have an idea of what they must be how substantial in their foundations—how vast in their proportions—how rich in their furnishings, to be fitting habitations for the immortals. Heaven comes nearer to us, and grows more attractive, as we think of the loved ones who dwell there.

My knowledge of that life is small,
    The eye of faith is dim,
But 'tis enough that Christ knows all,
    And I shall be with him.

                     —Richard Baxter

Degrees of Bliss in Glory

J. R. MacDuff

There are to be different degrees of bliss in a future heaven. One star is to differ from another star in glory. There are to be rulers over five, and rulers over ten cities—those who are to be in the outskirts of glory, and those basking in the sunlight of the Eternal Throne! Is this no call on us to be up and doing? Not to be content with the circumference, but to seek nearness to the glorious center—not only to have crowns shining as the brightness of the firmament, but to have a myriad of stars in that crown? It is the degree of holiness now that will decide the degree of happiness then—the transactions of time will regulate the awards of eternity.

425

The King Calls His Children

Cotton Mather

he King of kings hath sent for our children to confer a kingdom on them. They are gone from a dark vale of sin and shame. They are gone into the land of light, and life, and love. There they serve the Lord day and night in his temple having all tears wiped from their eyes, and from there methinks I hear them crying aloud unto us, "As well as you love us we would not be with you again. Weep not for us, but for yourselves, and count not yourselves at home till you come to be, as we are, forever with the Lord."

Seeing Friends Again

Cyprian

e ought not to mourn for those who are delivered from the world by the call of the Lord, since we know they are not lost, but sent before us; that they have taken their leave of us in order to precede us. We may long after them as we do for those who have sailed on a distant voyage, but not lament them. We may not here below put on dark robes of mourning, when they above have already put on white robes of glory. We may not give the heathens any just occasion to accuse us of weeping for those as lost and extinct, of whom we say that they live with God, and of failing to prove by the witness of our hearts the faith we confess with our lips. We, who live in hope, who believe in God, and trust that Christ had suffered for us and risen again; we, who abide in Christ, who through him and in him rise again—why do we not ourselves wish to depart out of this world?—or why do we lament for the friends who have been separated from us, as if they were lost?

Would You Call Him Back?

S. I. Prime

s if an angel had lost his way, and for a few days had wandered among the sons of men, till his companions suddenly discovered him in this wilderness and caught him, and bore him off to his native residence among the blessed; so the child is taken kindly in the morning of its wanderings, and gathered among the holy and brought home to his Father's house. How pure his spirit now; how happy he is now?

Apostles, martyrs, prophets, there around my Savior stand, and among them I behold the infant forms of those whose little graves were wet with the tears of parental love. I hear their infant voices in the song. Do you see in the midst of that bright and blessed throng the child you mourn? I ask not now if you would call him back again. I fear you would! But I ask you, "What would tempt him back again?" Bring out the playthings that he loved on earth, the toys that filled his childish heart with gladness and pleased him on the nursery floor; the paradise that was ever bright when he smiled within it; hold them up, and ask him to throw away his harp, and leave the side of his new found friends, and the bosom of his Savior! Would he come, to be a boy again, to live and laugh, and love again, to sicken, suffer, die, and perhaps he lost I think he would stay. I think I would shut the door if I saw him coming.

GOD BLESS YOU, best and noblest brother; and if God permits you still longer to live, forget not that tie that binds us, which will be just as agreeable to us in heaven as it has been useful to the church on earth.

—*John Calvin (in a letter to his dear friend William Farel)*

Death of a Good Man

Charles Haddon Spurgeon

hen you see the body of a saint, if he has served God with all his might, how sweet it is to look upon him—ah, and to look upon his coffin too, or upon his tomb in after years!

Go into Bunhill-fields, and stand by the memorial of John Bunyan and you will say; "Ah! There lies the head that contained the brain which thought out that wondrous dream of the *Pilgrim's Progress* from the City of Destruction to the "better land." There lie the fingers that wrote those wondrous lines which depict the story of him who came at last to the land of Beulah, and waded through the flood, and entered into the celestial city. And there are the eyelids which he once spoke of, when he said; "If I lie in prison until the moss grows on my eyelids, I will never make a promise to withhold from preaching." And there is that bold eye that penetrated the judge, when he said; "If you will let me out of prison today, I will preach again tomorrow, by the help of God."

If he had written nothing else but that, I would say; "John Bunyan, be honored forever."

Sir Isaac Newton

Philip Doddridge

ccording to the best information, whether public or private, I could ever obtain, his firm faith in the Divine Revelation discovered itself in the most genuine fruits of substantial virtue and piety, and consequently gives us just reason to conclude that he is now rejoicing in the happy effects of it, infinitely more than all the applause which his philosophical works have procured him, though they have commanded a fame lasting as the world.

Echoes From Heaven

John Cumming

n the shores of the Adriatic, the wives of fishermen whose husbands have gone far out upon the deep, are in the habit, at eventide, of going down to the seashore and singing, as female voices only can, the first stanza of a beautiful hymn. After they have sung it, they listen till they hear, borne by the winds across the desert sea, the second stanza, sung by their gallant husbands as they are tossed by the gale upon the waves. Perhaps, if we would listen, we too might hear on this desert world of ours, some sound, some whisper, borne from afar, to remind us that there is a heaven and a home.

Assurance of Present and Future Happiness

William McEwen

he assured Christian is a rare and happy person,, whose conscience bears him witness in the Holy Spirit, that his faith is immovable, his love sincere, his fear filial, and his repentance evangelical. And being pleasantly conscious of those prints of divine grace in his own heart, which are the fruits of past election, and the buds of future glory, firmly concludes that he is in a state of favor with God, and an heir of the heavenly inheritance.

Repine at death? Why should the mournful prisoner take badly the kindly office that unties his chains and overturns the walls of his dungeon? Why should the child not seek to burst the narrow confinement of the womb and salute the rejoicing light of day? Ought not the weary pilgrim bless the day which returns him to his Father's house? And the espoused bride to rejoice in the hour when she is presented to her faithful Bridegroom without spot, or wrinkle, or any such thing?

Death Has Lost its Terror

Philip Schaff

o the Christian this present life is simply a pilgrimage to a better country and to a city whose builder and maker is God. Every day he moves his tent nearer to his true home. His citizenship is in heaven, his thoughts, his hopes, his aspirations, are heavenly. This unworldliness or heavenly-mindedness, far from disqualifying him for the duties of earth, makes him more faithful and conscientious in his calling; for he remembers that he must render an account for every word and deed at a bar of God's judgment! Yea, in proportion as he is heavenly-minded and follows the example of his Lord and Savior, he brings heaven down to earth and lifts earth up to heaven, and infuses the purity of and happiness of heaven into his heart and home. Faith unites us to Christ, who is life itself in its truest, fullest conception—life in God, life eternal. United with Christ, we live indeed, shedding round about us the rays of His purity, goodness, love and peace. Death has lost its terror; it is but a short slumber from which we shall awake in His likeness and enjoy what eye has not seen, nor ear heard, nor even entered the imagination of man. "Because I live, ye shall live also."

AH, BELIEVER, it is only heaven that is above all winds, storms, and tempests; God did not cast man out of paradise, that be might be able to find himself another paradise in this world. The world and you must part, or Christ and you will never meet. "Ye cannot serve God and Mammon."—*Thomas Brooks*

Splendor of Eternal Glory

James McConkey

ho has not marked even here the glory of God as seen in a great sunset. Rivers of glory wind through meadows of gold. Lakes of glory lie embedded in the evening sky. Seas of glory lap eternal shores with their shimmering waves. Mountains of glory rear themselves to the heavens with cloud-capped summits tipped with the splendor of the dying day. Earth too is flooded with the glory. It falls in the dim aisles of great forests and illumines them with its splendor. It dances among the wind-tossed leaves. It splotches the trunks of giant trees. It bathe's in light the upturned faces of those who watch and worship as the climaxing splendor of earth, sea, and sky turns the heart to God our Father who is Himself the glory of all creation and who deigns to give us, in the lavish, golden glory of the sunset the faint forth-shadowing of the glory of the Father's House.

But if the earthly glory is such, what must be the glory of the heavenly city? It needs no sun, for the glory of God lightens it. The nations of the earth walk in the glory of it. Its foundations can only be likened to the glory of the diamond, the sapphire, the amethyst, the topaz, and like precious stones of earthly glory. Its gates are pearls—each wondrous gate a single pearl. The city and its street are gold. But it is gold which the earth knows not. For it is called "gold like unto clear glass" (Rev. 21:18), and "transparent glass" (Rev. 21:21). That is—it is the glory-gold. It is gold through which the glory of God can shine forth in crystal splendor. God uses this earthly imagery as the nearest symbolism by which He can give us any glimpse of the glory of His House prepared for us. But when all has been said it is as nought to that glory of which He says—"Eye hath not seen nor ear heard, neither have entered into the heart of man, the things which God hath prepared for them that love Him."

Heaven in My Heart

Richard Baxter

f heaven dwell in my heart, shall I not desire to dwell in heaven? If Divine love would more plentifully pour itself upon my heart, how easy would it be to leave this flesh and world! Death and the grave would be a triumph for victorious love. In this world I have known many of God's mercies and comforts, but their sweetness was their taste of Divine love and their tendency towards heavenly perfection.

We Reap What We Sow

J. C. Ryle

he life that we live upon earth is short at the very best, and soon gone. "We spend our days as a tale that is told." "What is our life? It is a vapor: so soon passeth it away, and we are gone." (Psalm 90:9; James 4:14) The life that is before us when we leave this world is an endless eternity, a sea without a bottom, and an ocean without a shore. "One day in Thy sight," eternal God, "is as a thousand years, and a thousand years as one day." (2 Pet. 3:. 8.) In that world time shall be no more. But short as our life is here, and endless as it will be hereafter, it is a tremendous thought that eternity hinges upon time. Our lot after death depends, humanly speaking, on what we are while we are alive. It is written, God "will render to every man according to his deeds; to them who by patient continuance in well-doing seek for glory and honor and immortality, eternal life; but to them that are contentious, and do not obey the truth, but obey unrighteousness, indignation and wrath." (Romans 2:6-8)

We ought never to forget, that we are all, while we live, in a state of probation. We are constantly sowing seeds which will spring up and

bear fruit, every day and hour in our lives. There are eternal consequences resulting from all our thoughts and words and actions, of
which we take far too little account. "For every idle word that men
speak they shall give account in the day of judgment." (Matt. 12:36)
Our thoughts are all numbered, our actions are weighed. No wonder
that Paul says, "He that soweth to the flesh shall of the flesh reap corruption; but he that soweth to the Spirit shall of the Spirit reap life
everlasting." (Gal. 6:8.) In a word, what we sow in life we shall reap after
death, and reap to all eternity.

Eternal Life in Christ

J. R. Miller

The resurrection is not far away, for it is all in Christ's hands.
When His believing ones die they sleep in Him. They are
not really dead. Those believing on Him never die at all. What
we call dying is only passing through the gate into the immediate presence of Christ. Christ has abolished death. To Him death was
real and full of terrors. But because it was so terrible to Him, it is only
an entrance of glory for His people. He absorbed the blackness and the
gloom in His own soul, as He passed through the valley, and left it a
vale of brightness for His followers.

If we could all get into our hearts the truth of the immortal life as
revealed in the gospel, it would take away all the gloom from the graves
of our dead. Those who live here are in Christ, and those who have
passed over are with Christ, thus in Him we are still united. There is
only one family in Christ—part gone over, part crossing now, soon all
to be together. This truth of the endless life is one of marvellous power
when we have, even in the least measure, realized it. Death is not the
end of anything but of mortality, imperfection, and sin. Life goes on

fuller, richer, nobler, with enlarged capacities, beyond the incident which we call death. We shall never die.

The Little Girl and the Ferryman

Dwight L. Moody

he story is told of a father who had his little daughter out late in the evening. The night was dark, and they had passed through a thick woods to the brink of a river. Far away on the opposite shore a light twinkled here and there in the few scattered houses, and farther off still, blazed the bright lamps of the great city to which they were going. The little child was weary and sleepy, and the father held her in his arms while he waited for the ferryman, who was at the other side. At length they saw a little light; nearer and nearer came the sound of the oars, and soon they were safe in the boat.

"Father," said the little girl. "Well, my child?"

"Its very dark, and I can't see the shore; where are we going?" she said. "The ferryman knows the way, little one. We will soon be over."

"I wish we were there, father!"

Soon in her home, loving arms welcomed her, and her fears and her tremor were gone. Some months pass by, and this same little child stands on the brink of a river that is darker and deeper, more terrible still. It is the River of Death. The same loving father stands near her, distressed that his child must cross this river and he is not be able to go with her. For days and for nights he and her mother have been watching over her, leaving her bedside only long enough for their meals, and to pray for the life of their precious one. For hours she has been slumbering, and it seems as if her spirit must pass away without her waking again, but just before the morning watch she suddenly awakes with the eye bright, the reason unclouded, and every faculty alive. A sweet smile is playing upon her face.

"Father," she says, "I have come again to the riverside, and am again waiting for the ferryman to come and take me across."

"Does it seem as dark and cold as when you went over the other river, my child?"

"Oh no! There is no darkness here. The river is covered with floating silver. The boat coming towards me seems made of solid light, and I am not afraid of the ferryman."

"Can you see over the river, my darling?"

"Oh yes, there is a great and beautiful city there, all filled with light; and I hear music such as the angels make!"

"Do you see any one on the other side?"

"Why yes, yes, I see the most beautiful form, and He beckons me now to come. Oh, ferryman, make haste! I know who it is! It is Jesus; my own blessed Jesus. I shall be caught in his arms. I shall rest on his bosom—1 come—I come."

And thus she crossed over the river of Death, made like a silver stream by the presence of the blessed Redeemer.

Present, Past and Future

Daniel Webster

t is a noble faculty of our nature which enables us to connect with our thoughts, our sympathies, and our happiness, with what is distant in place or time; and looking before and after, to hold communion at once with our ancestors and our posterity. Human and mortal although we are, we are nevertheless not mere insulated beings, without relation to the past or the future. Neither the point of time, nor the spot of earth, in which we physically live, bounds our rational and intellectual enjoyments. We live in the

past by a knowledge of its history, and in the future by hope and anticipation.

As it is not a vain and false, but an exalted and religious imagination, which leads us to raise our thoughts from the orb, which, amid
this universe of worlds, the Creator has given us to inhabit, and to send
them with something of the feeling which nature prompts, and teaches, to be proper among children of the same Eternal Parent, to the contemplation of the myriads of fellow-beings, with which His goodness
has peopled the infinite space. So neither is it false or vain to consider
ourselves as interested and connected with our whole race, through all
time; allied to our ancestors; allied to our posterity; closely compacted
on all sides with others; ourselves being but links in the great chain of
being, which begins with the origin of our race, runs onward through
its successive generations, binding together the past, the present and
the future, and terminating at last with the consummation of all things
earthly, at the throne of God.

The Whole Family in Heaven

John Angell James

ne of the most exquisite delights which we ever experience
on earth, is the enjoyment which springs from the first
interview with a friend from whom we have been separated.
And this delight is in proportion to the length of time, and
greatness of distance, and magnitude of danger, which have intervened
between the separation and the meeting. What language can describe
the thrill of transport, the almost agony of rapture, which the wife
experiences in that moment when she receives a husband back again to
her arms, who has been away from home for months, who has been
separated from her by half the circumference of the globe, and threat-

438

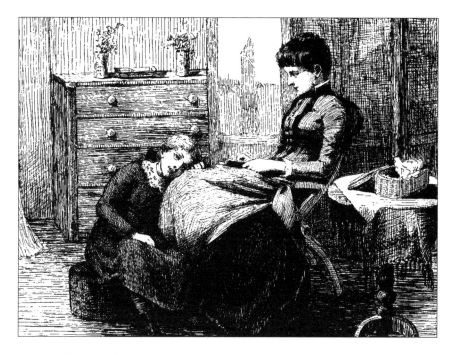

ened to be torn from her forever, by the dangers of shipwreck or of battle? Or who shall set forth that scene of domestic bliss which is exhibited when the sailor-boy, after having been absent for years, returns
from the dangers of the sea, and the horrors of captivity, to the bosom
of his family, and exchanges ecstatic greetings with his parents, and his
sisters, and his brothers, till all seem ready to dissolve with excess of
joy? What then must be the meeting of these same relatives in heaven,
after having been separated by worlds and ages?—that meeting when a
mother receives her children to the skies from this degenerate earth,
and the father hails his offspring from the world of death to the region
of life and immortality? Here imagination confesses its weakness. It is
a scene we have never witnessed ourselves, nor have we ever conversed
with one who has. My heart, while I write, seems to beat quicker at the

thought; and the very anticipation raises a commotion of pleasurable feelings in my bosom, which no words could enable me to express.

Then remember this meeting is not for a mere transient interview, but for an eternal association. it is to take place in a world where adieus and farewells are a sound unknown. What an interruption does it now form to the enjoyment of domestic intercourse, that the different branches of the family cannot always live beneath the same roof, or in the vicinity of their parents. One member after another goes from the paternal abode, and settles at a distance, till counties and perhaps kingdoms separate them from each other. Rarely does it happen, where the children are numerous and grown to maturity, that they can all meet together. Occasionally this does happen, perhaps on a parent's birthday, or at the festive season of the year, and then home puts forth all its charms, and pours out in copious streams its pure and precious joys. Such a circle is a resort of peace and love, where friends and dear relations mingle into bliss. The parents look with ineffable delight upon their children and children's children, and see the smiles of love reflected from the happy group. Piety gives the finishing touch to the picture, when, ere they part, they assemble round the domestic altar, and after reading in that Book which speaks of the many mansions in our Father's house above where the families of the righteous meet to part no more, and after blending their voices in a sacred song of praise to him who bath united them, both by ties of nature and of grace, they receive the benedictions, and join in the prayers of their saintly and patriarchal father, who over the scene that surrounds him, feels a divided heart. One moment thinking he has lived long enough in that he has been permitted to witness it, but the next, breathing an aspiration to heaven for permission to witness it a few years longer.

This scene, and it is not an uncommon one, is one of the purest to be found on earth. It is, as nearly as it can be, paradise restored; or, if it be, as it certainly is, still without the gates of Eden, it is near enough to the sacred enclosure to receive some of the fruits that drop over the wall. What is wanting here? I answer, continuance. It is bliss only for a season. It is a day that will be followed with a night. And the heart was often checked in the full tide of enjoyment, in the very meridian of its delights, by looking at the clock and counting how rapidly the hours of felicity were rolling away, and how soon the signal of parting would be struck. But the meeting in heaven shall be eternal. The family shall go no more out forever from the mansion of their Father above. Their interview shall not be measured nor limited by time. They shall meet for one day, but then that day will be everlasting—for "there is no night there." They shall spend eternal ages together. Neither the fear nor the thought of parting shall ever pass like a cloud over the orb of their felicity, nor let fall a passing shadow to disturb the sunshine of their breast. "We are met," shall they say one to another, "and we shall part no more. Around us is glory, within us is rapture, and before us is eternity!"

Happiness of Heaven

William McEwen

lorious things are spoken of you, O city of God! Of the happy beings who walk the golden streets and dwell in ivory palaces, they are all kings and priests unto God. Hail, you highly favored of the Lord, who have now received a crown, not of flowers which fade, not of gold which is also a corruptible thing; but of glory and righteousness in which you shall flourish. The throne of Christ receives you. Eternity shall be your triumph, O happy victors, who have more than conquered. Therefore, you are arrayed in white robes, with palms in your hands, and blessings of salvation in your mouths.

441

Christ First!

Charles Dickens (from Life of Our Lord, *written to his children)*

emember!—It is Christianity to do good, always—even to those who do evil to us. It is Christianity to love our neighbors as ourself, and to do to all men as we would have them do to us. It is Christianity to be gentle, merciful, and forgiving, and to keep those qualities quiet in our own hearts, and never make a boast of them, or of our prayers or of our love of God, but always to show that we love Him, by humbly trying to do right in everything. If we do this, and remember the life and lessons of our Lord Jesus Christ, and try to act up to them, we may confidently hope that God will forgive us our sins and mistakes, and enable us to live and die in peace.

Heavenly Thoughts

Dwight L. Moody

here are men who say that there is no heaven. I was once talking with a man who said he thought there was nothing to justify us in believing in any other heaven than that we know here on earth. If this is heaven, it is a very strange one-this world of sickness, sorrow and sin. I pity from the depths of my heart the man or woman who has that idea.

This world that some think is heaven, is the home of sin, a hospital of sorrow, a place that has nothing in it to satisfy the soul. Men go all over it and then want to get out of it. The more men see of the world the less they think of it. People soon grow tired of the best pleasures it has to offer. Some one has said that the world is a stormy sea, whose every wave is strewed with the wrecks- of mortals that perish in it. Every time we breathe someone is dying. We all know that we are going to stay here but a very little while. Our life is but a vapor. It is only a shadow.

"We meet one another," as some one has said, "salute one another, pass on and are gone." And another has said; "It is just an inch of time, and then eternal ages roll on;" and it seems to me that it is perfectly reasonable that we should study this Book, to find out where we are going, and where our friends are who have gone on before. The longest time man has to live has no more proportion to eternity than a drop of dew has to the ocean.

Always Ready!

J. R. Miller

he criticalness of life should lead us to be always ready for death. Though we are plainly taught by our Lord not to be anxious about anything that the future may have in store for us, we are as plainly taught to live so as to be prepared for any event which may occur. Indeed, the only way to eliminate care from our present is to be ready for any possible future. Death is not merely a possible, but is an inevitable, event in every one's future. We can live untroubled by dread of it only by being ever ready for it. Preparation for death is made by living a true Christian life. If we are in Christ by faith, and then follow Christ, doing his will day by day, we are prepared for death and it can never surprise us unready.

True preparation for death is made when we close each day as if it were the last. We are never sure of tomorrow. We should leave nothing incomplete any night. Each single separate little day should be a minia-ture life complete in itself, with nothing of duty left over. God gives us life by days, and with each day be gives its own allotment of duty—a portion of his plan to be wrought out, a fragment of his purpose to be accomplished by us. Says F. W. Faber, "Every hour comes with some little portion of God's will fastened upon its back." Our mission is to find that bit of divine will and do it. Well-lived days make completed years, and the years well lived as they come make a life beautiful and full. In such a life no special preparation of any kind is needed. He who lives thus is always ready. Each day prepares for the next, and the last day prepares for glory.

Present With the Lord

Isaac Watts

> And is this heaven? And am I there?
> > How short the road! How swift the flight!
> I am all life, all eye, all ear:
> > Jesus is here—my soul's delight.
> Is this the heavenly Friend who hung
> > In blood and anguish on the tree,
> Whom Paul proclaim'd, whom David sung,
> > Who died for them, who died for me?
>
> How fair, thou Offspring of my God!
> > Thou first-born Image of his face!
> Thy death procured this blessed abode,
> > Thy vital beams adorn the place.
> Lo, he presents me at the throne
> > All spotless; there the Godhead reigns
> Sublime and peaceful through the Son:
> > Awake, my voice, in heavenly strains.

My Soul!

George Matheson

y soul, why are you perplexed about the future? Do you see clouds in tomorrow's sky which your present strength is inadequate to meet? God has not given you your present strength to meet the future, but to meet the present. When tomorrow shall become today you shall learn to have power over it. Why are you distressed about the unborn sorrow? You are born anew for each new day. Your armor is freshly burnished to fight each rising sun. In the hour of battle you will laugh at the memory of your fears. You will say even of the last enemy that shall be conquered, "Oh, death! Where is thy sting? Oh, grave! Where is thy victory!" You shall marvel at yourself when you pass through the valley. You shall tread it so lightly, so easily. You shall ask, "Can this be death?"

You shall wonder to hear its desert break into singing, to see its wilderness blossom like the rose. You shall be surprised to find so many lights gleaming in the valley. But the lights will not be in the valley but in you. God will Illuminate you for the dark day, and what shadows shall abide the blaze of His illumination? The light will not come till the shades come. Weaken not your spirit by forebodings before battle, for in a moment, in the twinkling of an eye, when the battle-trump shall sound, your power shall be raised incorruptible, and "as your days, so shall your strength be."

Where Will You be?

J. C. Ryle

I leave the subject of eternity here, and pray that God may bless it to many souls. In conclusion, I offer to every one who reads this volume some food for thought, and matter for self-examination.

(1) First of all, how are you using your time? Life is short and very uncertain. You never know what a day may bring forth. Business and pleasure, money-making and money-spending, eating and drinking, marrying and giving in marriage,—all, all will soon be over and done with forever. And you, what are you doing for your immortal soul? Are you wasting time, or turning it to good account? Are you preparing to meet God?

(2) Secondly, where shall you be in eternity? It is coming, coming, coming very fast upon us. You are going, going going very fast into it. But where will you be? On the right hand or on the left, in the day of judgment? Among the lost or among the saved? Oh, rest not, rest not till your soul is insured! Make sure work! Leave nothing uncertain. It is a fearful thing to die unprepared, and fall into the hands of the living God.

(3) Thirdly, would you be safe for time and eternity? Then seek Christ, and believe in Him. Come to Him just as you are. Seek Him while He may be found. Call upon Him while He is near. There is still a throne of grace. It is not too late. Christ waits to be gracious. He invites you to come to Him. Before the door is shut and the judgment begins, repent, believe, and be saved.

(4) Lastly, would you be happy? Cling to Christ, and live the life of faith in Him. Abide in Him, and live near to Him. Follow Him with heart and soul and mind and strength, and seek to know Him better every day. So doing you shall have great peace while you pass through things temporal, "and in the midst of a dying world shall never die." (John 11:26.) So doing, you shall be able to look forward to "things eternal" with unfailing confidence, and to feel and "know that if our earthly house of this tabernacle be dissolved we have a building of God, a house not made with hands, eternal in the heavens." (2 Cor. 5:1)

446

FINIS.